GOING NORTH

Migration of Blacks and Whites
from the South, 1900 — 1950

This is a volume of
Quantitative Studies in Social Relations
Consulting Editor: Peter H. Rossi, University of Massachusetts,
Amherst, Massachusetts

GOING NORTH

Migration of Blacks and Whites
from the South, 1900 — 1950

Neil Fligstein
Department of Sociology
University of Arizona
Tucson, Arizona
and
National Opinion Research Center
University of Chicago
Chicago, Illinois

ACADEMIC PRESS
A Subsidiary of Harcourt Brace Jovanovich, Publishers
New York   London   Toronto   Sydney   San Francisco

ACADEMIC PRESS, INC.
111 Fifth Avenue, New York, New York 10003

United Kingdom Edition published by
ACADEMIC PRESS, INC. (LONDON) LTD.
24/28 Oval Road, London NW1   7DX

Library of Congress Cataloging in Publication Data

Fligstein, Neil.
    Going north, migration of Blacks and whites from the
South, 1900-1950.

    (Quantitative studies in social relations)
    Originally presented as the author's thesis.
    Bibliography: p.
    Includes index.
    1. Rural-urban migration--United States--History--
20th century. I. Title. II. Series.
HT361.F55 1981   304.8'0975   81-14901
ISBN 0-12-260720-1   AACR2

PRINTED IN THE UNITED STATES OF AMERICA

81 82 83 84   9 8 7 6 5 4 3 2 1

To My Parents

Contents

Preface

Vast changes transformed America from a colony of the British empire to a power in its own right. This transformation entailed a shift from a predominantly rural, extractive economy to an urban, industrial, and service economy. This study attempts to understand this transition and its effects on the rural population of the South. The key argument is that the emerging business interests in the northern United States came to dominate the South and West politically and economically after the Civil War. This domination made the South an internal colony that was used for its natural resources and cash crop production. The migrations from the rural South to the towns and cities of the South and North in this century should be understood in this context. Before 1930, the migrations of blacks and whites reflected the expansion and contraction of cotton agriculture in the South. After 1930, the major cause of black and white migration was the transformation of cotton agriculture from a labor-intensive tenant economy to a capitalist machine-oriented economy. This was achieved by the self-conscious political activity of the organized farm owners who benefited from the Agricultural Adjustment Act of 1933. Farm owners restricted acreage, released their tenants, and invested their subsidy payments in machines, thereby reducing their need for tenant labor even further.

The following piece of research can be considered a hybrid. It reflects thinking on a topic that is, at once, historical, demographic, sociological, and economic. The coherency of this endeavor rests in understanding what constitutes an answer to the question I am asking. In this research, I have taken a tack that can be called "social — structural" or, perhaps more simply, "sociological." Thus, historians may view this work as glossing over contradictory evidence and taking a position on issues that are presently being argued without adding much evidence to those arguments one way or another. However, every social scientist must choose the set of facts upon which he or she wishes his or her argument to rest. The "truth" or "value" of the argument is related directly to the organization of ideas and facts. I leave the reader with the responsibility of deciding how well I have organized my facts and ideas. Of course, I am responsible for any errors of commission and omission.

Acknowledgments

Books are social projects that reflect the social and intellectual circles of their authors. Without the aid, advice, and support (both financial and emotional) of one's friends, advisors, and colleagues, such projects would be impossible. This manuscript has evolved over four years and three places. Each of these places has contributed positively to this project. Here, I would like to acknowledge those contributions.

This book began as a dissertation. My advisor on this project was Hal Winsborough. Without his encouragement, trust, and advice, I would never have gotten this far. The other members of my committee, Mike Aiken, Karl Taeuber, Ron Aminzade, and John Sharpless, have all contributed useful criticisms, ideas and suggestions. Professor Aiken first sensitized me to the importance of the historical conjuncture and encouraged me to place this project in the relatively broad historical context that prevades this text. At various times, I have received insightful criticism from Jim Baron, Bill Frey, Alex Hicks, David James, Rob Mare, Ed Nelson, Bill Roy, Michael Sobel, Mette Sorenson, Wendy Wolf, Erik Wright, Glenn Yago, and Maurice Zeitlin. I would like to thank Larry Bumpass, head of the Center for Demography and Ecology at the University of Wisconsin, and the Center itself for providing access to a computing facility, a library, an office, as well as financial support during the time I worked on the dissertation. My support came from a NRSA training grant award (HD-07014) given by the National Institute of Child Health and

Human Development. Computing was made possible by a grant from the National Institute of Child Health and Human Development to the Center for Demography and Ecology (HD-05876). Some of the data used in this project were obtained from the Data and Academic Computing Center's library at the University of Wisconsin. I would like to thank Anne Cooper, data librarian, for her help in the use of the various data tapes. Ruth Rabelais performed an enormous keypunching job on some of the data used in this project and deserves thanks for the care with which she performed her task. Gordon Caldwell provided programming expertise at critical moments. Sandy Goers did a very impressive job of typing the manuscript and Renette Saunders aided in the proofreading. I would also like to thank Sandy Goers for drawing the figures.

This work was continued at the University of Arizona. My colleagues there provided much stimulation and a fair amount of insight. I would like to thank Al Bergesen, Diane Bush, Richard Curtis, Michael Hout, and Stan Lieberson. I completed this work while I was at the National Opinion Research Center at the University of Chicago. NORC provided me with an environment where it was possible to grind out the final details of this book. For that freedom, I wish to thank Norman Bradburn, Bill McCready, and Bob Michael.

Finally, I wish to thank Eileen Mortensen-Fligstein for putting up with me, keeping me high, and helping me over the rough spots.

Chapter 1

Migration of Blacks and Whites: An Overview

Theoretical work then, whatever the degree of its abstraction, is always work bearing on real processes. Yet since this work produces knowledge, it is wholly situated in the process of thought: no concepts are more real than others. Theoretical work proceeds from a raw material, which consists not of the "real – concrete," but of information, notions, etc. about this reality, and deals with it by means of certain conceptual tools: the result of this work is the knowledge of an object.
– NICOS POULANTZAS
Political Power and Social Classes (1968:12)

The most important change in the distribution of the American population since 1850 is the shift from rural to urban areas. This rural – urban migration has been viewed as primarily a function of industrialization. Industrial development, as the story goes, caused the substitution of machines for men in the countryside, which created a surplus population in rural areas. Industrialization implied the creation of new jobs in cities, both in industry and services, and these new jobs lured the rural population to the city (Kuznets, 1966:113 – 127; Fulmer, 1950:60 – 134; Davis, 1973:369 – 389).

The primary goal of this study is to go beyond this model of American development and to demonstrate that the causes of the most important population movement of this century in America, the movement of blacks and whites from the South to the North and West, are not consistent with this characterization. Two interrelated themes emerge from this study. First, the process of proletarianization (i.e., the shift from rural, tenant labor to urban, wage labor) of blacks and whites who lived in the South is explicated. The central point is that the rural population was displaced and forced to become an urban "surplus population." While this theme has been prominent in writings about Western Europe and the Third World, it has received little attention in the American context. The second theme is that the economic development of the United States and its concomitant effects on the distribution of the population have

1

reflected the uneven regional development of the United States. Many view the United States as a developed country with relatively homogeneous wage rates and industrial distribution (see Lee *et al.*, 1964, for a statement of this position, and Holland, 1976, for a rebuttal). In reality, the United States continues to have pockets of underdevelopment, and the large corporations continue to exploit that fact (witness the return migration to the Sunbelt). The process of underdevelopment is not just international; it is also interregional. This study attempts to understand the subtlety of these processes and how they worked in the South. The migrations from the South resulted from a complex set of interactions between many layers of social relations. The opportunity structure of the southern population was determined by the southern organization of cash crop production, its dependence on credit, northern control over the South, and the South's place in the world commodity markets. It is the goal of this study to demonstrate how these processes structured the migrations from the South. Toward this end, this chapter consists of (a) a presentation of the economists' version of American development and their account of the causes of black and white migration from the South; (b) a general theoretical and methodological discussion of the model of migration used here; and (c) a concrete theoretical, methodological, and empirical discussion of the causes of black and white migration from the South from 1900 to 1950.

Economists' Version of American Development and Migration

Before proceeding to establish the general notions underlying this study, it is of some value to consider briefly the dominant version of American development and migration. This view is based on economic theory and tends to underlie most work in the study of migration. The economists' theory is presented here because it represents the major theory that purports to account for the migration of blacks and whites from the South.

The economists' view of American development can be summed up in the following way. In the early stages of American history, most people lived in rural areas and were subsistence farmers. The urbanization of America proceeded as the result of two forces: mechanization in agriculture and industrialization in cities (Lee *et al.*, 1964:2). The mechanization of agriculture began first, and the major result was the reduced need for manpower in the countryside. Industrialization, which can be characterized as the growth of the factory system, drew people to the cities.

From a sociological point of view, this implies that the technical relations of production caused shifts in the social relations of production. Technical innovation is viewed as the primary causal factor in the transformation of America from a rural, subsistence, agricultural economy to an urbanized, industrial economy.

Economists view migration as a result of the impact of wage rate differentials (Eldridge and Thomas, 1964; Sjaasted, 1962; Todaro, 1969; Vickery, 1977). The theory suggests that people move in response to wage differences; that is, they move from areas of low income to areas of high income. The economic version of the move of blacks and whites from the South is a straightforward application of the development and wage rate theories. It is thought that before 1930, opportunities in industry and in cities were the main causes of black and white migration, whereas after 1930, the substitution of machines for men in southern cotton agriculture forced people off the land and made the opportunities offered by both southern and northern cities more attractive. Tractors and later, mechanical cotton pickers made large numbers of agricultural laborers surplus population. The two world wars and sustained economic growth offered people opportunities in the cities. The higher wages offered in the cities of the South and North, along with the decline in demand for agricultural labor in the South due to the mechanization of agriculture, caused the migrations of blacks and whites (Dillingham and Sly, 1966; Eldridge and Thomas, 1964; Fulmer, 1950; Kuznets, 1966; Street, 1957; Vickery, 1977).

Methodologically, this theory implies a constant shift from a rural to an urban population. The technology was developed and applied, and the accompanying shifts in the distribution of the population followed. The theory suggests that where technology did not have an impact, there must have been either a social or a political blockage (Fulmer, 1950; Street, 1957). Traditional modes of cultivation could persist only because cultural norms prevented the implementation of new technology. Street (1957), for example, argues that it was the *culture* of cotton cultivation that prevented the South from mechanizing. The basic assumption in such an argument is that farmers, for instance, will constantly try to increase profits by applying new technologies. Farmers who do not choose to use such technologies are then seen to be irrational, and we must look elsewhere (e.g., to culture) to explain their actions.

Most economic models of migration begin with the wage rate differential (Eldridge and Thomas, 1964; Todaro, 1969; Vickery, 1977; for a review, see Greenwood, 1975). Empirical studies based on this notion usually find that migration is responsive to wage rate differences: People migrate from areas of low income to areas of high income. Indeed, Vickery (1977) concludes that the major cause of the migration of blacks in this century is the wage rate differential. Other studies (notably Mandle, 1978) implicitly accept such a conclusion, but stress the mechanization of agriculture as well.

A General Theoretical and Methodological Discussion

The central criticism of the economists' approach to American development and migration centers on the technological determinism implicit in the economic approach. The key counterargument is that the social relations of production will place limits on and shape technological innovation. From this point of view, the urbanization, industrialization, and mechanization of American society resulted from the underlying struggles between various groups and from the economic, political, and ideological solutions to such struggles. The economic transformation of America required that a dominant set of interests be imposed on the bulk of the population through economic and political activity. At each stage of this process, those who were dominated protested, and at every point they were defeated politically and economically.

To clarify this argument, it is of value to present a general model of rural – urban migration in a capitalist social formation. This will allow consideration of a variety of key theoretical and methodological notions to emerge. Figure 1.1 presents a schematic diagram of that model. In trying to understand migration, it is necessary to consider two periods of time in the social formation: (a) a time period previous to the study; and (b) a time period relevant to the study. The history of structures reveals where previous crises emerged, how they were resolved, and how new crises are likely to result. Once armed with a knowledge of history, it will be possible to proceed to an interpretation of the time frame under study.

The second aspect of the model to be discussed is the separation of social relations of agriculture from conditions exterior to agriculture; that is, the rest of the social formation and the world market for the commodity produced. By virtue of different social relations of production and exchange, agriculture forms a meaningful sector of the economy. At the economic level, production in any agricultural system revolves around ownership of land, use of wage labor, use of various technologies, and the goal of production (subsistence or commodity production for the market). The ties between these various economic features are relatively loose, although subsistence agriculture tends to be small scale with primitive technology and little use of wage labor, and commodity production tends to be large scale production utilizing high technology and

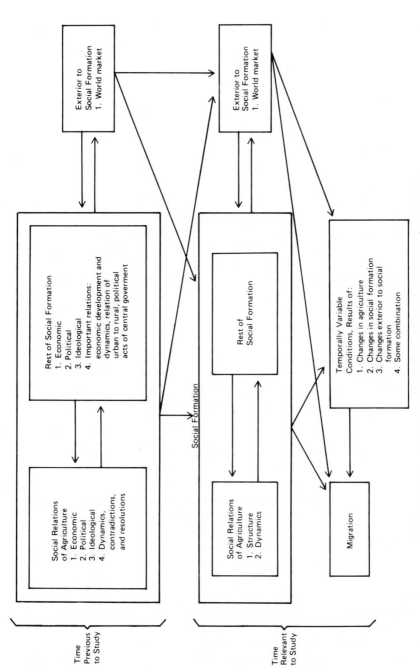

FIGURE 1.1. *A model of rural–urban migration in a capitalist social formation.*

the use of wage labor. Of course, any real agricultural system will have elements of both commodity and subsistence production. The economic crises of farmers will depend on the class structure of agriculture and the dynamics of production and price.

The relations between the agricultural sector and the rest of the social formation will depend on (a) the dynamics of class structure and capitalist accumulation in the rest of the economy; and (b) the relation between agriculture and the rest of the economy at the political and economic levels. At the economic level, farmers can be dependent on the industrial and finance sectors for credit, supplies, transportation of commodities, organization of markets, and demand for commodities. The state also provides a link between agricultural and industrial accumulation. If the state favors industrial over agricultural production, the agricultural sector can be dominated by capitalist production, which has been the case to a large extent in the United States. The state can also take actions to help farm owners maintain their position in production.

The next element to consider is the role of the world market for commodities. Once farmers shift from subsistence to cash crop or commodity production, it is the price of the commodity in the market that determines whether they prosper as farmers. The relation to local, national, or world commodity markets can undermine local class relations and cause crises that may result in political action or reorganization of production.

In the time period relevant to the study, three factors need to be considered in order to specify a model of migration. First, one needs to understand the social relations of agriculture in the period (i.e., the class structure, its shifts, and the dynamics of production). These relations and rhythms are a direct outgrowth of previous relations and crises. Second, one needs to see how these dynamics are affected by and affect conditions in the rest of the social formation and conditions exterior to the social formation. In the South, for example, despite falling prices, the basic credit mechanism put farmers in the position of having to produce more cotton. This dynamic was integral to the social relations underlying agriculture. If at the same time the demand for the product decreased in the social formation or the world market or production in other countries increased, the result would be a drop in price. If the price remained low for a long period of time, a serious crisis would develop. The third factor to consider is temporally variable conditions. These are unique factors that, when introduced into the situation, undermine the farmers' ability to produce. The boll weevil infestation in the early part of this century is one example of such a condition.

The social relations of agriculture affect migration in the following ways:

1. In periods of expansion, migration follows opportunities.
2. In periods of contraction, crisis, or transformation, people are forced off the farms.

There is an implicit assumption in this study that local conditions are most important in migration decisions. Individuals will tend to remain where they are until social relations make it difficult to continue. Events in other parts of the social formation and in the world economy will impinge on the migration process, but one must focus on the implications of these events at their points of origin. From a social psychological point of view, people are unlikely to leave an area unless (a) they are forced out by lack of opportunities; (b) the possibilities for work elsewhere are known and offer good alternatives; or (c) both a and b. Individuals are involved in the social relations at the point of origin. These relations themselves are affected by other more distal social relations, but the important effects must have implications at that point of origin (i.e., where the actors are). For this reason, this study is biased toward understanding the events that occurred in the South and, in particular, in southern cotton agriculture. The central argument is that conditions in the rural South made the cities and towns of the South and North attractive places.

Conditions external to agriculture also affect migration in a number of ways. General economic conditions in cities and towns can operate as factors causing migration from rural areas. When demand for agricultural commodities is strong, agricultural production itself can expand. Political decisions concerning agricultural prices, exports, and imports will affect the social relations of agriculture and, hence, opportunities. The world market for commodities could also affect the migration process by affecting rural class structure and the general profitability of production. Temporally variable conditions can affect migration by (a) facilitating production; or (b) hindering production. The transformation of southern agriculture was the result of a political response to a severe crisis in the 1930s, and this transformation had profound effects on migration as it took away the ability of most tenant farmers to earn a living.

In this model, it is important to attempt to locate mechanization. The argument initially presented was that mechanization was the result of shifts in the social relations of production. In practice, this means that the process of mechanization must be located in the structure and dynamics of the social relations of agriculture. Mechanization in the South was not held back by tradition-bound white landlords and uneducated tenants. Rather, the absence of machines reflected the lack of liquid capital in the region and the social organization of agriculture into a landlord—tenant relationship. Since most farm owners operated through the use of credit, it was difficult for them to find money to invest in machines. The landlord—tenant relationship was highly dependent on the landlord's extracting money from the tenant for food, seed, fertilizer, and, of course, rent. From the landlord's point of view, supplying tenants was more profitable than buying machines. The mechanization of agriculture in the South required a crisis whereby capital became available and tenant farming was no longer profitable for the landlord. From the perspective presented here, this means that mechanization resulted from the resolution of a crisis generated in the social relations of agriculture.

The theoretical model just outlined has a number of methodological implications. The model focuses on three aspects of social relations that underlie any migration process: (a) the social relations of agriculture; (b) these relations and the rest of the social formation; and (c) these relations and the world market. To understand migration from the point of view outlined here, one must (a) view the historical crises of a given society and (b) produce an account of how and why these crises came about and what their implications were for migration. The model of migration that emerges must stress the disjunctures, contradictions, and crises and must be sensitive to the economic and political activities of important groups. In sum, understanding migration from rural to urban areas in capitalist social formations requires a model that is historical and structural. One can note that this methodology is applicable to most processes (e.g. fertility, mortality, industrialization, and urbanization in capitalist social formations).

The Causes of the Migration of Blacks and Whites from the South, 1900—1950

The model of migration in a capitalist social formation that has been explicated is mainly a formal model with very little content. This is because the model depends very much on the concrete social formation for its context. The purpose of this section is to provide that context and offer a schematic overview of the causes of the migration of blacks and whites from the South by using the theory and method of the previous section.

A statement of the key question of this study is in order: What were the causes of black and white migration from counties of the South from 1900 to 1950? Three questions immediately spring from such a question.

1. Why the South?
2. Why this period?
3. Why blacks *and* whites?

The South has been chosen because its development since 1865 has been slow and stunted. The effects of capitalist development in America are expressed in the South in roundabout ways. The South of 1900 was primarily rural, and its economy depended on cash crops—mainly cotton, sugar, and tobacco. The social relationships in the growing, marketing, and processing of these crops have their histories shaped by ante- and postbellum experiences. The examination of these experiences causes us to consider the relation of the South to the world market, the increasing dominance of northern capital in the South following the Civil War, and the social relations within the South (big farm owners/ merchants versus tenants/small farm owners and blacks versus whites). These social relations and their contradictions and fluctuations are both the heart of the development process and the driving force of the eventual out-migration.

The period was chosen as it was a time of great flux. In 1900, the South was only 18% urban, which was less than half that of the country as a whole (Taeuber and Taeuber, 1958:122). In 1950, the South was 49% urban, which was about 80% of the national figure. The twentieth century has witnessed great changes in American society. The emergence of modern America began in the 1870s, but it was not until 1915 that southern agriculture lost its momentum and began to lose its rural population. In 1850, the southern population was 8.3% urbanized, and by 1900 it was only 18% urbanized. In this period, the northeastern states moved from 26.5% urbanized to 66.1%, while the northern central states began with 9.2% and ended with 38.2% urbanized. The burgeoning capitalist development and its concomitant urbanization did not affect the South. This raises a series of related questions. Why did industrial development and urbanization come so late to the South? What were the features of the southern economic environment that were not conducive to northern capitalist penetration? In what ways did the North come to control the economic development of the South and further stultify southern industrialization and urbanization? The basic answer to these questions revolves around viewing the South as an internal colony (Hechter, 1975; Woodward, 1974). As a result of northern control over southern development, the South provided the raw materials and cash crops but did little of the processing of these products.

Blacks and whites will be considered separately because each group's experiences were different in the South. Blacks had fewer options than whites in the South and would be expected to respond differently to social conditions. While there has been a fair amount of speculation about why blacks left the rural areas (Eldridge and Thomas, 1964; Farley, 1968; Scott, 1920; Street, 1957; Vance, 1929, 1945; Woofter, 1969), there is very little written about the experiences of whites. It is the argument here that whites reacted to the declining southern agricultural system in very much the same way that blacks did (i.e., they migrated).

One restriction is placed on the scope of this study. For the most part, the concern here is with the cotton growing region of the South. While corn, tobacco, and sugar were important southern crops, cotton was the basis of the southern economy until quite recently (Fulmer, 1950; Hoover and Hatchford, 1951:89—110; Street, 1957; Vance, 1945:154—231). In this study, attention is focused on the states of North Carolina, South Carolina, Georgia, Alabama, Mississippi, Arkansas, Louisiana, Oklahoma, and eastern Texas. These states encompass most of the cotton belt in the South. Virginia, Tennessee, Missouri, Florida, and Kentucky all planted negligible amounts of cotton (Fulmer, 1950:6; Watkins, 1908:30) and therefore are excluded from this analysis.

Given this motivation and the theoretical model proposed earlier, the approach that will be taken here can be summarized in the following way. In order to understand the movement of blacks and whites out of the rural South from 1900 to 1950, a real event in a real social formation, one must understand the social relations that existed in 1900 and how they came to be. This requires giving an account of (a) the changes in the social relations of production following the Civil War; and (b) the implications for the organization of southern society from 1865 to 1900 at the economic, political, and ideological levels. From this, a model of why groups move at different points in time can be constructed. After these models are constructed, an attempt will be made to test them and ascertain the magnitude of the effects of the various factors involved.

The first task is to define the relevant periods of study more precisely. There are three key periods: 1865—1900, 1900—1930, and 1930—1950. The dates used are approximate as they reflect the shortcomings of using census data to describe the structure of the social relations underlying southern agriculture. The period 1865—1900 began with the end of the Civil War and ended with the demise of populism, the disenfranchisement of poor blacks and whites, and the beginning of Jim Crow laws which elevated racism to state policy. These events circumscribe a time when the basic dynamics of post-Civil War southern agriculture became established. The period 1900—1930 was a time when there were no threats to the social relations of agriculture. Migration in this period was more a result of the dynamics of cotton production. The period 1930 – 1950 circumscribed the transformation of southern agriculture from a labor intensive tenant system to a mechanized capitalist agriculture. This transformation had profound effects on the opportunity structure of blacks and whites and therefore is highly related to migration.

1865 – 1900

With the end of the Civil War, the Confederate states found themselves in the position of having most of their cities devastated, most of their land in disarray, and the basic social mechanism underlying production (i.e., slavery) destroyed. Within the South there was very little capital to reconstruct southern agriculture and infrastructure. In order to start producing crops, two major obstacles needed to be surmounted: labor needed to be controlled, and capital needed to be found. Part of the solution came in the form of crop lien laws. These laws allowed producers to take loans on crops that were in the fields. The development of sharecropping and other tenant farming arrangements allowed large landowners to secure a stable labor force. The capital for loans came through merchants who got their capital from the North. As long as the farmer produced cotton, there was money available to grow it.

The international market after the Civil War was very good for American cotton (Hammond 1897:120 – 141; Watkins, 1908:18 – 20). The Civil War disrupted the major source of cotton for England, and although some cotton was grown in India, Egypt, and Turkey, American cotton was more suitable for making thread (Hammond, 1898:346). There was a pent-up demand for cotton in the United States and abroad, and so it was in the economic interests of the northern mill owners and merchants as well as the southern planters to begin growing cotton immediately.

At the political level, the post-Civil War struggle can be characterized as an attempt to settle the issue of the role of blacks and their status in the South. The results of this struggle went through two phases. The first occurred from 1865 to 1877. As most historians have argued, the end of Reconstruction brought back into power the planters, the newly rich merchants, and a nascent capitalist class (Arnett, 1922:23 – 25; Going, 1951:27 – 40; Hicks, 1931:51 – 53; Stampp, 1966:186 – 205; Weiner, 1976; Williamson, 1965; Woodward, 1974:51 – 74). The second phase of this struggle was more complex. While the crop lien system brought about the revitalization of cotton production, it brought into the forefront a new kind of struggle. At the economic level, small yeoman farmers and tenant farmers were in conflict with the merchants and large planters. The crop lien system led to impoverishment of many farmers. For these farmers, the central issue was cheap money for loans. Their indebtedness to the merchants (or planters, if they were tenants) only seemed to worsen as the price of cotton fluctuated in the period 1873 – 1890. The decade of the 1880s saw the rise of radical farmers' movements.

When this struggle reached the political level, the planter/merchant class clearly felt threatened (Hicks, 1931:153 – 181; Woodward, 1974:235 – 263). In fact, a number of elections that would have put Populist elements into power in state governments were rigged by the dominant class (Arnett, 1922:153 – 155; Woodward, 1974:257 – 263). The role of the blacks in the Populist movement was severely limited. At an early point, blacks joined the Colored Farmers' Alliance which was the black man's adjunct to the Farmers' Alliance, the largest of the southern farmers' organizations. Blacks were not allowed in that organization because racism ran deep among white yeoman and tenant farmers (Hicks, 1931:96 – 98; Saloutos, 1960). As time went on, it was clear that many blacks were in the camp of the conservative Democrats (the planter/merchant/capitalist fraction of the Democratic party). This was because many blacks were sharecroppers working for white planters. The planters controlled votes through black self-interest, fraud, threats, and sometimes bribery (Going, 1951:32 – 40; Hicks, 1931:231 – 234; Woodward, 1966). In the end, the Populist party was defeated at the polls.

The southern Democrats had two political strategies that worked to secure their position against possible future resurgence of anti-southern Democratic and third party activity—disenfranchisement and fusion. In 1896, the Populist party and the Democratic party fused with the nomination of William Jennings Bryan for president. The effect of this fusion was the destruction of the Populist party as the Democratic party took certain key Populist demands (such as silver-based currency) and made them part of the party's platform.

The disenfranchisement of blacks was a complex phenomenon that reflected the racism sweeping the South in the 1890s as well as the self-conscious action of southern Democrats to preserve the status quo in the political and economic systems. Southern Democrats were interested in preventing an alliance between blacks and poor whites. To do this, the southern Democrats relatively self-consciously brought about the disenfranchisement of the blacks and poor whites across the South (Kousser, 1974:238 – 265). This had the effect of destroying the potential political clout of both blacks and poor whites. The issue of race was the ideological tool used to achieve this domination. Poor whites were removed as a political force and blacks were made permanent, powerless scapegoats as racism became part of state policy with the advent of Jim Crow laws. After this point, the difficulties of the poorer classes in the face of a cyclical economy no longer threatened to become a political issue. Capitalist growth and planter/merchant domination were insured and insulated from possible hostile political actions. Tenant farming, sharecropping, and the crop lien laws were firmly in place. Racism developed its most insidious forms—separate restaurants, hotels, and places in theaters and schools as well as frequent lynchings and public beatings of black men and women.

This system of southern agriculture began its slow decay in the twentieth century. The creation of one-party politics along with the rise of anti-black feelings left intact an agricultural system that was increasingly oppressive and unprofitable for more and more people. There was a continued increase in the number of tenant farmers (especially among whites), a general insolvency of most farmers, and competition in a world market that caused the price of cotton to stay relatively low. The migrations of the twentieth century must be viewed from this vantage point.

Since the turn of the century, many writers have suggested that the South needed to diversify its crop system and create a large class of yeoman farmers in order to destroy the tenant system (Fulmer, 1950; Johnson et al., 1935; Vance, 1935, 1945; Watkins, 1908), but there was no impetus for this kind of reform for two reasons. First, cotton was a cash crop and loans could be secured for its cultivation. For tenant farmers, there was no choice. If they were to survive, they needed to grow cotton. For plantation owners and merchants, the cash crop was essential to maintain profits and cash flow. The entire credit system and much of the farm land were tied up in cotton, and without it southern agriculture would have crumbled. Second, when the price of cotton was high, profit could be made. DeCanio (1974) has shown that cotton farming was profitable intermittantly through the period 1890–1920, despite a major depression in the 1890s. All in all, the entire southern agricultural system was tied to the production of cotton and the credit system that supported it. Furthermore, the political system buttressed the agricultural system with one-party politics and discriminatory policies. Only the collapse of the credit system in the early 1930s brought change to the South.

It is useful to consider the relative social and economic positions of blacks and whites in the South in 1900. There were basically two classes in the rural South—those who owned land and those who did not. Most of those who owned land farmed anywhere from 20 to 200 acres. The bulk of the farmers who owned land held relatively small amounts of acreage and have been called yeoman farmers. Plantation owners who had large holdings were a small proportion of all land owners. Those farmers who did not own land were cash or share tenants, sharecroppers, or wage laborers. These various statuses reflected different rental arrangements or forms of wage payment and a differential amount of supervision. In

1865, most white farmers were not involved in cash crop production. By 1900, many white yeoman farmers were growing cotton and a fair proportion of whites were tenants. At the end of the Civil War, on the other hand, most blacks were, at best, wage hands. In 1900, about 60% of the white farmers were owners and 40% tenants, while 80% of the black farmers were tenants and only 20% were owners. Blacks were also more likely to be sharecroppers than whites. This implies that at the turn of the century a majority of whites were farm owners and, therefore, were in control of their labor power. For blacks, just the opposite was true. Blacks, by virtue of race and class, were most susceptible to the vagaries of the cotton economy.

It should be noted that by 1930, the majority of white farmers were tenants. This suggests that whites were also vulnerable to the ups and downs of the cotton economy. But the fact that many whites still tended to have more money and be land owners suggests that the general socio-economic condition of whites was better than that of blacks. These differential economic positions will be important in considering what caused black and white migration.

The Causes of Migration: An Introduction

To assess the causes of black and white migration empirically, one needs two devices: (a) a model that incorporates in it the various theoretical and historical factors that affected migration; and (b) a way to operationalize such a model in order to bring data to bear on the causal assertions implicit in the model. It is obvious that each of these devices will have real effects on the other. For the moment, we should accept the fact that such a model can be generated from an understanding of the social formation of the South in 1900 and from the subsequent events that have altered that formation. The operationalization of the model is more difficult. In this study, counties are used as the units of analysis and the dependent variable is the net migration rate of blacks and whites at the county level. The basic analytical strategy is an attempt to explain variations in net migration rates of blacks and whites from counties of the South as a function of the various factors that have been proposed as causes of the migrations. Appropriate measurement of these factors takes place at the county level. The critical theoretical question of this study can be restated in a more empirical fashion: "What caused the black and white net migration rates from counties of the South from 1900 to 1950?" In the statistical analysis that follows, each decade is treated separately and a final piece of analysis treats the entire period. The statistical technique used to analyze the data is a version of weighted least squares regression. This technique and the logic of the analysis will be explained in greater detail in other chapters. The results discussed here are based on models taking the form just described.

1900—1930

The decade 1900—1910 was the final decade of the westward expansion of cotton production in the South. Migration in the South was in response to new opportunities for cotton cultivation in Arkansas, Mississippi, Texas, Louisiana, and Oklahoma. The decade also offered substantial growth in southern industrialization and urbanization. The boll weevil infestation began in this decade and started the eastern movement that took it across the South by 1922. During the period, blacks left highly tenantized counties to become tenants elsewhere. Blacks continued their westward movement as cotton production expanded over the decade into new fields in the western half of the South. Blacks also left rural counties for opportunities in the towns and cities of the South and they were particularly attracted to counties with large cities or counties next to large cities. Blacks were quite affected by the boll weevil infestation, for they were forced to migrate from counties infested in this era. Differential black repression was not a cause of black migration from 1900 to 1910.

The white net migration rate was caused by slightly different factors. Whites were attracted to counties with high and increasing levels of tenantry as well as counties that were experiencing expansion of cotton production. This reflects the continued influx of whites into tenant farming and cotton farming. Whites, unlike blacks, were also migrating to counties where white land ownership was increasing. This reflected the differential class composition of blacks and whites. Whites also were attracted to the cities and towns of the South and, like blacks, were especially attracted to the large cities. On the whole, whites were not displaced by the boll weevil infestation. This was probably the result of the fact that the majority of the white population were farm owners, and the boll weevil did not force them off the land, it only forced them to produce other crops.

The decade 1910—1920 marked the first decade in which new cotton lands were not being planted in the South. By approximately 1915, cotton was being grown in about as many places as it could be grown. Furthermore, the boll weevil infestation had swept across the South, causing much hardship. Meanwhile, World War I produced many opportunities in the cities and towns of the North and South. Blacks, because they were mostly tenants, were severely affected by the lack of new opportunities in cotton production. Many blacks were migrating, and the war was producing opportunities for them in the cities and manufacturing industries of the South and North. Many whites continued to become tenants and owners, while others were drawn to the cities and towns. With cotton at a high price from 1915 on, those blacks and whites who could grow cotton were doing fairly well. Those who could not (because of the boll weevil infestation) were being forced off the land.

The decade 1920 – 1930 produced a severe agricultural depression owing to an overproduction of cotton in America and around the world. The effects of this overproduction worsened because the crop lien system forced many farmers to produce more cotton in order to pay off debts. By the end of the decade, many farm owners lost their land because they were unable to get out of debt. For whites, losing farms and being forced to become tenants were the greatest forces affecting out-migration. For blacks, high levels of tenancy and loss of farm ownership meant worsening conditions and, thus, out-migration. Both blacks and whites were attracted to opportunities in the cities and towns of the South and North.

1930 – 1950

When the decade of the 1920s ended, the southern agricultural system was in trouble. The early 1930s witnessed a precipitous decline in the price of cotton and an intensification of the crisis. By 1932, most farmers, including plantation owners, were nearly bankrupt. In 1933, the federal government intervened in the production of cotton by using subsidy payments to curtail cotton acreage and to raise prices. This solution was enacted with the approval and support of farm organizations representing the interests of farm owners and commercial farmers.

The implementation of acreage reductions, subsidy payments, and the control of the price of cotton all worked to the advantage of the farm owner and commercial producer. Tenants, both black and white, were forced off the land as cotton acreage was curtailed and as farm machinery was brought in to further intensify production on land still planted in cotton. Displaced tenants had two choices: They could stay nearby and become part-time wage hands or migrate. The impetus for the transformation of southern agriculture was relatively self-conscious political action taken by the large farm owners.

The analysis done on the decades 1930 – 1940 and 1940 – 1950 provides evidence that the out-migrations of blacks and whites during these decades were caused to a large degree by acreage reductions and agricultural subsidies. The introduction of tractors did not force black and white tenants off the land. What did force them out was acreage reductions in cotton and the presence of agricultural subsidies that allowed the mechanization to proceed. Because the 1930s was an era of depression, cities and towns offered few opportunities to blacks and whites displaced from the land. The 1940s and World War II changed that, as both blacks and whites streamed into the towns and cities of the North and South to escape the decay and decline of the rural areas. A number of whites who could get capital became farm owners who produced for local markets. Many blacks left the rural areas altogether and began to seek opportunities in the towns and cities.

One final piece of analysis is performed that attempts to assess the impact of the level and change in level of income per capita in the north-eastern United States on the net migration rate of blacks and whites from counties of the South from 1900 to 1950. The result of this analysis is that the pull of the North had a small but significant effect on black and white net migration rates. This effect was nowhere as large as the effects related to the expansion and contraction of tenantry, ownership, cotton acreage, and urbanization, as well as the level of agricultural subsidy payments. This suggests that migration is most sensitive to the conditions that exist where the potential migrant originates. The pull of opportunities in the North was a result of the decline and transformation of southern cotton agriculture. Migrations from counties of the South were timed and conditioned by an agricultural system that drifted in and out of crisis and was finally transformed by the intervention of the federal government.

The results of this study suggest three major conclusions. First, in general, the net migration rates of blacks and whites from counties of the South were determined by the dynamics of cotton agriculture, the differential class position of blacks and whites, and the urbanization and industrialization of the South and, to a lesser degree, the North. Second, the transformation of southern agriculture from a system dependent on tenant farming and crop liens to a large-scale mechanized capitalist agriculture was the result of political activity on the part of organized farm owners and the federal government. Blacks and whites who were tenants were forced off the land, for the most part, by cotton acreage reductions and subsidy payments. These payments allowed large producers to increase their incomes, buy machines, and further displace tenants. The migrations of blacks and whites from 1930 to 1950 were to a large degree caused by this transformation.

Finally, it is not strictly the pull of the North that caused blacks and whites to leave the South. Most blacks in the South in 1930 were living in rural areas and were tenant farmers. Cotton acreage reductions hit the black population the hardest. Because of a lack of opportunities, many left for the cities and towns of the South and North. Those who stayed made their living mainly by picking cotton. With the advent of mechanical cotton pickers in the early 1950s, those blacks remaining in rural areas lost their most important means of support. The cities and towns of the South had some opportunities for blacks, but, for the most part, discrimination and segregation were rampant. The decision to move North represented a kind of last option. The proximate conditions of the South offered the black man few opportunities. The pull of the North was only operative given the bleakness of life for blacks in the South. For whites who were tenants, there were other options. Some became farm owners and produced dairy products, produce, and meat for local markets. Others took jobs in the cities and towns of the South that were growing and had opportunities. Still, many moved North (and West) to find better opportunities. In summation, black and white migrations were most responsive to the existing conditions at the migrant's place of origin, and the pull of a better life somewhere else was only operative when no other options existed.

The migrations from the South can be characterized as forced migrations. Because the large-scale producers in the South were able to secure their own positions and profits, blacks and whites had to leave. The modernization of agriculture caused the rural population to drift to the cities. The rural population then became an urban surplus population who were chronically unemployed and were placed in low-paying jobs.

Structure of the Study

It has been asserted that an historical, social account stressing the social relations of agriculture and their dynamics, is needed in order to produce an account of the migration of blacks and whites from the South. The rest of this book is oriented toward convincing the reader that the summary discussion in this chapter is valid. Chapter 2 presents the history of the social formation from 1865 to 1900. It is an attempt to give the reader a sense of how things developed in the South from 1865 to 1900 and what the results of these developments were for the South circa 1900. Chapter 3 presents ways in which other writers have viewed migration and its causes and how migration and its causes are conceptualized in this study. The general analytic strategy of this project is presented, as is the precise measurement of net migration utilized here. Chapter 4 is a descriptive chapter describing the net migration of blacks and whites from counties of the South from 1900 to 1950. It also presents relevant data on the changes in farm ownership and tenantry for blacks and whites, cotton acreage, and cotton production, as well as the increase in the use of tractors. These patterns provide the backdrop for the historical discussions that follow.

Chapters 5 — 9 are the heart of the study. Chapter 5 presents a relevant history from 1900 to 1930 as it impinged on southern agriculture. It also contains relevant hypotheses as to when and why black and white migrations occurred. Chapter 6 is a decade-by-decade consideration of the causes of net migrations of blacks and whites from 1900 to 1930. Chapter 7 presents the history of the transformation of southern agriculture from 1930 to 1950, and it also suggests relevant hypotheses concerning the causes of black and white migration. Chapter 8 is a decade-by-decade analysis of the causes of the net migration of blacks and whites from 1930 to 1950. Chapter 9 is an analysis that attempts to assess the effects of the level and changes in level of per capita income in the northeastern United States and the effects of cotton prices on the net migration rates of blacks and whites from counties of the South from 1900 to 1950.

Chapter 10 offers conclusions and reflections on the migrations of blacks and whites. Five technical appendices follow Chapter 10. These contain data sources, sample selection, data coding, migration measurement, and an explanation of the weighted least squares technique utilized in this study.

Chapter 2

Agriculture in the South, 1865 – 1900

The high price of cotton [after the Civil War] thus aided in establishing that credit system which has been the main feature of southern agriculture since the war, as slavery was previous thereto and which has been the chief cause retarding the economic development of the cotton states and the betterment of their agriculture. Had the price of cotton been low in 1865 – 6, the revival of the farming industry of the South would doubtless have been less rapid, but it would probably have taken a different direction, leading to the production of larger food crops, and a more moderate increase in the production of cotton, and would thus have prevented many farmers from falling into that state of peonage to factors and merchants in which the majority of the cotton growers are today to be found.

—MATHEW HAMMOND
The Cotton Industry (1897:122)

The key to understanding the migration of blacks and whites from the South in this century lies in the events that occurred from 1865 to 1900. During this period, the dynamics of southern agriculture and the basic social relations of production and exchange were shaped. The purpose of this chapter is to trace how these relations developed, to gain an understanding of the opportunity structure people faced in the South in 1900, and to comprehend the dynamics underlying this structure.

Given the theoretical perspective outlined in the first chapter, there are three interrelated sets of social relations to consider: (a) the organization of southern agriculture; (b) the relation between the South and the North at the economic, political, and ideological levels; and (c) the relation between southern cotton agriculture and the world market. The basic theme is that the development of southern agriculture following the Civil War must be viewed as the result of the political victory of the North over the South. The domination of the South was first sealed at the political level, and it was only over the course of the following 50 years that the North came to dominate the South economically.

The problems of the South must be viewed in the context of the various conflicts in the United States and their conjunctural solutions. The northern industrialists defeated the southern planters in the Civil War. The struggle over the federal government was won by the industrial, banking, and merchantile interests of the North. The federal government then forced the South to undergo economic reorganization by not allowing the planters to reenslave the blacks. The South formally capitulated to the North's domination with the Compromise of 1877. In exchange for local political autonomy in the South, the planter/merchant class in the South and the rejuvenated Democratic party accepted northern economic domination. This domination, in accord with the dynamics of the "New South" agricultural system, eventually brought about severe hardship for the bulk of the population. The small farm owners of the South organized and attempted to overcome both northern economic domination and southern planter/merchant political domination. The resolution of these struggles brought about a final victory for the planter/merchant class. This resulted in the ascendance of racism as state policy and the disenfranchisement of poor blacks and poor whites. The state governments throughout the South insulated themselves from the vagaries of the cotton economy, and the South remained an underdeveloped country in the early part of the twentieth century.

It is not the concern here to add detail to the historical record. Instead, the purpose is to attempt to synthesize events and give a coherent sociological account of them. Toward this end, the focus is on (a) the crisis in southern agriculture following the Civil War; (b) the rise of crop liens, tenant farming, and merchants; (c) the class structure of the rural South; (d) the role of the world market and northern control over the South; (e) the dynamics of southern agriculture; (f) the political events in the social formation during two periods (1865 – 1877 and 1878 – 1900); and (g) the South in 1900.

The Crisis of Southern Agriculture following the Civil War

The end of the Civil War left the South destroyed, disorganized, and destitute. Since the South had been primarily agricultural before the war, the impetus was to restore crop production as rapidly as possible. The high price of cotton after the Civil War made this restoration all the more attractive (Brooks, 1914:19; Hammond, 1897:122). In 1865, the average price for cotton on the New York Exchange was over 83¢ per pound (Watkins, 1908:30). Before the Civil War, the price of cotton fluctuated from 9.5¢ per pound in 1852 to 13.5¢ per pound in 1857, and it did not drop this low again until 1876. Production of cotton was profitable for those who could grow it.

The problems facing potential planter/farmers were twofold. First, there was very little money available to plant crops and pay laborers.

Second, blacks, who were the major part of the labor force, were enjoying their new freedom, and getting them to submit to the work gang system was nearly impossible (Coulter, 1947:92 – 112; Hammond, 1897:120 – 126; Ransom and Sutch, 1977:44 – 47; Stampp, 1966:120 – 126).

The problem of securing capital in the South was quite severe. Most banks went bankrupt following the war because the securities they held were, on the whole, worthless (Coulter, 1947:4 – 5). Farmers had little to offer as collateral for loans. Land prices after the Civil War plummeted, and plantations that sold for $100,000 to $150,000 before the war sold for $5000 to $10,000 after the war (Hammond, 1925:427; Nevins, 1927:22 – 24). Before the war, planters used men (called "factors") in the cities to market their crops and supply them with goods (Gray, 1957:409 – 433; Hammond, 1897:108 – 112; Woodman, 1968:8 – 42). The factor was a banker, merchant, and commodity seller. To get loans to plant the crop and sustain the plantation, the planter committed his crop to a certain factor. He would use his slaves, land, and the growing cotton as collateral for the loan. After the war, the planter no longer had slaves, and the land was almost worthless. The only valuable possession the planter had was the growing cotton.

The problem of securing a stable labor force was also vital. Before the Civil War, plantation owners had a guaranteed labor force. Through close supervision, frequent threats, and physical abuse, slaves were made to work in the cotton fields. Slaveholders constituted only 18% of the farmers in 1860 (Gray, 1957:529). Twenty-five percent of the slaves were owned by farmers who had less than 10 slaves, 50% were controlled by farmers with holdings of 10 to 25 slaves, and the remaining 25% were owned by farmers with holdings of 50 slaves or more (Gray, 1957:530 – 531). These slaves, and the plantations they worked, produced the bulk of the cash crops in the South (Gray, 1957:706 – 710). Freeing the slaves destroyed the social relations governing the production of cash crops in the South. The rights of newly freed blacks and the reorganization of southern society were complexly linked. Day-to-day relations between blacks and whites needed to be redefined, just as relations between landholders and freedmen needed to be clarified.

C. Vann Woodward (1966:44 – 64) argues that there were four main philosophies of race relations put forward during the period 1865 – 1895. The first was extreme racism, which demanded total segregation, disenfranchisement, and ostracism of the black population in the South. This view, of course, eventually won out. Another approach was the conservative philosophy. Those who held this position believed that blacks were inferior to whites, but they did not advocate the ostracism or humiliation of the black population. This point of view held an implicit paternalism and suggested that whites needed to help and to control blacks since they were incapable of doing so themselves. This conservative philosophy was tried out over a considerable period of time (Woodward, 1966:45). A third approach, that of the southern Populists, was a radical egalitarianism based on the notion that poor whites and blacks were in the same economic position. The rights of small landowning or of renting white farmers were related to the rights of blacks. As a Texas Populist put it, "They are in the same ditch as we are" (Woodward, 1966:61). The fourth philosophy was a liberal philosophy which had proponents but was never a serious rival of the other three positions (Woodward, 1966:47). It called on the government to treat all citizens equally and give protection to all citizens. Furthermore, it was explicitly against discrimination and objected to segregation, paternalism, and other forms of degradation. The advocates of this philosophy never really had a following until the twentieth century.

At the end of the Civil War, the governments of the South were in the hands of the northern military. The period witnessed a fair amount of disorder, and at the center of the disorder was the black man (Woolfolk, 1957; Coulter, 1947:92 – 112; DuBois, 1964; Reid, 1965:42 – 56). It is clear that blacks took advantage of their new freedom as they left the plantations, congregated in the small towns of the South, or migrated to the Southwest and the border states (Woolfolk, 1957:94 – 95). Those who stayed behind were not inclined to resume working for their former masters. "Basically the Negro did not like to take orders; that reminded him of slavery [Coulter, 1947:92]."

Crop Liens, Tenant Farming, and the Rise of the Merchants

The high price of cotton following the Civil War stimulated a resurrection of the plantation system. While capital was forthcoming, the stability of the labor force never materialized. This section attempts to describe how the plantation system was transformed into the sharecropping and tenant farming system and how crop liens and the emerging merchant class played a role in this transformation.

The capital for postwar expansion of southern cotton crops came from cotton factors. These factors received money from people in the cotton trade in New York and in Europe. In order to lend money, factors needed collateral or some guarantee of payment. This guarantee came in the form of a crop lien which had its origin in antebellum times. The first postwar crop lien laws were passed in 1867 (Banks, 1905:46 – 47; Brooks, 1914:32 – 36; Coulter, 1947:211 – 233; Hammond, 1897:154 – 160; Woodman, 1968:255 – 268; Woodward, 1974:179 – 184), and their major function was to allow planters to get credit. These laws allowed farm owners to mortgage their growing crops and give the first claim on harvested crops to the factors or others who advanced supplies.

By 1868, however, the plantation system was failing. Blacks did not want to be treated as slaves and participate in gang labor. Attempts to legislate gang labor (i.e., the black codes) had failed because the right of blacks to move freely was protected by the federal government. The wages and forced labor of the plantation system could not compete with the option of moving West or of taking up residence on farms where land was rented or operated under a share system. With bad crop years and the price of cotton falling, more and more planters found they could not pay off their crop liens. The system of factors and planters declined, and a new farming system arose to take its place (Ransom and Sutch, 1977:56 – 80).

Concurrent with the decline of the old plantation system was the increase in the number of farms in the South. Large plantations that were sold off were often bought in small pieces by white and black farmers, but most of these new farmers were white. Before the war, only 17% of those engaged in cotton farming were whites; by 1876, 40% were white. Whites were lured into cotton farming because they believed it was profitable. The idea that the laborer should have a share of the crop was being experimented with in South Carolina as early as 1866 (Hammond, 1897:132). By 1868, an almost wholesale abandonment of the wage system had taken place in Georgia (Brooks, 1914:47) and sharecropping or some other form of tenant arrangement was the rule. The revolution that took place from 1868 to 1874 was mainly a revolution in terms of the organization of labor and the securing of capital. For blacks, the key issue was control over their own labor process (Banks, 1905:78 – 79; Brooks, 1914:48 – 50; Wharton, 1947:58 – 60; Williamson, 1965:64 – 95). Throughout the Old South, blacks were holding the upper hand. They tended to work when they wanted to, migrate when they wanted to, and gravitate to the farm situation that offered them the most freedom. The planter had no labor alternatives, although a number of schemes were tried in the hope of attracting immigrants to work in the cotton fields (Coulter, 1947:102 – 105; Hammond, 1897:96 – 97; Shugg, 1939:244 – 249; Woodward, 1974:297 – 299). Therefore, the planter could either rent the land, sell it, or leave it fallow, and though all three options were utilized, tenant arrangements won out.

The growth in the number of tenants and small farm owners brought the need for more credit (Hammond, 1897:144 – 145). This credit did not come from factors because it was unprofitable for them to seek the business of small farm owners and tenants whom they could not supervise or judge the ability of (Woodman, 1968:282 – 284). Massive changes in transportation and communication were occurring which also undercut the position of the factor. Railroads were built through the entire South, and the need to move cotton to large cities from where it would then be shipped to factories was unnecessary (Woodman, 1968:270 – 271). The major effect of the railroads was to open up cotton marketing and make much of the trade move inland. Using the telegraph, farmers in small towns could find out the price of cotton and sell their crops at the closest railroad junction. This saved them the expense of selling to a middleman and thus increased their profits. By 1880, direct shipping and interior buying had almost replaced the factorage system. Every stop on the railroad became a market where the grower could sell his crop (Ransom and Sutch, 1977:126 – 148; Woodman, 1968:274).

The changes in crop marketing and the need of small farm owners and tenant farmers for credit and supplies brought about the rise of the small town merchant. The small-town merchant knew the people he was dealing with and was able to keep track of their crop and supply needs. The rise of the merchant is linked to the development of tenant farming, the rise of new small farms, and the changing uses of the crop lien. The crop lien was originally used only to mediate the relationship between the factor and the planter. As time went on, the planter found that it was easier and cheaper to take a crop lien from a local merchant. Supplies from a local merchant were close at hand, and directly marketing the crop was certainly more profitable for the planter (Woodman, 1968:295 – 314).

The Class Structure of the South

It is of some value to present the workings of the class structure of the rural South. This structure and its dynamics were set in place by 1877, and they persisted until the transformation of southern agriculture in the early 1930s. This section describes the class structure of the South and gives an overview of what each class position entailed. Census data showing gross changes in this class structure between 1860 and 1900 will then be presented. There are many descriptions of the southern agricultural system, and this discussion draws heavily on these sources: Arnett (1922); Banks (1905); Boeger and Goldenweiser (1916); Brooks (1914); DeCanio (1974); Goldenweiser and Truesdell (1924); Hammond (1897); Hicks (1931); Raper (1936); Saloutos (1960); Schwartz (1976); Shugg (1939); Vance (1935, 1945); Woodman (1968); Woodward (1974); Woofter (1936, 1969).

Figure 2.1 presents a diagram of the social relations underlying southern agriculture. The basic class distinction in the South revolved around the ownership of land. Those who owned land were in control of their labor power and source of livelihood. There were two categories of landholders—small farm owners and plantation owners. Small farm owners have been separated from plantation owners since they really occupied different social positions. The small farm owner, who owned 20—200 acres, worked the land with his family and possibly one or two wage hands, tended to be white and, before the Civil War, was mainly a subsistence farmer. After the Civil War, high cotton prices and crop liens from merchants convinced many small farm owners to produce cotton.

Large plantations were operated in one of four ways. In one, the owner lived on the plantation and worked part of the land with wage labor. The rest of the land either lay fallow or was operated by sharecroppers, share

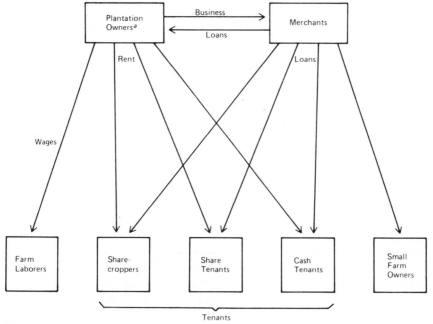

^a Types of plantation owners:
1. Operators
2. Absentee landlords
3. Corporation
4. Merchants

FIGURE 2.1. *Class relations underlying southern cotton agriculture. Arrows indicate direction and form of domination.*

tenants, or cash tenants. It was not unusual for plantations to have mixed arrangements or, for that matter, to have blacks and whites working on the same plantation (Woofter, 1936:10 – 11). The second type of operation was the absentee landlord situation. Here, the landowner moved to the city and rented the land either to share or cash tenants. His contact with the tenants was occasional, and tenants were left largely unsupervised. The third arrangement occurred as merchants began to own land. If a planter could not repay the merchant after a number of years, the merchant sometimes took control of the land. The merchant then rented the land out, and supplied those working the land with food, clothes, and goods while holding a crop lien on the growing crop. Because the merchant owned the land, he supervised the tenant fairly closely. The fourth situation involved corporate or bank ownership of land. If a planter was unable to pay a loan back, the bank took control of the land. The bank might then sell the land to a corporation which would rent out plots.

The nonowners of land formed a rough status ranking from lowest to highest, that was determined by the degree of close supervision or control that existed over the nonowners. The classifications were (from lowest rank to highest) farm laborers, sharecroppers, share tenants, and cash tenants.

The farm laborer is the simplest status to describe. These people were wage laborers and worked under the direct supervision of a farm owner. If the farm was big enough, laborers were organized into work gangs. Farm laborers were at the bottom of the social structure since they controlled neither the land nor their labor.

Sharecroppers were distinguished in a number of ways. They worked about 20 – 30 acres of land, and the landlord usually supplied the sharecroppers with land, housing, fuel, tools, work stock, seed, one-half of the fertilizer, and feed for the work stock. The sharecropper supplied the labor and one-half of the fertilizer. At the end of the year, the crop was split; half went to the landlord and half went to the tenant (Woofter, 1936:10). Central to the sharecropper's situation was the amount of supervision imposed by the landlord. The landlord told the sharecropper what to plant and when to plant it (Brooks, 1914:66 – 68). The landlord controlled the fertilizer allotment, and often the sharecropper was almost in the position of the wage hand except for the fact that he worked a separate plot of land.

Share tenants, on the other hand, were closer to being true renters (Woofter, 1936:92). The landlord supplied the tenant with land, housing, fuel, and one-third or one-fourth of the fertilizer. The tenant supplied labor, work stock, feed for work stock, tools, seed, and the rest of the fertilizer. The landlord received one-fourth or one-third of the crop, while the tenant received the remainder. If the share tenant raised cotton and corn, as was often the case, the landlord received a third of the cotton and a fourth of the corn. The share tenant was a renter, and therefore the landlord did not have the right to supervise his daily activity.

Cash tenants had an arrangement with the landlord similar to that of the share tenant. Typically, the landlord furnished only the land, housing, and fuel while the tenant was responsible for labor, work stock, feed for work stock, tools, seed, and all of the fertilizer. The landlord received a fixed rent in cash or cotton lint, and the tenant took the remaining crop. This tenant status had the most independence, and because the tenant owned all crops produced above the rent, he was motivated to raise more crops.

The discussion now turns to the role of the local merchant in the rural class structure. The furnishing merchant in the South almost always sold goods to farmers on credit. The merchant kept track of transactions, and a credit limit was set by the crop lien (Clark, 1944, 1946; Woodman, 1968). That is, credit was determined by how much cotton was planted. The insidious circle that the farmer was caught in began here. Since cotton was the only commodity the farmer could sell, it was the only commodity he could take a loan on. Merchants got most of their supplies on loans using crop liens for collateral, so both farmers and merchants were caught in the need to produce cotton in order to make money. The crop lien became the institutional tool that allowed southern agriculture, in its cash crop form, to survive.

The major sources of profit for the merchants were the food and supplies they sold to the farmers at very high prices and the loans they gave at high interest rates (Clark, 1944, 1946; Ransom and Sutch, 1972; 641 – 669; Woodman, 1968). Since the merchant kept track of all transactions, the farmer rarely knew how much he was paying for any given commodity or how much interest was being charged. It was not uncommon for the farmer to come out and the end of the year with little money or even to find himself in debt.

The relations between the merchant, planter/landlord, and tenant were problematic. The issue was twofold. If the renter was allowed to give the crop lien to the merchant, the planter or landlord would not get first claim to the crops. This placed planters and merchants at odds with one another (Brooks, 1914:35 – 36; Hammond, 1897:193 – 195; Schwartz, 1976:57 – 63; Woodman, 1968:295 – 314). The other issue was who should supply the tenant with food, seed, and fertilizer. If the merchant did so, the planter lost control over the tenant and lost potential profit as well. These issues were resolved in one of three ways. Sometimes planters and merchants worked out an arrangement. For instance, the planter would tell the merchant how much credit the tenant could have and the planter was thereby able to control the indebtedness of the tenant (Brooks, 1914:34). More common, however, was domination by either the planter or merchant (Brooks, 1914:36; Hammond, 1897:195; Schwartz, 1976:57–63; Woodman, 1968:310–314; Woodward, 1974:180–184). Often, the planter became a merchant and supplied the tenants, thereby making a profit not only on the rental of the land but also on the tenant's subsistence. Similarly, where absentee landlords abounded, the merchant was the sole source of credit for tenant farmers.

Given this description of class relations underlying southern agriculture, it is useful to consider trends in the formation of classes from 1860 to 1900. The division of southern cropland into smaller units after the Civil War was a phenomenon upon which a number of writers have commented (Banks, 1905; Brooks, 1914; Saloutos, 1960; Shugg, 1939; Hammond, 1897; Woodward, 1974). This division was the result of two forces. First, some amount of redistribution of land was occurring. As the plantation system broke down and land values plummeted, smaller parcels of land became available for the use of the small farmer. The second force, of course, was the rise of the sharecropping and tenant systems. Table 2.1 contains the number of farms and their average sizes in the nine states under consideration here from 1860 to 1900. A quick glance reveals a large increase in the number of farms throughout the period and a decrease in the average farm size throughout the period. It should be noted that here *farm* refers to any piece of land larger than 3 acres that was worked by a farmer and his family. If a 1100-acre plantation had 30 sharecroppers, each working 30 acres, and the plantation owner was working the remainder of the land with wage hands, it would appear in the census as 31 farms with an average size of 35.5 acres. This table does not demonstrate that the concentration of land was decreasing over time; rather, it shows only that the subdivision of land was occurring very rapidly.

It is of interest to assess the extent to which this subdivision was due to tenantization and the extent to which it was due to new farm ownership. This question is difficult to answer since data on tenure status were collected only from 1880 forward. Table 2.2 shows the number (per state) of owner-operated and rented farms in 1880, 1890, and 1900. Table 2.3 presents calculations that attempt to reveal how much the increase in the number of farms was due to the growth of tenant arrangements. In 1860, there were almost no tenant farms in the South, and so the number of farms in 1860 is treated as coterminous with the number of farm owners. By 1880, all states had a sizable number of tenants. From 1860 to 1880, over 65% of the growth in the number of farms was attributable to

TABLE 2.1
The Number of Farms and Average Farm Size in Acres
in Selected Southern States, 1860–1900

State	1860	1870	1880	1890	1900
Alabama	55,128[a] (349)[b]	67,438 (272)	135,864 (139)	157,772 (126)	223,220 (93)
Arkansas	39,004 (591)	49,333 (301)	94,433 (128)	124,760 (119)	178,694 (93)
Georgia	62,003 (430)	69,964 (338)	138,626 (188)	171,071 (47)	224,691 (117)
Louisiana	17,328 (537)	28,444 (247)	48,292 (171)	69,294 (138)	115,969 (95)
Mississippi	42,840 (370)	67,985 (193)	101,772 (156)	144,318 (122)	220,803 (83)
North Carolina	75,203 (316)	93,565 (212)	157,609 (142)	178,359 (127)	224,637 (146)
South Carolina	33,171 (488)	52,383 (233)	93,864 (143)	115,008 (115)	155,355 (90)
Texas	42,891 (591)	61,125 (301)	174,184 (208)	228,126 (225)	352,190 (257)
Oklahoma	--	--	--	8,826 (182)	62,495 (368)

[a]Number of farms.

[b]Average farm size.

SOURCE: U.S. Census.

the growth in tenant farming. Between 1880 and 1890, and 1890 and 1900, tenant farming accounted for over 75% of the growth in the number of farms in each decade. In all states, the percentage of owners declined over the period 1860–1900. By 1890, tenants were the majority of farmers in South Carolina, Georgia, and Mississippi. By 1900, the majority of farmers in Alabama, Texas, and Louisiana were also tenants. Over the 40-year span the number of farms increased by 1,432,574, and 1,017,687 of these were operated by tenants. Therefore, over 71% of the new farms were the result of tenantization. This tenantization grew most rapidly in the old South, and by 1900, the majority of farmers in six of the eight states considered here were tenants. It can be concluded that even though some new land ownership occurred, by far the most important change in land tenure was due to the introduction of tenant farming. The increase

TABLE 2.2
*A Comparison of the Number of Farms Rented and Owned
by State for 1880, 1890, and 1900*

State	Owner operated			Number of renters		
	1900	1890	1880	1900	1890	1880
Alabama	94,346	81,141	72,215	128,874	76,631	63,649
Arkansas	97,554	84,706	65,245	81,140	40,054	29,188
Georgia	90,131	79,477	76,451	134,560	91,594	62,275
Louisiana	48,735	38,539	31,286	67,234	30,755	17,006
Mississippi	82,951	68,058	57,214	137,852	76,260	44,558
North Carolina	131,629	117,469	104,887	93,008	60,890	52,722
South Carolina	60,471	51,428	46,645	94,884	63,580	45,219
Texas	177,199	132,616	108,716	174,991	95,560	65,468
Oklahoma	30,750	8,761	--	31,745	65	--

SOURCE: U.S. Census, 1900.

in the number of tenants was the result of a startling development that can be termed, without overstatement, a revolution.

The relationship between cotton-growing and the growth in tenant farming will now be considered. Table 2.4 shows the crop production for the years prior to the census from 1860 to 1900 by state. Table 2.5 gives the rank order of states in terms of cotton production and proportion of farmers who were tenants. Of the top six producers in 1880, only one was not in the top six in tenantization. In 1890 and 1900, all of the top six in cotton production were in the top six in tenantization. The Pearson correlation coefficient between the rank orders is .64 in 1880, .78 in 1890, and .76 in 1900. This result suggests that cotton growing and the development of the tenant system were intimately related.

The next issue to be discussed is a consideration of the relative proportions of blacks and whites who were cotton producers and/or tenants and when they came to occupy those roles. In 1860, only one out of every six people who worked in the cotton fields was white (Hammond, 1897:130). But the high price of cotton and the end of the plantation system brought whites into the cotton fields. Table 2.6 attempts to piece together the rate at which whites entered into cotton production. In 1876, whites outnumbered blacks in cotton production only in Texas and Arkansas. However, a substantial number of whites had moved into the cotton fields in every state except Louisiana by this time. By 1900, whites had narrowed the gap between themselves and blacks and were producing cotton almost as frequently as blacks. In Texas, the largest cotton producing state by 1900, whites outnumbered blacks four-to-one.

As has been shown, most new farm operators were tenants. Furthermore, the number of tenant farmers was related to cotton production. It follows that if whites were entering cotton farming, they must have occupied the tenant status. Table 2.7 presents the number (by state) of white as compared to black farmers who held tenant status in 1900. Forty-four percent of the farmers were white owners, while 27% of the farmers were white tenants. This is compared with 6% of the farmers who were black owners and 23% of the farmers who were black tenants. A glance through the table reveals that blacks were much more likely to be tenants than whites. Seventy-eight percent of the blacks were tenants while 38% of the whites were tenants. The largest number of white tenants were in South Carolina, Georgia, Texas, and Oklahoma, while large concentrations of black tenants lived in South Carolina, Georgia, Alabama, Mississippi, and Louisiana.

The period 1860 – 1900 witnessed an incredible agricultural change as tenant farmers went from 0% of the farm population to nearly 60%. While there was a growth in the number of farm owners, most of the new farms (over 71%) were operated by tenants.

The Role of the World Market and the North

In the theoretical model proposed in Chapter 1, it was argued that the social relations of agriculture needed to be linked to those in the rest of the social formation and those in the world market. This section of the chapter is oriented toward these linkages. Figure 2.2 presents a summary of the relevant social relations. The discussion here presents the world market first and the role of the North second.

The South was the largest producer of cotton in the world before the Civil War (Hammond, 1897:291; Watkins, 1908). The British, who were the largest users of raw cotton, had tried numerous times to find other sources for their cotton supply prior to the war (Hammond, 1897:339), and during the war they turned to using Indian, Egyptian, and Brazilian cotton. After the Civil War, however, American cotton was again in demand. This was because Indian cotton, the largest source of imports for

TABLE 2.3

An Attempt to Assess the Change in Number of Farms and the Component of That Change due to the Increase in Farm Owners and Tenants in Southern States, 1860–1900

State	Total farms	% owners	% tenants	Change in farms	% change due to ownership	% change due to tenantship	Number of new owners
Alabama							
1860	55,128	100	0	--	--	--	--
1880	135,864	53	47	80,736	21	79	17,087
1890	157,772	51	49	21,908	41	59	8,926
1900	223,220	42	58	65,428	20	80	13,205
Arkansas							
1860	39,004	100	0	--	--	--	--
1880	94,433	69	31	55,429	47	53	26,241
1890	124,760	68	32	30,327	64	36	19,461
1900	178,694	54	46	53,934	23	77	12,848
Georgia							
1860	62,003	100	0	--	--	--	--
1880	138,626	55	45	76,623	19	81	14,448
1890	171,071	46	54	32,445	9	91	3,026
1900	224,691	40	60	53,620	19	81	10,654
Louisiana							
1860	17,328	100	0	--	--	--	--
1880	48,292	65	35	30,964	45	55	13,958
1890	69,294	56	44	21,002	35	65	7,253
1900	115,969	42	58	46,675	21	79	10,196
Mississippi							
1860	42,840	100	0	--	--	--	--
1880	101,772	56	44	58,932	24	76	14,374
1890	144,318	47	53	42,546	25	75	10,844
1900	220,803	37	63	76,485	18	18	14,433

North Carolina							
1860	75,203	100	0	--	--	--	--
1880	157,609	67	33	82,406	36	64	29,684
1890	178,359	66	34	20,750	61	39	12,582
1900	224,627	58	42	46,278	30	70	14,160
South Carolina							
1860	33,171	100	0	--	--	--	--
1880	93,864	50	50	60,693	22	78	13,474
1890	115,008	45	55	21,144	23	77	4,783
1900	155,355	38	62	40,347	22	78	9,043
Texas							
1860	42,891	100	0	--	--	--	--
1880	174,184	62	38	131,293	50	50	68,825
1890	228,126	58	42	178,006	13	87	23,900
1900	352,190	50	50	124,064	35	65	44,583

*Data Source: U.S. Bureau of the Census.

TABLE 2.4

Cotton Production by State in Bales (400 lb)
in Year Previous to Census

State	1859	1869	1879	1889	1899
Alabama	989,955	429,482	669,654	915,210	1,089,519
Arkansas	367,393	247,968	608,256	691,494	705,583
Georgia	701,738	473,934	814,441	1,191,846	1,231,060
Louisiana	777,738	350,832	508,569	659,180	700,352
Mississippi	1,202,507	564,938	963,111	1,154,725	1,237,666
North Carolina	145,514	144,935	389,598	336,261	440,400
South Carolina	353,412	224,500	522,548	747,190	837,105
Texas	431,463	350,628	805,284	1,471,242	2,609,018
Oklahoma	--	--	--	425	71,983

SOURCE: U.S. Bureau of the Census

TABLE 2.5

Rank Order of States by Amount of Cotton Produced
and Proportion of Tenants

State	1880		1890		1900	
	(1)[a]	(2)[b]	(1)	(2)	(1)	(2)
Mississippi	1	4	3	3	2	1
Georgia	2	3	2	2	3	3
Alabama	3	2	4	5	4	4
Texas	4	5	1	4	1	6
Arkansas	5	8	6	8	6	7
South Carolina	6	1	5	1	5	2
Louisiana	7	6	7	6	7	5
North Carolina	8	7	8	7	8	8
Oklahoma	9	9	9	9	9	9

[a] Rank order of amount of cotton produced.

[b] Rank order of proportion tenantized.

TABLE 2.6
Proportion of Blacks and Whites Cultivating Cotton, by State

State	1860[a]		1876[b]		1900[c]	
	Blacks	Whites	Blacks	Whites	Blacks	Whites
Alabama	83	17	59	41	43	57
Arkansas	83	17	40	60	--	--
Georgia	83	17	66	34	36	64
Louisiana	83	17	77	23	51	49
Mississippi	83	17	68	32	59	41
North Carolina	83	17	65	35	--	--
South Carolina	83	17	65	32	55	45
Texas	83	17	38	62	19	81

[a]SOURCE: Hammond, 1898.

[b]SOURCE: Commissioner of Agriculture, 1876.

[c]SOURCE: U.S. Bureau of the Census; states included were over 70 percent of
the farms cultivated cotton in 1889. Figure is based on assumption
that black and white farmers are cultivating crop equally.

the British, was short stapled, which made it more difficult to spin
(Hammond, 1897:326). The British immediately began buying long staple
American cotton when it became available.

The price of cotton after the Civil War was quite high, and as American
production geared up, the price dropped rapidly from about 83¢ per
pound in 1865 to roughly 24¢ per pound in 1870 (Watkins, 1908:30). During the decade of the 1870s, the price dropped to around 10¢ per pound.
While the price of cotton dropped, the number of countries using cotton
increased as did the amount of cotton they used. In 1860, Great Britain
took 55% of the American crop and by 1895 took only 33% of the American
crop (Hammond, 1897:340). This percentage decrease occurred while Britain increased its usage of American cotton from roughly 1.2 billion
pounds to 1.6 billion pounds (Hammond, 1897:Appendix 1). The European continent was absorbing increasing quantities of cotton, and the
decade of the 1880s witnessed some very large crop years with the price
of cotton hovering at around 10¢ per pound. The 1890s saw the price of
cotton plunge to a low of 6¢ per pound in 1899. World consumption of
cotton increased roughly 28% from 1880 to 1890, while world production
of cotton increased by about the same amount during this period. Pro-

TABLE 2.7
Owners and Tenants in Southern States by Race in 1900

	Whites		Blacks	
State	Owners	Tenants	Owners	Tenants
Alabama	79,362 (.61)[a] (.36)[c]	48,973 (.39) (.22)	14,110 (.15)[b] (.06)	79,901 (.85) (.36)
Arkansas	84,794 (.64) (.48)	46,178 (.36) (.26)	11,941 (.25) (.07)	34,962 (.75) (.29)
Georgia	77,154 (.54) (.35)	63,317 (.46) (.28)	11,375 (.13) (.05)	71,243 (.87) (.32)
Louisiana	38,323 (.67) (.33)	18,531 (.33) (.16)	9,378 (.16) (.09)	48,703 (.84) (.42)
Mississippi	61,048 (.66) (.28)	30,253 (.34) (.14)	20,973 (.16) (.10)	107,599 (.84) (.48)
North Carolina	113,052 (.64) (.46)	63,148 (.36) (.27)	21,443 (.32) (.09)	44,139 (.68) (.18)
South Carolina	40,447 (.58) (.26)	38,633 (.42) (.19)	18,970 (.22) (.12)	66,251 (.78) (.43)
Texas	154,500 (.54) (.44)	129,685 (.46) (.37)	30,139 (.30) (.06)	45,306 (.70) (.13)
Oklahoma	50,018 (.53) (.46)	44,265 (.47) (.41)	10,191 (.77) (.10)	2,985 (.23) (.03)

[a] Percentage of whites in each status.

[b] Percentage of blacks in each status.

[c] Percentage of total number of farmers in each status.

duction of cotton increased 12% in the period 1890 – 1895, while consumption did not increase at all (Hammond, 1897:337). By 1896, there were roughly 3.9 million bales of cotton unsold.

Much of the increased production of cotton from 1880 to 1895 occurred in the United States. In 1880, the United States produced 7.5 million bales of cotton, while the rest of the world produced 1.8 million

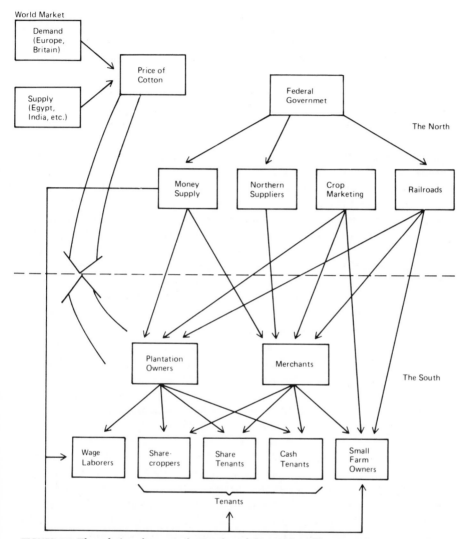

FIGURE 2.2. *The relations between the South and the North and between the South and the world market, circa 1880. Arrows show connections.*

bales. In 1895, the U.S. produced 10.1 million bales, and the rest of the world produced roughly 2 million bales. While the U.S. production increased roughly 30%, the rest of the world's production increased only 11%. Thus the drop in cotton prices affected American farmers the most.

While the world price of cotton was of immense importance to the fiscal well-being of the farmer, capitalist development in America impinged directly and indirectly on the farmer's life. This development reflected both political and economic processes. The ascendancy of the Republican party has been associated with the rise of northern business. The sense in which the party was the "party of business" was that it organized the interests of different fractions of the capitalist class and placed legislation favorable to those interests on the agenda. The success of this organization was reflected only later (i.e., from 1870 – 1890). With the proper, enabling legislation, and a South that was forced to accept its position in the newly emergent capitalist order, northern development proceeded rapidly. Spokesmen for the "New South" felt the future of the South was with northern business. Indeed, without the capital of the North, the New South's dream of an industrialized land could not emerge. As Woodward (1974) has argued, "With the aid of the New South propagandists, however, and by frequent resort to repressive or demagogic devices, the rightforkers contrived to keep the South fairly faithful to the Eastern alignment until the advent of the populists [p. 50]." The northern economic control over the South began *after* the political domination of the South was completed. With the reemergence of the southern Democratic party, an indigenous organized party existed in the South in the 1870s to promote peace with the North and to oversee the beginning of the capitalist control over the South at the economic level.

The discussion now turns to the ways in which the North and West came to dominate southern agriculture. Most of these were tied up in supplying the cotton farmer with food, supplies, seed, and fertilizer, and also in marketing the crop. The crop lien system encouraged farmers to plant as much cotton as possible. This was because the only way the farmer could make money for goods or get out of debt was to grow cotton. One major result of this system was that farmers did not grow their own food (Arnett, 1922:53 – 60; Banks, 1905:36 – 38; Hammond, 1897:151 – 160; Hicks, 1931:45 – 46; Vance, 1929:200 – 201; Woodman, 1968:308 – 314), which meant that food needed to be imported into the South. The major source of this food was the Midwest, which produced grain, beef, and pork. To buy food from the furnishing merchant, farmers needed a crop lien that was large enough to pay off debts and buy supplies and food for 8 months. The beneficiaries of this system were the midwestern farmers (who benefited the least), the railroad owners (who did the shipping at high rates), and the local merchants (who charged high interest rates and prices).

The merchant got his money on credit also. This credit was extended from two sources: the supplier of the goods and the cotton merchants in New York or Europe. Most of the goods were supplied by northerners, and they profited handsomely from their loans (Woolfolk, 1957; Woodman, 1968). The local merchant was interested in securing the largest crop lien available, since that gave him greater ability to get supplies as well as get a firmer grasp on farmers and on the possibility of making more profit. Cotton merchants extended credit because local merchants promised to market the crop with those who lent them the money. The entire crop lien system was integrated into the expanding northern business system.

There are two other elements that eventually helped the North to control the marketing of the cotton crop—railroad expansion and the consolidation of the cotton market. Stover (1955:37−38), in his monograph on southern railroads, argues that after the Civil War, southern railway expansion was controlled almost entirely by southerners and as late as 1875, southerners still controlled the southern railways. Northern capitalists were reluctant to invest large sums of money in the South due to the general lack of financial security there and to the presence of better investment opportunities in the rest of the United States (Stover, 1955:55). But the late 1870s and early 1880s brought an end to this. New railroad building and the consolidation of railroad lines brought northern capital into southern railroads. This trend was gradual, and by 1890, 43 of the 58 companies with more than 100 miles of track were dominated by northern interests. These railroads accounted for 88% of the total rail mileage (Stover, 1955:279). The depression of the 1890s brought about further mergers, and by 1900, northern-dominated firms controlled 96% of the total rail mileage (Stover, 1955:282). While this was occurring, the number of miles of track increased from 9167 after the Civil War to 29,263 in 1890 (Stover, 1955:5, 193). The transportation revolution that destroyed the factor system was related to this increase in railroads, and it is not surprising that the northerners who began to control the railway system directed cotton away from the southern ports and toward the Northeast.

The actual marketing of the cotton crop also underwent consolidation. With the decline of the factorage system and the rise of the local merchant, a new form of cotton-buying evolved. Cotton buyers had representatives all over the South; often they were local merchants or men who ran cotton gins. As time went on, cotton buying became concentrated in the hands of a few large American and European firms. By 1921, 24 firms handled 60% of the southern crops (Woodman, 1968:289). These firms tended to be located in New York City, although they had representatives all over the South. The postbellum era also saw the development of a cotton futures market. Merchandise purchased in one market often changed hands several times before delivery, and speculation was common (Woodman, 1968:289).

The issue of money supply affected the farmers and merchants throughout the South. The problem centered on the fact that there was a fixed quantity of money circulating in the economy. Indeed, from 1865 to 1895, the dollar appreciated almost 300% (Arnett, 1922:69). Meanwhile, the actual amount of money in circulation declined, and this meant that high interest rates abounded. Most farmers paid off their debts in crops and, as money appreciated and the price of crops decreased, farmers ended up paying even more to settle their debts.

The Dynamics of Southern Agriculture

The broad outline of southern class structure and its relation to the world market and the North is complete. The South, as a region, was like an underdeveloped country with the problems of (a) lack of capital; (b) industries mainly extractive in nature; and (c) development that was limited and controlled by outside forces (in this case, the North). To complete this picture, one only needs to see how these various social structures combined to produce the dynamics of southern agriculture.

Cotton producers were in the position of trying to maximize their profits. To do this, farmers planted as much cotton as they could and took crop liens in order to buy food for themselves and for their animals. If farmers grew their own food as well as feed for the animals, they had to cut down on available acreage for cotton. If a farmer was in debt, it was a perfectly rational response to plant as much cotton as possible in order to get out of debt or keep from starving.

When the price of cotton was high, many people made money under this credit system. However, as the price of cotton dropped, tenant and yeoman farmers often found themselves in debt. So the next year, the farmer would plant even more cotton in order to try to get ahead. As crop prices dropped, the farmers' position continued to deteriorate, and, naturally, the only response to their improverishment was to continue to plant cotton.

Tenant and yeoman farmers were in no position to escape this cycle. If tenants stopped growing cotton or started growing food, the landlord would force them off the land. In order to maximize their share of the crop, landlords made sure to keep cotton production high. If the landlord was furnishing his tenants, he did not want them to grow food because that would cut into his profits. It was in the interest of the landlord to keep the tenant growing cotton and only cotton. The yeoman farmer also found it difficult to stop growing cotton because the merchant he owed money to would only give him a crop lien to grow cotton. If yeoman farmers were in debt and the merchants saw them growing food, thus cutting down cotton production, the merchant could foreclose on the yeoman's land. After they were in debt, yeoman farmers could not afford to stop producing cotton. The price they had to pay was high—the land. So both tenants and yeoman farmers were caught in a dynamic where their only recourse was to grow cotton. Debt, the lien system, merchants and landlords, and the plummeting world price of cotton placed small farm owners and tenants in a position where they had to produce more cotton. That production caused prices to decrease further and their position became even more desperate. Many modern writers have chastised the southern farmer for his dependency on cotton (Goodrich, 1934; Vance, 1935; Woofter, 1969). Once the farmer went into debt, however, there were powerful forces preventing him from changing farming practices. The entire social structure of the South depended on this newly emergent system of agricultural production (Ransom and Sutch, 1972:641 — 669).

History in Periodization

The account presented so far has been relatively static. In order to get a sense of the development of class arrangements in the South and their consequences for persons laboring under them, it is necessary to consider the interplay between various real structures and their agents at different points in time. There are two periods of interest: 1865 — 1877 and 1878 — 1900. The first time period circumscribes the initial crises within the South and outside of the South following the Civil War. The resolution of these crises brought about an economic and political reemergence of planter domination. The crisis of the second period was a direct result of the reorganization of southern agriculture, and this period ended, again, with planter/merchant/capitalist domination.

1865 — 1877

Following the Civil War, the most pressing problem for the federal government was to decide how to bring the southern states back into the Union. The political struggle throughout the South was centered on blacks and their rights. In the classic accounts of Reconstruction, the era is associated with evil and is viewed as a time when power was abused for personal promotion (Bowers, 1929; Coulter, 1947; Dunning, 1907; Rhodes, 1902). Other historians have questioned this account (Arnett, 1922; DuBois, 1964; Shugg, 1939; Stampp, 1966; Wharton, 1947; Woodward, 1974). Here the argument follows Stampp's (1966) and Woodward's (1951, 1974) interpretation.

After the Civil War, President Andrew Johnson tried to reconstruct the

South according to his vision (Stampp, 1966:50 – 82). His major difficulty was that he had to deal with the elements of the Republican party who controlled Congress. Johnson was a Democrat who ran with Lincoln in 1864 in order to present a presidential ticket that was bipartisan and unequivocal in its support of the Civil War. He always remained a Democrat, which created a natural tension between him and a Republican Congress. The Republican version of Reconstruction differed from Johnson's, and ultimately they came into conflict.

Lincoln's plan for Reconstruction would have restored the southerners' rights very rapidly and would have promoted southern development. The radical Republicans, however, were determined not to lose the war through an easy peace that would allow southern rebel leaders to regain the positions of political and economic power that they had held before the war, and therefore Republicans were against such a reconstruction (Stampp, 1966:50 – 51). When Andrew Johnson became president, it appeared as though he would accept the radicals' terms, for he was a vociferous opponent of the planters, who controlled the political system of the South. In 1865, Johnson appeared interested in bringing prominent southerners to trial and even considered measures to redistribute the land of the planters (Stampp, 1966:60 – 70). He also had the apparent support of the radical Republicans in these endeavors (Stampp, 1966:52).

Radical Republicans wanted to make reentry into the Union difficult for the South. They wanted to check southern political influence and try to consolidate the Republican party in America. They supported the civil and political rights of blacks for reasons that were both political and idealistic (Woodward, 1974:43 – 44; Stampp, 1966:89 – 109). While they were very interested in maintaining political control, they were also concerned with the situation of the blacks. They felt that the only way to control the South was to destroy the planter class and its power.

Johnson's point of view was quite different. While he wanted to destroy the planter class, he did not want to replace southern society with an equalitarian society (Woodward, 1951:14; Stampp, 1966:51 – 82). Rather, he wanted to remove the southern gentry from power and replace them with white small farm owners each controlling the labor of a few blacks. While Johnson believed the planter class needed to be controlled, he did not see the elevation of blacks as the key issue. Instead, he felt that the defeat of the southern planters in the Civil War was complete and that the natural heirs to power were the white small farm owners who would come to control southern governments with his help.

In 1865, Johnson began the Reconstruction of the southern states. Conventions were held, elections followed, and governments were formed. Johnson decided to go ahead with his notion of Reconstruction without the support of Congress. All over the South old Confederate officers and officials were elected into positions of power. The basic attitude in the South was that although the South had lost the war, the "cause" was still valid (Coulter, 1947; Woodward, 1974; Stampp, 1966). Congressmen and senators were sent to Washington to convince Johnson that the South had suffered enough and that no further penance should be done (Stampp, 1966:68−70). Consequently, Johnson was swayed from attempting to destroy the planter class to attempting to secure its position. He decided against land redistribution in the South and, further, he spoke out against guaranteeing black rights with a constitutional amendment. He became committed to a return to black repression and did not oppose the black codes, which helped planters secure their labor forces (Stampp, 1966:80).

The radical Republicans in Congress were outraged by this, and the Republican party united for the sake of survival (Stampp, 1966:82−90; Woodward, 1951:16−17). The key to their survival lay in forcing the planters to surrender political power and in upholding the rights of blacks. The motives of the Republican party were complex. The core of their position was the place of the free black in American society. Racial equality was the central ideology involved, for it was thought that blacks should have equal protection under the law which meant all the political rights of other citizens, including the right to vote. The Johnsonians and classic historical schools of thought had never taken these arguments seriously since they believed that the motives of the radical Republicans were more political (Coulter, 1947). It was clear that the radical Republicans thought that the best basis on which to maintain political power was to organize blacks, but not all Republicans felt comfortable in an alliance with the blacks. More moderate members of the party dreamed of an alliance with the southern planters that would promote economic expansion and control black labor. In 1865, however, the Republicans were afraid of a southern and western political alliance that would subvert the Republican cause. As a result, they sought to prevent this by organizing southern governments that would be friendly to the Republican party. In part, their alliance with blacks was the result of their desire to maintain political power, but even more practically, the Republican party was the party of northern business (Stampp, 1966:95; Woodward, 1951:246). It was important to control Congress since aspects of the business environment (laws concerning development, tariffs, incorporation and money supply) could not be promoted in a Congress dominated by planters and farmers. Stampp argues that all of these motives were present in the actions of radical Republicans. Perhaps more importantly,

Stampp suggests that if the radical Republicans had not taken this position, the political, legal, and economic rights of blacks in the South would have been circumscribed (Stampp, 1966:82). If Andrew Johnson had had his way, the plantation system in its postbellum form would not have been in crisis.

The congressional election of 1866 produced a tremendous victory for the radical Republicans and a tremendous defeat for Johnson (Stampp, 1966:117). The major issues in the election were clear-cut. Johnson attempted to portray Republicans as supporters of blacks and used the banner of racism to denounce the programs of the Republicans. The Republicans countered with arguments that Johnson was going to let the South win the peace by letting it establish measures to control blacks and restore governments controlled by disloyal (Confederate) men. The Republican arguments prevailed, and in 1867 Congress shaped its own plan for southern reconstruction.

This program had three major parts: (a) it outlawed the black codes; (b) it passed constitutional amendments guaranteeing black rights; and (c) it established southern state governments that would accept federal rule and promote the rights of blacks. Consideration was given to breaking up southern plantations and to giving the land to blacks (Stampp, 1966:124–130; Coulter, 1947:66–69, 107–112). This program did not pass Congress because many Republicans who supported black political and legal rights did not understand the need to give the freedmen economic support. It would have violated the American principle that one's economic status must be determined by one's enterprise (Stampp, 1966:130). Redistribution of land would have been an attack on property and inconsistent with Republican morality (Coulter, 1947:112; Stampp, 1966:130).

While some Reconstruction governments were corrupt, they were no more corrupt than state and city governments in the rest of the country in the period 1865–1873 (Nevins, 1927:178–202). In fact, some of the Reconstruction governments were less corrupt than the Democratic party-controlled governments that followed them (Woodward, 1974:1–23). In Mississippi, for instance, it is clear that this was the case (Wharton, 1947). This was, however, the era of "Grantism," as the Democrats called it (Woodward, 1974:53). There were railroad scandals, cases of state officials embezzling large amounts of money, and the wholesale giving of public land to speculators and other persons in the private sector to exploit (Woodward, 1974:51–74; Coulter, 1947:126–142).

The major positive accomplishment of the Reconstruction governments was the guaranteeing of the rights of blacks (Stampp, 1966:184–185). The black codes were abolished and blacks were guaranteed freedom of movement. This political accomplishment forced the plantation system into a crisis because protection of black rights made it impossible for planters to coerce black labor into the fields. The racial policy of the Reconstruction governments, as well as the corruption of those governments, became the central ideological issue in the struggle over state power in the South.

The top half of Figure 2.3 summarizes the political relations in the South during Reconstruction. The Republican party, with the support of blacks, white northerners ("carpetbaggers"), and a few white southerners, controlled the state governments while the bulk of the white population was not politically involved.

The end of the radical Republican governments in the South was brought about by two major forces. First, the radical Republican leadership was declining as early as 1868. Power in the party was shifting from the idealistic, abolitionist elements to the more moderate elements which supported the status quo (Woodward, 1974, 1951; Stampp, 1966). The result of this shift was an increasing uneasiness with the union of "carpetbaggers" (northerners who went South to take advantage of the political and economic chaos), "scalawags" (white southerners who supported the Republican party), and blacks in the South. "The party of abolitionist radicalism had now become the party of vested interests and big business. Yet in the South, the party still appealed to the votes of a propertyless electorate of manumitted slaves with a platform of radical equalitarianism. The contradiction was obvious [Woodward, 1974:28]."

Second, the southern Democratic party was experiencing a resurgence. Its platform was essentially anti-black and anti-carpetbagger, and southern Democrats argued that the North was imposing racial equality and a corrupt government of outsiders on the South. Their racial philosophy was the conservative philosophy spoken of earlier. They did not want blacks to be a brutalized lower caste, and they exhibited a paternalistic attitude toward blacks, feeling that the inferior black man needed to be led by his superiors (Woodward, 1966:42 – 60). The resurgence of the southern Democratic party was also helped by another force—extreme racism in the South (Coulter, 1947:162 – 183; Woodward, 1966:85 – 86, 1974:55 – 57; Stampp, 1966:199 – 202). The Ku Klux Klan and its supporters were terrorizing black and white Republicans throughout the South (Horn, 1939; Tannenbaum, 1969). The group and its supporters called for total separation of the races and for total subjugation of the black man. Poor whites believed that the essential fact of life was skin color. "That I am poor is not as important as that I am a white man and no Negro is ever going to forget that he is not a white man" (quoted in Stampp, 1966:196). Throughout the South, acts of violence and force were

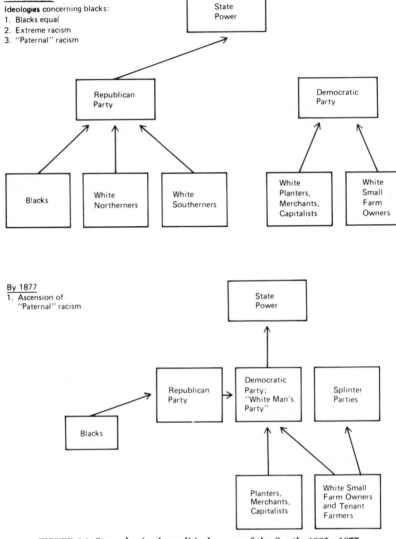

FIGURE 2.3. *Struggles in the political arena of the South, 1865–1877.*

perpetrated against blacks to prevent them from voting, organizing politically, and meeting in large groups.

As soon as southern governments were reconstructed, there was agitation throughout the South to end radical Republican rule. The political force in the South that organized to do this was the newly revived Democratic party. The leaders of this party tended to be wealthy landholders, merchants, and a number of capitalists who had interests in factories and railroads (Coulter, 1947:366 – 391; Woodward, 1951:40 – 50, 1966:48 – 59, 1974:1 – 23; Stampp, 1966:193 – 195; Shugg, 1939:211 – 212; Arnett, 1922:23; Kirwan, 1951:18 – 26; Going, 1951:27 – 41; Ezell, 1963: 101 – 114). Some of these men had been in the Confederate government or army. This party campaigned on the platform of white supremacy and, as such, elements of the entire white population were members of this party. By 1876, only Louisiana, South Carolina, and Florida remained in the hands of the radical Republican governments, and by 1878, these three states also had governments controlled by the Democratic party.

As southern Democrats took power all over the South, blacks were becoming more and more isolated. The climax of this isolation came with the Compromise of 1877. At this time, the Republican party officially withdrew its support of the struggle of blacks, and it became committed to a policy of conciliating the South. The policy toward the South originated among men whose primary motive was to destroy the planter class while elevating the freedmen to the status of legal and political parity with whites. This policy failed to jell a cohesive political force, so the Republicans abandoned the blacks and attempted to gain favor with forces in the South that accepted northern domination and capitalist development. The Compromise of 1877 sealed this pact (Kousser, 1974:11; Stampp, 1966:210 – 211; Woodward, 1951:246, 1974:23 – 50).

The crisis which prompted the Compromise of 1877 was precipitated by the election of 1876. Samuel Tilden, the Democratic candidate for president, was one electoral vote shy of victory and led the popular vote by over a quarter of a million votes (Woodward, 1951). Rutherford Hayes, the Republican candidate, was behind Tilden in the electoral vote count and claimed the votes of the three states which had not been decided— South Carolina, Florida, and Louisiana. The compromise entailed a bargain between Hayes and southern Democrats. Hayes told the southern Democrats that he would remove the remaining troops from the South, thereby ending Reconstruction as well as withdrawing support from the remaining Republican governments in the South. The southerners, in return, promised to insure Hayes's election (Woodward, 1951:1 – 21, 1974:24). Hayes felt that by turning southern governments back to indigenous southerners, he would attract white conservatives to the Republican cause. As it turned out, these conservatives remained Democrats (Woodward, 1951:244). The implication of the compromise for settling the regional differences was immense (Woodward, 1951):

> The Compromise of 1877 did not restore the old order in the South, nor did it restore the South to parity with the other sections. It did assure the dominant whites political autonomy and nonintervention in matters of race policy and promised them a share in the blessings of the new economic order. In return, the South became, in effect, a satellite of the dominant region. So long as the Conservative redeemers held control they scotched any tendency of the South to combine forces with the internal enemies of the new economy-laborites, western agrarians, reformers. Under the regime of the Redeemers, the South became the bulwark instead of a menace to the new order [p. 246].

It is necessary to consider the meaning of redemption for the blacks during this time. The national Republican party's desertion of blacks left blacks with no congressional clout and put them at the mercy of the southerners. With the withdrawal of radical Republican support, the political and legal equality of blacks was being threatened. White supremacy was being touted as the racial solution, and blacks everywhere were intimidated by whites. The only whites who did not want to place blacks in a caste from which they could not rise were the upper-class southerners. While this group believed in white supremacy, they felt that blacks had rights and could be convinced to support conservative Democrats (Stampp, 1966:196–197; Woodward, 1974:79). Black votes were likely to be won by this group as blacks had no one else to deal with. Planters in black areas gained control of black votes, and by 1880, blacks were supporting the southern Democratic party, the party of white supremacy (Woodward, 1974:79). This transition is not hard to understand. The planter faction in the Democratic party, although paternalistic, wanted to maintain political and legal rights for blacks (at least for the time being). Blacks had two choices—either support the southern Democrats or be at the mercy of more racist elements.

These shifts are summarized in the bottom half of Figure 2.3. The Democratic party, backed by most whites, controlled the state governments of the South, while blacks were the major members supporting the Republican party. At the local level, black Republicans worked with the Democratic party. There were also a number of splinter parties, although at this point in time they were not large.

1878–1900

The dynamics of the southern agricultural system produced a serious crisis for southern society at both the economic and political levels during this period. As southern Democrats took complete control over all southern governments in 1877, the farmers' movements to dethrone them were already taking shape. The goals of this section are: (a) to characterize how farmers expressed their positions on "what was wrong" in America; (b) to discuss the various struggles on the economic and political levels; and (c) to present the resolution of these struggles. Many excellent studies exist on various aspects of farmers' movements in the South and the rest of America, and here they are cited liberally (Arnett, 1922; Goodwyn, 1978; Hicks, 1931; Kirwan, 1951; Saloutos, 1960; Schwartz, 1976; Simkins, 1947; Woodward, 1938).

In the late 1870s, farmers in the West and South were becoming increasingly angry. Wheat, corn, and cotton prices all dropped from 1870 to 1890. Hammond (1897:160) estimated that cotton could be produced for 8¢ a pound. As the price dropped, the profit on the crop became negligible. In the South, the enemy was the credit system, which put more and more people into debt. As long as the price of cotton was high, grievances against merchants, railroads, and tariff-protected manufacturers were muted. When the price of cotton declined to the point where it was no longer profitable to grow it, the protest began.

The oppression and the struggle that ensued must be considered a class struggle (Arnett, 1922:81; Hicks, 1931:404 − 408). As has been suggested, there were essentially two sets of superordinate − subordinate relationships governing the production of cotton in the South. These were the merchant − small farm owner and the landlord − tenant relations. The uniting dynamic in the social system was twofold; (a) the expansion of the world market for cotton and (b) the availability of credit with which to grow cotton. Once caught in this dynamic, small farm owners became subject to the same ills that affected tenants—the high price of credit and the cyclical price of cotton.

During booms and busts, people could change their positions in the class structure. Shifting statuses within the tenant system did not imply a radical shift in social status since the individual was still operating within the landlord − tenant structure. A shift from one tenant status to another (or even from being a sharecropper to being a wage hand) implied that one was still working someone else's land and therefore was still subject to a landowner's will. However, the shift from farm owner to tenant status (or vice versa) implied a shift in class. Small farm owners were always in a very vulnerable position because they lacked the money and financial resources to save their land in hard times. At the same time, losing the land forced landowning farmers to migrate or become renters. This entailed a real loss of independence for the farmer and forced a substantial loss of social status.

It is not surprising, then, that many of the farmers' movements sprang from groups of small farm owners who were faced with loss of land and a change in class during a time of depression (Farmer, 1930; Hackney,

1969:vii–xii; Hicks, 1931:104–112; Hunt, 1934:27–31; Saloutos, 1960:70–78; Woodward, 1938:188, 1974:193). The political movements of the South always reflected this concern and were, in this sense, conservative. The small farm owner wanted to maintain his social position—his land—in the face of capitalist development, a development which caused the prices of goods (including loans) to increase while it decreased the prices for his product. Agrarian movements, then, tended to be correlated with the economic pressure that the small farm owner felt. The object of the rural class struggle in the South was often implicitly the preservation of the independent small farm owner in the face of the domination of merchants, railroaders, and capitalists. The political program of the organization of small farm owners was liberal in that it only wanted to mitigate some of the emerging industrial capitalist system's most blatant excesses. The struggle of the tenant farmer fit into this only insofar as the tenant was the victim of these same forces (i.e., the crop lien system and capitalist development).

The period from 1874 to 1889 was a classic low point in the cotton cycle. As the price of cotton dropped, individual producers went further into debt. This indebtedness caused a further increase in production. By the late 1870s and into the 1880s, many small farm owners lost their land and lapsed into tenantry (Arnett, 1922:22; Hackney, 1969:vii–xii; Hicks, 1931:85; Hunt, 1934:27–31; Schwartz, 1976:73–89). It is not surprising that in various rural areas farmers' organizations with names such as the "Farmers' Alliance," the "Wheel," and the "Farmers' Union" began. These organizations multiplied and grew until 1889, at which time the Wheel and the Alliance merged to form the Farmers' Alliance and Industrial Union (Arnett, 1922:77). By 1889, these organizations claimed three million members in the South alone.

On the whole, members of the Alliance were small producers or tenant farmers (Saloutos, 1960:76). The role of the large planters in the movement was relatively clear. In most states, planters were in favor of capitalist development since it implied more business opportunities and more effective exploitation of the land (Saloutos, 1960:57–68). These planters had diversified interests because they invested heavily in land, lumber, railroads, and manufacturing. Virginia provided an exception to this as some of the Alliance's strongest supporters were planters. In most states, however, planters tended to be against this revolt because they supported the New South policy of the southern Democrats.

What were the goals and activities of these organizations? First and foremost, they were concerned with economic matters. One function of these organizations was educational. The organizations spread information on the use of fertilizers, machines, and seed selection, as well as attempting to teach sound business management (Arnett, 1922:78). More importantly, farmers' organizations set out to make the farmers' position more stable in the face of those who were their enemies—bankers, merchants, manufacturers, railway directors, and speculators. Two general strategies were employed in this endeavor: cooperation among farmers and political action. In the early period, cooperation was the major strategy; political action only came into play after 1889.

In order to cut the costs of purchasing, cooperatives were formed to buy fertilizer and other supplies, and some crops were sold in the same way. By 1887 it became apparent that a larger scale of business would cut costs even further, and state exchanges were formed in most cotton states (Arnett, 1922:79; Hicks, 1931:133−140). These exchanges dealt in almost every commodity that farmers bought and sold. "Encouraged by the success of these enterprises, cooperative stores, cotton warehouses, and gins sprang up like mushrooms over the South [Arnett, 1922:80]." While only members of the various organizations could use the cooperative stores, the effect of the "co-ops" was felt by all farmers when merchants in competition with the co-ops were forced to cut prices in order to retain customers.

The rise of the cooperatives was met by opposition from those who had a stake in the old system. Wholesalers, railroads, and money-lenders all charged higher prices and rates for farmers' ventures (Arnett, 1922:80; Hicks, 1931:138−140). Eventually, a large number of the cooperatives went bankrupt often because the farmers' exchanges were undercapitalized and poorly managed. Merchants in competition with the exchanges would drastically lower prices and the exchanges were unable to hold farmers' loyalty in the face of cutthroat competition (Hicks, 1931:140).

By 1889, the stage was set for political activity. The founders of the Alliance stressed that the organization had economic and not political goals. As time went on, it became evident to Alliance leaders that economic reform would occur only with political reform (Arnett, 1922; Goodwyn, 1978; Hicks, 1931; Kirwan, 1951; Saloutos, 1960). Alliance members met in St. Louis to develop a political platform in 1889, and at this meeting they decided to support only those candidates who accepted the principles in the Alliance's platform. That platform had the following goals: (a) to abolish national banks and substitute treasury notes "in sufficient volume to do the business of the nation on a cash basis [Arnett, 1922:84]," as well as to expand the volume of money as business grew; (b) to outlaw commodity dealing in futures; (c) to promote free and unlimited coinage in silver; (d) to have laws passed outlawing alien ownership of land; (e) to make people work for taxation and not "build up one interest or class at the expense of another [Arnett, 1922:84]"; (f) to have Congress issue paper currency in a large enough amount to allow exchange through the mail; and (g) to nationalize communications and transportation.

These goals were centrally concerned with increasing the money supply, ending the use of government revenues for railroad and manufacturing development, and nationalizing the railroad and telegraph systems. This program spoke directly to the articulated needs of the small farm owner. In each state, the local Alliance might have modified the platform and sought to legislate to specific needs. The Arkansas Wheel, for instance, called for repeal of crop lien legislation (Hicks, 1931:142–143).

When the Farmers' Alliance decided to adopt a political strategy, there was some disagreement over how to implement that strategy. In the South, the Alliance stayed with the Democratic party and supported anyone who accepted its platform. In the Midwest, the Alliance was unable to come to an agreement with the Democrats; therefore, in 1890, the Populist party was formed (Woodward, 1974:233–263; Hicks, 1931:205–237). Whites in the Alliance in the South wanted to remain in the Democratic party since it was an established party and was the party of white supremacy. It appeared as though the southern Farmers' Alliance strategy worked better than the third party's (i.e., the Populist's) strategy because, in 1890, those who professed the Alliance platform were elected all across the South. As it turned out, Democrats who were elected did not support the Alliance program after all. Once in office, they did little to further the interests of Alliance members (Hicks, 1931:248–250; Woodward, 1974:235–242).

The final blow that caused certain Alliance supporters to join the Populist party came in 1892 with the Democratic party's nomination of Grover Cleveland as its presidential candidate. Cleveland was a conservative Democrat who supported northern business development and was opposed to the easy money policies supported by the Alliance. At this point in time, southern Democratic Alliance members left the Democratic party and joined the Populist party. Hicks (1931) estimates that roughly half of the Alliance membership joined the Populist party. The members of the Populist party were mostly white small farm owners and tenant farmers. Most were quite poor and saw the Populist movement as a way to circumvent the worst causes of their poverty (Arnett, 1922:76–79; Hicks, 1931:85–88; Kirwan, 1951:85–93; Woodward, 1974:192–194).

The role of blacks in this struggle was pivotal. In 1877, with the rise of the southern Democratic party as the "white man's party" and the decline of the Republican party, blacks were politically isolated. While most blacks initially remained Republican, the period 1877–1896 witnessed an increasing crossover of the black vote to the Democratic party. The southern Democrats came to control the black vote through one of four methods: coercion, ballot box stuffing, the actual buying of black votes, and fusion (Kousser, 1974:36; Woodward, 1966:54–57).

The white southern Democrats, however, were wary of this alliance. They were always afraid that the blacks would split off from them and ally themselves with more radical, agrarian white elements. The conservative southern Democrats were fearful because they saw that the whites could split over fundamental economic issues and that the blacks would hold the controlling votes (Arnett, 1922:153–155; Hicks, 1931:334–339; Kousser, 1974:11–38; Rice, 1971:86–112; Woodward, 1966:78–80). Because the white small farm owners and tenants would have a program that would appeal to the blacks, the black vote could swing away from the southern Democrats, and the poorer white elements would rule in coalition with the blacks.

As it turned out, the role blacks played in the Populist party was minimal. The Populist leaders, notably Tom Watson in Georgia, tried to appeal to the blacks on the basis of self-interest (Hicks, 1931:114; Woodward, 1938:216–244, 1966:60–64; Arnett, 1922:153–155). The Populist argument was that poor whites and blacks were in the same social position, and the only way they could get out of the grasps of landlords, merchants, and railroad industrialists was to band together and execute legislative action to relieve their mutual ills. The philosophy of race relations underlying this argument was quite radical; it suggested that whites and blacks were equal by virtue of their common oppression (Woodward, 1966:61).

This potentially radical alliance never quite became reality for two reasons. First of all, much of the hard-core support of the Populist movement was among those who were most prejudiced against blacks. Members of the Populist party who hated blacks always caused difficulty in sustaining relationships between blacks and whites in the party. The second difficulty lay in recruiting blacks into the party. At the outset, the Populists attempted to attract the black vote by ignoring established Republican leadership and by trying to appeal directly to the mass of black farmers. This strategy never worked very well, and in the end, it only alienated black Republicans from the Populist cause (Woodward, 1966:77–80; Kousser, 1974:35–36; Arnett, 1922:155). Eventually, the Populists tried to adopt the strategies of the southern Democrats, and attempts were made at "fusion." While these attempts were a bit more successful, black support of the Populist movement was still not great.

The top half of Figure 2.4 contains a diagram that illustrates the basic political conflict in the South from 1889 to 1896. The white small farm owners and tenant farmers divided into the Populist and Democratic

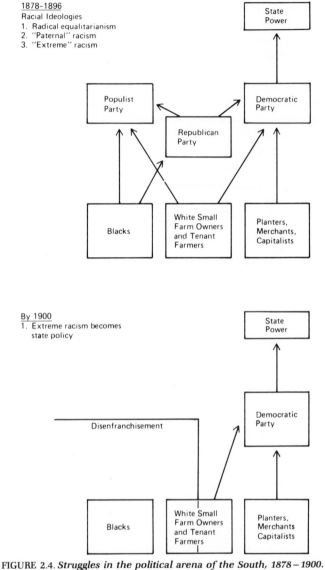

FIGURE 2.4. *Struggles in the political arena of the South, 1878–1900.*

parties. The white planter/merchant/capitalists controlled the Democratic party and blacks played the pivotal role in the elections of 1894 and 1896.

The elections of 1894 and 1896 were the climax of the struggle between Populists and conservative Democrats. The elections were bitterly fought battles and violence was common (Hicks, 1931:321–329; Woodward, 1974:264–290; Kousser, 1974:29 – 44; Arnett, 1922:183–185). The Populist party only took control of one state government in the South—North Carolina. In Georgia and Alabama in 1894, very blatant vote fraud prevented Populists from taking power (Arnett, 1922:183–184; Hicks, 1931:334–336). Ballot box stuffing in the black counties prevented the Populists from taking control of the state governments. Southern Democrats weathered the Populist assault, but it took tremendous illegalities to do it.

The Populist revolt lost steam after 1896, and the movement was absorbed by the Democratic party. Populist leaders became part of the Democratic party in order to support the issue of silver-based currency which would increase the amount of money in circulation. In 1896, the nomination of William Jennings Bryan as the Democratic party's candidate for president drew the support of the Populists, but fusing the Populists with the Democrats had the effect of destroying the third party machinery of the Populists and the party never recovered (Hicks, 1931:378).

While political efforts of tenant and yeoman farmers were being thwarted, a new movement was afoot to split the agrarian radicals and ally all whites against blacks. Woodward (1966) argues that the South was in just the state of mind to react strongly against blacks:

> Economic, political, and social frustrations had pyramided to a climax of social tensions. Hopes for reform and the political means employed in defiance of tradition and at a great cost to emotional attachments to affect reform had likewise met with cruel disappointments and frustration. There had to be a scapegoat. And all along the line signals were going up to indicate that the Negro was an approved object of aggression [p. 81].

The black man would serve as the scapegoat to conciliate the white classes. "The only formula powerful enough to accomplish that was the magical formula of white supremacy, applied without stint and without any of the old conservative reservations of paternalism [Woodward, 1966:82]."

This backlash against blacks took two forms: disenfranchisement and Jim Crow laws. Who was behind the Jim Crow laws and the disenfranchisement movement? Kousser (1974), in his study of southern politics between 1890 and 1910, concludes,

> The new political structure was not the product of accident or other impersonal forces, nor of decisions demanded by the masses, nor even the white masses. The system which insured the absolute control of predominantly black counties by upper class whites, the elimination in most areas of

parties as a means of organized competition between politicians and, in general, the nonrepresentation of lower class interests in political decision-making was shaped by those who stood to benefit most from it—Democrats, usually from the black belt and always socioeconomically privileged [p. 238].

Kousser goes on to argue that disenfranchisement operated not only against blacks, but also against whites. He argues convincingly that at the center of the movement to remove blacks from the political arena were whites (the planter/merchant/industrialists) who wanted to preserve the Democratic party from further threats to its conservative form.

While the southern Democrats did not invent the extreme racist attitudes sweeping the South in the 1890s, it is clear that they were quite willing to use them in order to rebond the poor whites into the Democratic Party—the white man's party. The social function of the Jim Crow laws and disenfranchisement was to establish the social order once and for all. The class struggle of the 1880s and 1890s was resolved ideologically by the emergency of extreme racist pronouncements that were to be made into law. The political domination of the southern Democrats became a fact, and the crisis in the agricultural system was offered no real relief. The bottom half of Figure 2.4 illustrates this graphically.

The South in 1900

The depression of the 1890s ended by 1900. The price of cotton rose and record-breaking crop harvests occurred (Watkins, 1908:30). For the first time since the 1870s, farmers found cotton production profitable. The world demand for cotton was rising and record world production was all that was keeping the price of cotton from going higher. In America it was evident that two areas of cotton growing existed—the old South and the Southwest. The old South consisted of North Carolina, South Carolina, Georgia, Alabama, Mississippi, Louisiana, and Arkansas, while the Southwest consisted of Texas and Oklahoma. Production in the Southwest was more profitable since (a) the land was planted on a larger scale; and (b) soils were less worn out which meant that less fertilizer was required and production costs were lowered. Cotton production was, therefore, expanding rapidly in the Southwest.

Social relations in 1900 were the same as those in the 1890s. The major groups were still farm laborers, sharecroppers, share tenants, cash tenants, small farm owners, and plantation owners, and the dynamics of the crop lien system did not lessen. The people from the rural areas of the South were caught in the cotton system. In order to get money to farm and subsist, they had to take crop liens. To take crop liens they needed to grow cotton, and this meant that more and more cotton was produced. If the price of cotton dropped, farmers went further into debt with merchants or planters.

The social and political isolation of the blacks in the South after 1900 is a well-known phenomenon (Myrdal, 1944:573−667; Woodson, 1924:1−17; Scott, 1920; Woofter, 1969:105−121; Tindall, 1967:143−183; Woodward, 1974:369−395). The process by which this isolation took place, however, is less understood. The central issue was the dominant ideology in the Populist movement and the role the Democratic party in the South played in destroying both the Populist movement and the buffer it provided between the economic and political structures. The Populist movement primarily reflected the concerns of small farm owners who saw their way of life (and their land) threatened by merchants, capitalists, and large planters. The movement's ideology was, first of all, oriented toward self-help (i.e., educating farmers and starting cooperative buying and marketing in attempts to get around merchants, railroads, and cotton warehousing). When direct economic action failed, members of the Populist movement (in particular, the Farmers' Alliance, the Wheel, and the Colored Farmers' Alliance) began to take political action. The Populists developed political programs whose major goals were expansion of the monetary system, nationalization of railroads, support for the price of cotton, and an end to commodity speculation. These goals clearly reflected the interests of small farm owners and did not constitute an attack on the tenure system. Rather, they were oriented toward easing the burdens of the crop lien system and making more money for the farmer.

While the Populist party faced defeat at the polls, the southern Democrats had two political strategies that would secure their position against a possible future resurgence of anti-southern Democratic and third party activity. The first was the use of disenfranchisement and racism, and the second was fusion. Fusion of the Populists with the southern Democrats occurred in 1896, when the Democratic party nominated William Jennings Bryan for president. The Populist party supported Bryan because he took up the banner of silver-based currency, a central Populist demand. Other populist proposals were also taken up by the Democratic party.

The other strategy, disenfranchisement, was more insidious and helped to prevent new Populist movements from arising and upsetting the status quo in the political and economic systems. The southern Democrats were interested in preventing an alliance between poor whites and blacks. The disenfranchisement laws worked to prevent poor whites and blacks from voting (Kousser, 1974). A number of historians have argued that this was precisely the intent of these laws (Hackney, 1969:147–179; Kousser, 1974:238–265; Woodward, 1974:342–349). State policy made blacks the legitimate target for white frustration.

Socially, it is clear that blacks became extremely ostracized in southern society. They were not permitted to share trains, hotels, buses, and restaurants with whites. Violence against blacks was relatively frequent, and public lynchings or beatings with little or no provocation occurred throughout the South. The white domination of blacks extended to psychic as well as physical violence. Discrimination and oppression were obviously rampant at this time.

Politically, poor whites and blacks were in similar positions. Neither group voted or directly participated in the political process. Politics became, as Key (1949) concludes, "conducted without the benefit of political party or party competition. Rather, political battles were fought by whites who represented various interests under the rubric of the Democratic Party [pp. 11–12]." The white small farm owners and tenants lacked political organization and power.

Blacks and most whites were politically powerless. Both groups were at the mercy of the crop lien system, the world price of cotton, and continued capitalist expansion. Since the political participation of blacks and whites was co-opted and circumscribed, they had little possibility of changing their situations. The polity was insulated from the economy, and this insulation was held in place by the state policy that legitimated violence against blacks. The broad outlines of southern poverty in the twentieth century were set into place. Only the collapse of the credit system in the early 1930s brought change to the South, and it should be noted that this change came from the federal government and wealthy landowners. It was not a result of political action by the southern masses.

Chapter 3

The Causes of Black and White Migration

From the perspective of the theoretical model presented earlier, the time period previous to the study has been examined. Before considering the time period relevant to the study, it is necessary to consider more precisely how to conceptualize migration and its causes at the theoretical, methodological, and empirical levels. Toward this end, this chapter will discuss demographic, sociological, and economic approaches to migration and then critique each of these approaches. Finally, it will outline the conceptual and analytical strategies to be used.

Demographic, Sociological, and Economic Approaches

What is migration? "Migration is a geographic or spatial mobility involving a change of usual residence between clearly defined geographic units [Shryrock and Siegel, 1971:579]." While this definition seems straightforward, it harbors one major ambiguity; that is, what constitutes a "clearly defined geographic unit"? For the moment, this problem is put aside, the definition is accepted, and consideration is given to what constitutes a study of migration. Demographers, sociologists, and economists have all undertaken studies of migration, and the next few pages describe how they have gone about doing such studies.

Demographers use migration in a number of ways. First, migration is one of the factors, along with births and deaths, that determine change in the population of an area. Measures of births and deaths in an area are often available, and the residual difference in the population change is taken to be the net migration. An area may experience enormous in- and out-migration and the net migration could be quite small. Many studies of migration tend to concentrate on net migration since determining in- and out-migration separately can be difficult without a special survey. Studies of migrations between states do exist, and are based on census information showing place of birth. These issues will be considered again when the measurement of migration is taken up.

Demographers have also suggested rudimentary theories of migration. The first such theory was proposed by Ravenstein's (1885, 1889) *The Laws of Migration.* His laws were only partially causal, and they mostly reflected observations he made.

1. Migrants tend to move short distances.
2. If migrants move long distances, they tend to go to large cities.
3. Migrants tend to make a number of moves and these move   are to increasingly larger places.
4. Each stream of in-migration also has a stream of out-migration.
5. People in rural areas tend to migrate more frequently than those in urban areas.
6. As industrialization increases, migration increases.
7. Migrants move in response to economic conditions.

More recently, Everett Lee (1966) has proposed a commonsense approach to studying migration. He argues that there are four factors that enter into the potential migrant's decision-making process: (a) factors associated with the area of origin; (b) factors associated with the area of destination; (c) intervening obstacles; and (d) personal factors. Lee goes on to suggest hypotheses about the volume of migration, the way streams of migration operate, and the selectivity of the migrant population. In terms of the volume of migration, he argues that

1. A high degree of diversity (uneven economic development) in the areas of a territory will result in large movements in that territory.
2. The volume of migration varies with the diversity of groups— different ethnic and racial groups tend to gravitate toward situations that will be comfortable to them.
3. The volume of migration will depend on the number of obstacles the migrant must surmount.
4. Migration varies with fluctuations in the economy.

5. Both rate and volume of migration tend to increase with time.
6. The volume and rate of migration is tied to the amount of industrialization.

Lee (1966) goes on to argue that migration streams tend (a) to be well-defined (i.e., large numbers of people migrate at around the same time to a specific location); (b) to be two way (i.e., counterstreams develop); (c) to be one way if conditions at the origin are very bad; (d) to be selective if obstacles are high; and (e) to vary with economic conditions. Migrants are: (a) selective positively if migrants are responding to pull factors (i.e., highly educated people tend to move to opportunities); (b) selective negatively where people are being pushed out of areas; (c) dependent on pushes and pulls; (d) selective positively as intervening obstacles increase; (e) selective with respect to life cycle characteristics (e.g., youth and newlyweds); and (f) tend to be intermediate between the characteristics of the population at origin and the population at destination.

Sociological theories of migration tend also to focus on the factors just cited (Goldstein, 1958; Jansen, 1970; Peterson, 1969; Rossi, 1955; Speare, Goldstein, and Frey, 1975; Stouffer, 1940, 1960; Zipf, 1946). Often these theories are more explicit in trying to ascertain the social and psychological states of migrants before and after migration, and they sometimes attempt to focus on how people get information on where they move (Cherry, 1965; Omari, 1955). Zipf's (1946) model is an explicit mathematization of Ravenstein's argument that migration varies as a function of distance—the farther the distance between two points, the less likely people are to move. This model presents a difficulty in that there is no theoretical argument that explains it, although one could construct several explanations. Stouffer's (1940) model is related to this, but he suggests that "the number of persons going a given distance is directly proportional to the number of intervening opportunities [p. 846]."

The final consideration of theoretical approaches is the economic approach. The central tenet in an economic theory of migration is that migrants tend to be responsive to wage differentials—people move from areas of low income to areas of high income (Sjaastad, 1962; Thomas, 1958; Todaro, 1969; Vickery, 1977; see Greenwood, 1975, for an excellent review of all of the recent economic literature). Todaro (1969) argues that one must also include as a cause of movement the probability of employment at the area of destination. If that probability is low, then the wage differential will not cause movement. Vickery (1977) concludes that wage differentials were the primary cause of black migration between the South and the North from 1900 to 1960.

Critique of the Other Approaches

There are at least four major difficulties with these theories:

1. They posit that laws of migration exist.
2. They are ahistorical.
3. They have poorly developed notions of the ways in which social structure impinges on people.
4. They posit a model of human action that is based on perfect information, rational action in an economic sense, and a notion that individuals perceive "pushes" and "pulls" and act accordingly.

Underlying most demographic and sociological work is the idea that the ultimate goal of social research is to discover laws of social interaction that transcend time and place. From this perspective, all historical events are just examples of the ways these laws are applied. The problem with this approach is that it is unlikely to yield laws that will give us a sufficient understanding of a concrete event since the event will be too complex to be understood in such simple terms. The purpose of studying concrete societies at concrete moments in time is not to discover their general principles, but rather to discover their peculiar dynamics.

The goal of this study is to gain knowledge of something real and concrete. For the demographer or sociologist, the goal is to establish a set of laws or principles (i.e., abstractions). The former perspective is likely to produce a well-grounded historical account that relies on a knowledge of the dynamics of social relations in a particular social formation. Such an account will be sensitive to the unique crises and contradictions a real society engenders and, most importantly, their consequences for whatever the object of explanation is. The latter approach will miss the twists and turns of real societies and will offer explanations that may be elegant, but are irrelevant to understanding real events.

It should be noted that the approach to this study is not strictly historical. The historian's argument against the positivist sociologist is that all human societies are totally unique and therefore all events are unique. From this perspective, the only kind of knowledge left is knowledge of unique events. The argument being made here is materialist, realist, and structuralist (Keat and Urry, 1975:96−118). This argument is materialist in the sense that it seeks knowledge of a concrete object (i.e., a real society), realist because it posits underlying mechanisms that explain surface level phenomena, and structuralist because it holds the position that the social relations that underlie real societies construct (i.e., limit, mediate, and cause) the surface events. Because any set of structures which makes up a social formation has a unique history, it is certainly necessary to understand history. Knowledge of a society, however, is not limited to events. Rather, knowledge of a society explicitly implies understanding (a) the underlying sets of social relations and their dynamics and contradictions; and (b) how these are likely to affect future outcomes. From the perspective used in this project, it is useful to compare two societies in order to assess how the underlying social relations affected the outcome of each society. Such a comparison does not reap abstract laws which transcend time and space, but, rather, provides us with a knowledge of the differences or similarities between two social formations that have specific alignments among their underlying social relations.

Another problem with the three approaches outlined previously centers on the relationships between individuals and the social relations surrounding them. Demographers posit that an individual (a) has information concerning opportunities at both the point of origin and the destination; and (b) understands the obstacles to migration. From a demographer's point of view, individuals have no problem with gaining and understanding their options. There are objective factors called "pushes" and "pulls" that the individual understands and responds to by migrating in accord with whichever factor is strongest. Hence, many demographers have argued that blacks were "pulled" to opportunities in the North because everyone accepted and understood the fact that such opportunities existed. This model of human behavior is inadequate as it assumes a calculating individual with clear-cut choices. It does not emphasize the fact that individuals are enmeshed in sets of social relations at the point of origin. These relations not only structure what an individual's options are, but they structure an individual's *perception* of what his or her options are and, further, they control information about opportunities elsewhere.

The major difficulty with the demographers' view concerns how pushes and pulls work on the individual. In this study, it is assumed that persons will be most sensitive to conditions at the point of origin. Pulls (e.g., opportunities somewhere else) only become operative when conditions at the point of origin deteriorate or hold no promise. Another problem is the ambiguity implicit in interpreting a factor as a push or pull. A demonstration of this can be found in Lee's (1966) assertion that pulls are operating when the most highly educated people move. Educational selectivity of migrants could just as easily result from the most educated migrants understanding the opportunity structure at the point of origin and migrating because opportunities were declining. This implies that it is very difficult to tell a push from a pull if one is operating at the level of the individual. In sum, push—pull models of migration are inadequate in explaining migration since they (a) operate ambiguously (how does one tell a push from a pull?); and (b) require a model of human behavior that ignores the basic sociological fact that individuals are involved in sets of social relations that determine their options, shape their perceptions of options, and provide limited information about options in other places.

Sociological models have tried to incorporate motives or values into the decision to migrate. These models are more sophisticated, but they also suffer from underdeveloped notions of social structure. There is no sense of the dynamics of social structure nor is there an attempt to view migration as the result of sets of social relations presenting few options to actors. Sociologists, on the whole, have sought explanations in social psychology and have avoided consideration of social structure.

The position presented in this study can be summed up as follows:

1. The point of origin is most important because agents are involved in sets of social relationships at that point.
2. Agents in similar positions in social structures will behave similarly (i.e., they will migrate).
3. Discovering how the structures impinge on agents in various positions in the social relations of production is paramount to understanding migration.

For example, the black tenant in South Carolina in 1905 had four basic options. He could (a) accept the social and economic oppression in South Carolina; (b) move west to find a better tenant situation but probably an equally oppressive social situation; (c) move to a southern city or town to attempt to better his economic situation but still remain in an oppressive social situation; or (d) move north to try to escape the worst forms of racism and economic oppression. These choices were determined by the tenant's social and economic position, and whichever choice was made was probably determined to some degree by which presented the best option; that is, given the tenant's knowledge, which option was mostly likely to remove him from economic and social subjugation.

In summary, then, the most abstract logic of this analysis implies that the macro-social relations of production and the various changes in these social relations structure the choices and options of the inhabitants of the South. The process of migration, from this point of view, is thought to be an outcome of these various processes because the opportunities of blacks and whites were structured by these processes.

Conceptualization of Migration

The purpose of this section is to offer the analytic strategy of this study. This strategy must fulfill the goals already suggested as well as allow for the development of a quantitative model that will test the assertions put forward in the next few chapters. In this discussion the unit of analysis is defined, the relevant groups are defined, the general theoretical model is posed, the dependent variable is defined, and the basic empirical strategy is outlined.

Choosing a unit of analysis is extremely difficult. Theoretically, one would like data on properly sampled individuals, with complete information on migration and the social relations in which the individual was involved. This kind of study is not tenable, however, since no such data exist. Counties, then, have been chosen as the units of analysis here. Counties represent relatively homogeneous areas in terms of their economic and social characteristics. For instance, shifts in the class structures of counties can be measured, and the level of aggregation seems meaningful. Since 1900 the Census Bureau and the Department of Agriculture have collected an enormous amount of data relevant to the project at hand that are disaggregated at the county level. By using these data at the county level, the effects of various social and economic conditions on the migrations in question can be assessed.

The argument must be made that real social groups exist, and they are defined as having similar positions in social and economic relations (Weber, 1968:968). Different groups will react to changes in their respective situations in different ways. For instance, under different social conditions, blacks may be more likely to move than whites, tenant farmers more likely to move than farm owners, and rural dwellers who live closer to urban areas may be more likely to move than those who live farther away. This implicitly suggests that the study of migration is a study of social groups and of the effects that various social arrangements have on any given group's migration probability at any point in time.

The two groups that this study focuses on are blacks and whites. These groups have been chosen for a number of reasons. For one, race was the central ideological issue in the South after the Civil War. Black—white relations underwent a series of transitions that were a function of the political climate as well as the ongoing agricultural crisis. It was this racial division that helped heal the wounds of the white class struggle. As such, the black—white split is central to giving an account of migration. Questions of obvious relevance are: Did blacks migrate more frequently since they suffered from more overt repression? Did they migrate less frequently because they had few opportunities in the burgeoning towns? Did blacks and whites migrate at similar rates if one allows for the fact that blacks were more likely to be tenants and tenants were more likely to move? Hopefully, these issues and others will be resolved in the chapters ahead.

Figure 3.1 presents a model of the migration process that will be used here. This model is a further development of the model presented in the first chapter. Precise hypotheses about the relations between the various factors and migration must be guided by an historical analysis of the relevant dynamics in and outside the social formation. For instance, if the price of cotton increases and opportunities to grow cotton increase, then in-migration will occur. In a crisis of overproduction with farm owners losing their land, one would expect out-migration.

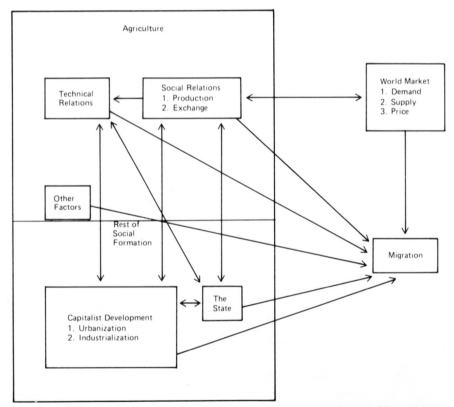

FIGURE 3.1. *A conceptualization of rural-urban migration in a capitalist social formation at a given conjuncture.*

There are six factors or sets of social relations that structured the opportunities of blacks and whites in counties of the South. The world market generally determined the price of cotton and, hence, the profitability of cotton production. Of course, this price was dependent on the amount of crop produced in the U.S. and the rest of the world and on the demand for the product. This factor structured migration because the amount of cotton production dictated the number of opportunities that were available. Capitalist development affected migration in that opportunities for employment in cities and towns operated as factors causing movement. This development also affected the social organization of agriculture since it (a) provided goods for the rural area; and (b) used the products of the rural areas. These two factors affected the profitability of cotton production and, hence, affected migration.

The state (be it a local, state, or federal government) had mainly indirect effects on migration. The state made decisions regarding capitalist development, agricultural prices, tariffs, and tax incentives and these all had effects on migration. The term "other factors" in Figure 3.1 refers to events that were not directly related to the other structures. The boll weevil infestation and the general repression of blacks are considered in this category. The general repression of blacks had its basis in the resolution of the Populist movement, but one can argue that repression had an independent effect on black migration.

The technical relations (Figure 3.1) of production refer to the way in which cultivation proceeded. The use of machines could have displaced labor, and this labor could have been forced to migrate; however, the social relations of production govern the technical relations. As has been argued, landlords would not mechanize because it was not profitable, and small farm owners could not mechanize because they could not afford machines. Only a shift in these social relations would bring about mechanization.

The social relations of production affected migration since these relations defined the options that individuals had. If opportunities for tenantry or for owning land increased in a county, one would expect in-migration. If such opportunities decreased, one would expect out-migration. The exchange relations (Figure 3.1) refer to relations between farmers, merchants, cotton markets, suppliers and railroads. These relations affected the amount of crop production and the distribution of crops. An indicator of exchange relations is the number of acres of cotton planted. The crop lien, which governed exchange and production relations, determined how much cotton was planted. When the price was high, farmers produced as much as possible and, hence, acreage increased. This implied that opportunities were expanding and in-migration resulted. Separating the effects of production and exchange relations is rather difficult and therefore they are considered together.

The strategy here is to attempt to piece together how these six factors structured the opportunities of blacks and whites in the South from 1900 to 1950. The ways that these factors worked at various moments in time are then tested by constructing indicators of the factors and by using multivariate models. This combination of an historical mode with an understanding of the dynamics of social relations enables us to test the entire argument empirically.

In terms of measurement, attention will be focused on all of the counties of North Carolina, South Carolina, Georgia, Alabama, Mississippi, Louisiana, Arkansas, Oklahoma, and the eastern half of Texas. These states were chosen because throughout the period they had large numbers of tenant farmers and considerable farm acreage planted in cotton. (More details on the sample selection are in Appendix B.)

Choosing counties as the units of analysis raises another very serious issue—it is impossible to assess the components of population change due to in- and out-migration because data are simply not available for the time period in question. The only measure that can be constructed is a measure of net migration. As has already been suggested, large amounts of movement could be taking place even when net migration is very small. This might not be very serious since the theoretical interest here is net migration. The goal of this analysis is to give an account of net in- and out-migration as a function of (a) the composition of the counties; and (b) the social and economic situation in each county and in surrounding counties. The net movement is a natural measure that suggests whether more people are being forced from or attracted to a county.

The measurement of net migration is now considered. From the demographic equation it is known that

$$M_{x+t} = P_x^t - P_x^0 - B_{x+t} - D_{x+t},$$

where M_{x+t} is net migration, P_x^t is the population at the second census interval, P_x^0 is the population at the first census interval, B_{x+t} is the number of births in the interval, and D_{x+t} is the number of deaths. The central difficulty is that in order to use this method one would need to know the number of births and deaths during the interval. Since this information is not available, net migration must be estimated by a more indirect technique. There are two basic ways to obtain such an estimate: (a) the national growth rate method; or (b) survival rate methods. The national growth rate method relies on the assumption that births and deaths are constant for the entire population. This method is not used because this assumption is over-restrictive and does not offer the best measure of net migration.

The measure used here is the forward census survival ratio method, which is a survival rate method. This method was chosen because it utilizes all of the available data in estimating net migration. While there are biases in this measure, it appears to be the most useful as well as one of the most common ways of attempting to estimate net migration (Shryrock and Siegel, 1971; Hamilton, 1959, 1964; Price, 1955; Lee et al., 1964). The formula for computing the forward census survival rate is

$$M_{x+t} = P^t_{x+t} - sP^0_x,$$

where x is an age group, t is the interval between censuses, P^0_x is the population aged x at the first census P^t_{x+t} is the population at the next census at age $x + t$, s is the survival rate from x to $x + t$, and M_{x+t} is the net migration for the $x + t$ age group.

The use of this method requires an estimate of s, the survival rate. The survival rate is a measure of the ratio of the number of persons in age group $x + t$ divided by the number of persons in age group x, assuming one has a closed population. This rate reflects the proportion of persons in the age cohort who survived to the second census interval. One can estimate s in two major ways—from life tables or from national censuses. Since life tables for the regions involved here are impossible to construct, the survival rates in this research are estimated from national censuses.

The survival rate method does not yield exact estimates of net migration because it fails to include an allowance for the net number of persons who migrated in or out and then died (Siegel and Hamilton, 1952). This can result in a biased estimate that is high or low depending on the conditions under which the deaths occurred. The survival rates are computed on the national population and represent the ratio of the number in the same national age cohort at successive censuses. Lee et al. (1964) estimated census survival ratios for the period 1870–1950 by race, sex, and age. These estimates will be relied upon in this analysis.

Consider the problem for a moment. The black and white populations in each county in 1900, 1910, 1920, 1930, 1940 and 1950 are known. In 1930, 1940, and 1950, the age, sex, and racial structures of each county are known. From the earlier censuses, only the number of persons residing in places with populations larger than 2500 is known. This information gives us insight into how urban or rural a county was. The problem, then, is to use the available information to estimate net migration from counties by using census survival ratios. Using the 1930, 1940, and 1950 censuses to estimate net migration will be rather straightforward. Appropriate survival rates will be applied to the distributions of age, sex, and race of each county's population. The major potential bias is due to the assumption that census survival rates apply uniformly to each county. Since race by urban−rural age distribution for each state is known, one can compute an average survival rate by race by urban−rural for each state. The urban−rural distinction is focused on because the age structure differs in urban and rural places. Since one can determine the urban and rural components of the county populations, one can use these average survival rates by race by urban−rural age structure to approximate rates of survival in counties. This rate is

$$s_{r,res} = \sum_{age} P_{r,res,age} \times s_{r,age}{,}$$

where $s_{r,res}$ is the weighted average survival rate by race by residential area (rural−urban), $P_{r,res,age}$ is the proportion of persons of a given age, race, and residential area at time 0, and $s_{r,age}$ is the survival rate in the state for race by age. This calculation weights the age-specific survival rates by the proportion in each age group in the residential areas (rural−urban). The composite rate which results from this calculation can be used to estimate net migration in each of the counties. To obtain the net migration in these counties, we use the following equation:

$$M_r = P_{x+t}^t - (s_{r,urb} P_{x,urb}^0 + s_{r,rur} P_{x,rur}^0),$$

where M_r is the migration by race by county, P_{x+t}^t is the population at time $x + t$ by race, $s_{r,urb}$ and $s_{r,rur}$ are the survival rates by race by rural and urban areas, and $P_{x,rur}^0$ and $P_{x,urb}^0$ are the populations which are rural or urban by race at time point 0. While the exact number of blacks and whites who were living in urban as opposed to rural places is not known, the proportion by race in the state is known and this is used as a proxy. This equation gives an estimate of migration for all counties.

In the later censuses, migration is estimated both ways in order to get a sense of what is lost by the second method of estimating net migration. (Details of these results are in Appendix C.) It can be stated that both methods produce almost identical results and are very highly correlated. The estimates of net migration are affected by the following difficulties:

1. Underenumeration of the black and rural population.
2. The inability to estimate "real" county-level survival rates. This results from our lack of sufficiently detailed county-level data.
3. Assumptions regarding the use of the census survival ratio and the forward residual method of computing migration.

4. Assumption of constancy of survival rates within and between states and counties.

Despite these caveats, the measurement problem here is no more serious than that involved in estimating such numbers in most developing countries. It can be argued that these measures are estimates and, as such, are fairly good estimates. Clearly, given the data limitation, they are the best that can be obtained. It should be noted that these net migration rate estimates concern the population that was born by the time of the first census and was 10 years old or older by the time of the second census. The net migration rates estimated here do not take into account the in- and out-migration of persons born during the decade. To reiterate, high rates of net out-migration do not necessarily imply a large change in the population of a county over the decade. This is because the birth rates of rural blacks and whites were quite high, and, thus, substantial population movements could be masked by a high replacement rate. (More details on the measure of net migration are available in Appendix C.)

One might argue that the analytic approach suggested here only explains intracounty movement within the South and ignores movement to the North. This objection would be misguided for the following reason. If one could decompose the net migration rates, one would find that a component of the movement is going North. One of the goals of this analysis is to figure out how much of that movement is accounted for by events in the North. Hence, this approach does not explain only the intracounty movement in the South, but, as the net migration rates reflect to some degree, the migration out of the South as well.

Chapter 4

Patterns of Net Migration and Changes in Social Organization

Before proceeding to an account of the South in the twentieth century, it is useful to present the basic patterns of change in migration from counties of the South as well as the patterns of change in the social organization of southern agriculture from 1900 to 1950. These patterns form a useful backdrop for the historical and causal analysis to come.

The first and most important trend is the pattern of net migration from counties of the South. In order to standardize the measure, all net migration measures have been transformed into net migration rates. The net migration rate is defined as

$$(NM_r/TP_r) \times 100,$$

where NM_r is the net migration for each race and TP_r is the total population for each race at the first point in time. The ratio can be interpreted as the percent increase or decrease in the population by race that is due to net migration. This ratio can take on a value of greater than or equal to -1 depending on the size of the numerator and the denominator. The percentage is multiplied by 100 in order to be interpreted as a rate. If 50 blacks move into a county where only 25 were before, the black population would increase by two times. This would mean the net migration rate was 200, which implies that for every 100 blacks in the county at the first point in time, 200 have now moved in. The net migration rate is a good measure because it standardizes the size of population movement and makes rates of migration between counties comparable.

TABLE 4.1
Average Net Migration Rates of Blacks
for Nine Southern States, 1900–1950[a]

State	1900–1910	1910–1920	1920–1930	1930–1940	1940–1950
Alabama[b]	-5.300	-8.968	-15.566	-11.820	-25.641
Arkansas	-7.529	-12.682	-22.068	-18.418	-19.506
Georgia	-8.172	-13.042	-27.436	-13.810	-26.804
Louisiana	-2.409	-11.038	-11.126	-8.263	-21.277
Mississippi	-4.409	-15.556	-11.834	-10.125	-27.062
North Carolina	-8.856	-8.925	-8.807	-10.878	-14.647
South Carolina	-10.902	-12.516	-26.420	-16.529	-24.520
Texas	-2.485	-4.704	-9.448	-10.251	-18.972
Oklahoma	--	-8.523	-12.591	-19.473	-11.567

[a]See Appendix B for details on the sample and Appendix C for details on the measure of net migration rates.

[b]The net migration rate is measured at the county level.

Table 4.1 contains the state-by-state average net migration rate of blacks over the period 1900–1950. The average net migration rate is precisely what it sounds like:

$$\frac{1}{C} \sum_{1}^{C} NM_r,$$

where NM_r is the sum of the net migration rates by race for each state and C is the number of counties in the state. A glance at Table 4.1 shows that the average net migration rate per state for blacks is always negative. This implies that blacks were, on the average, leaving more counties (and leaving them at greater rates) than they were moving into. The decade 1940–1950 appears to have the largest net out-migration rates followed by 1920–1930, 1930–1940, 1910–1920, and 1900–1910. The decade 1920–1930 was a decade of agricultural depression in the South, and the high net out-migration rate reflects opportunities outside of the agricultural sector as well as factors associated with the stagnant agricultural system. The decade 1930–1940 would have witnessed even more net out-migration had there been more opportunities outside the collapsing agricultural system. Notice also where the average rates are the lowest. Texas, Louisiana, Mississippi, Alabama, and Arkansas have the lowest out-migration rates, while Georgia and South Carolina have the highest rates. This reflects the fact that the black population in the South was gradually moving West to seek new agricultural opportunities.

Similar patterns emerge in the white average net migration rates presented in Table 4.2. Most of the white average net migration rates are negative. The only exceptions are Louisiana in 1900−1910 and 1920−1930, Texas in 1900−1910, and Oklahoma in 1910−1920. Over time, the decade 1940−1950 had the largest net out-migration followed by 1920−1930, 1910−1920, 1930−1940, and 1900−1910. The states with the lowest average net out-migration are those states in the West—Texas, Oklahoma, Louisiana, Mississippi, and Arkansas.

It is of some value to compare the patterns of black and white average net migration rates. Starting with the largest amount of net out-migration and working down to the smallest, the patterns are identical except for

TABLE 4.2

Average Net Migration Rates of Whites
for Nine Southern States, 1900−1950[a]

State	1900−1910	1910−1920	1920−1930	1930−1940	1940−1950
Alabama[b]	-7.664	-7.199	-8.094	-4.982	-12.224
Arkansas	-2.817	-5.773	-9.148	-5.077	-16.856
Georgia	-10.044	-7.261	-14.167	-3.712	-10.252
Louisiana	3.420	-6.041	6.241	3.298	-5.876
Mississippi	-4.902	-7.405	-1.356	-1.043	-11.551
North Carolina	-6.207	-6.247	-3.147	-.876	-6.916
South Carolina	-6.581	-4.507	-8.216	-.269	-5.807
Texas	30.730	-4.820	-11.555	8.889	-14.166
Oklahoma	--	3.134	-7.096	-5.513	-25.001

[a] See Appendix B for details on the sample and Appendix C for details on the measure of net migration rates.

[b] The net migration rate is measured at the county level.

the transposition of the 1910−1920 decade and the 1930−1940 decade. This suggests that whatever caused out-migration was affecting blacks and whites in similar ways. On the average, both blacks and whites tended to have lower net out-migration rates from counties in the western part of the South than from those in the eastern part. This implies that opportunities existed in the West. The major difference between these rates is that black rates tend to be higher than white rates in all decades. This difference reflects the greater mobility of blacks and suggests that blacks found themselves in worse situations than whites and probably responded by moving more frequently.

One difficulty with the average net migration rate is that each county is standardized. This is problematic because that average weights the rate in counties with small populations as much as it does the rate in counties with large populations. For instance, if one county has a net in-migration of 10,000 whites and a base population of 50,000, the net migration rate will be .20 or 20 persons entering per 100. Another county may have an out-migration of 100 whites and a base population of 200, thereby yielding a net migration rate of −.5 or 50 persons leaving per 100. The average net migration rate is $(-.5 + .2)/2 = -.3/2 = -.15$ or 15 persons per 100 leaving. The average net migration is $(10,000 + -100)/2 = 9900/2 = 4950$. Even though taken together these two counties are experiencing massive in-migration, in terms of their rates, it appears as if there is substantial out-movement.

Since a fair number of the counties in our sample (particularly in Texas and Oklahoma) had small base populations, it is useful to examine the patterns of black and white mean net migration to see if the patterns hold up in a less standardized metric. The mean net migration is defined as $(1/C) \Sigma_i^c NM_r$, where C is the number of counties and NM_r is the sum of the net migration by race per county. Table 4.3 presents these figures for blacks. Most of the signs in this table are negative. Only the counties of Arkansas in 1900−1910 and Oklahoma in 1910−1920 experienced average net in-migration of blacks. This differs from the table of net migration rates. However, the other patterns from the table of net migration rates appear to hold up. The greatest net out-migration occurred in 1940−1950, followed by 1920−1930, 1910−1920, 1930−1940, and 1900−1910. The states with counties losing, for the most part, the least black population were Texas, Oklahoma, Arkansas, and Louisiana, whereas South Carolina, Alabama, Mississippi, and Georgia lost the most. These conclusions suggest that despite the fact that the net rate weights each county equally, it is not an inaccurate representation of the average gross patterns for blacks.

Table 4.4 presents the mean net migration rates for whites. Again,

TABLE 4.3
Mean Net Migration Rates of Blacks
for Nine Southern States, 1900 – 1950[a]

State	1900-1910	1910-1920	1920-1930	1930-1940	1940-1950
Alabama	-455.485	-1046.328	-1623.925	-952.029	-2428.388
Arkansas	281.560	-19.587	-830.440	-441.787	-1535.773
Georgia	-350.175	-640.466	-1954.200	-574.547	-1197.390
Louisiana	-291.508	-1127.150	-747.969	-128.406	-1694.188
Mississippi	-584.227	-1943.278	-1182.158	-714.854	-3165.122
North Carolina	-318.742	-341.143	-327.470	-599.419	-1097.210
South Carolina	-2478.800	-2244.744	-4865.043	-2060.174	-3475.565
Texas	-179.077	-78.045	-271.282	-70.224	-587.583
Oklahoma		10.566	-41.195	-168.584	-487.234

TABLE 4.4
Mean Net Migration Rates of Whites
for Nine Southern States, 1900 – 1950[a]

State	1900-1910	1910-1920	1920-1930	1930-1940	1940-1950
Alabama	-603.424	-641.910	-518.074	-1510.149	-1432.522
Arkansas	-648.920	-905.667	-1452.960	-1271.240	-1923.787
Georgia	-495.854	-423.103	-857.548	-275.641	-149.893
Louisiana	402.118	-1006.050	468.000	222.109	251.313
Mississippi	-484.293	-1002.861	-124.085	-391.597	-636.293
North Carolina	-572.206	-545.969	419.050	-253.320	-260.700
South Carolina	-604.050	-341.977	-696.869	-174.782	-55.522
Texas	-144.838	-123.474	-1875.243	-244.981	67.442
Oklahoma	--	643.553	-268.468	-3327.896	-3453.493

there are a few more positive signs than the average net migration rate table showed, but, still, similar conclusions emerge. Net out-migration was greatest in 1940–1950, followed by 1920–1930, 1930–1940, 1910–1920, and 1900–1910. The states in the West (Texas, Oklahoma, Mississippi, and Louisiana) appear to have had slightly less net out-migration, although the patterns are not as clearcut as those shown in the average net migration rate table.

All in all, it appears that the general patterns in the average net migration rate tables are similar to those in the mean net migration tables. This suggests that the use of migration rates does not misstate the gross patterns of net migration.

Tables 4.5 and 4.6 give a better sense of the spread and variation of net migration rates. These tables show the number and percentage of counties in each state that had net migration rates of (a) less than −10; (b) greater than −10 and less than 0; (c) greater than 0 and less than +10; and (d) greater than +10.

Table 4.5 presents these breakdowns for blacks. One should note that except for the cases of Georgia and Mississippi in 1940–1950 and South Carolina in 1900–1910, 1920–1930, 1930–1940, and 1940–1950, there are counties in every classification. The most impressive feature, however, is the overwhelming preponderance of counties that experienced net out-migration rates. In the 1940–1950 period, for instance, the state with the lowest proportion of counties experiencing a net migration rate of less than −10 for blacks was Texas, and yet over 77% of the counties in Texas had this high a rate. The general patterns in this table confirm what the average rates by state show. Table 4.5 displays similar patterns for all states at all points in time as do Tables 4.1 and 4.3. In all cases but two, the net rate of "less than −10" has a plurality of the counties, and in nearly 75% of all the states, counties in this category form a majority over a period of time.

The patterns of net migration per state for whites are in Table 4.6. Again, this table reveals similar patterns to Table 4.2. In all cases, there are counties applicable to each of the four categories. The differences between black and white patterns is quite telling. While most states experienced net out-migration in most counties, the number of counties in the "less than −10" category is far lower for whites than blacks. This implies that whatever was pushing or pulling was a stronger force for blacks than for whites. While rural poverty in the South may have had similar causes for both groups, it is likely that blacks faced more severe crises and, in most cases, were an underclass that took a disproportionate share of hard times. This disadvantage manifested itself in a relatively higher rate

TABLE 4.5

Number and Percentage of Counties in Each State Experiencing
Black Net In- and Out-Migration Rates

State - rate	1900-1910 #	1900-1910 %	1910-1920 #	1910-1920 %	1920-1930 #	1920-1930 %	1930-1940 #	1930-1940 %	1940-1950 #	1940-1950 %
Alabama										
Lt -10	27	40.9	39	58.2	52	77.6	46	68.7	61	91.0
-10 - 0	18	27.3	15	22.4	8	11.9	16	23.9	4	6.0
0 - 10	9	13.6	8	11.9	2	3.0	2	3.0	1	1.5
10+	12	18.2	5	7.5	5	7.5	3	4.5	1	1.5
Arkansas										
Lt -10	32	42.7	40	53.3	54	72.0	56	74.7	66	88.0
-10 - 0	16	21.3	19	25.3	8	10.7	10	13.3	3	4.0
0 - 10	8	10.7	4	5.3	5	6.7	6	8.0	1	1.3
10+	19	25.3	12	16.0	8	10.7	3	4.0	5	6.7
Georgia										
Lt -10	59	43.1	89	61.0	139	89.7	117	73.6	141	88.7
-10 - 0	47	34.3	38	26.0	8	5.2	28	17.6	14	8.8
0 - 10	24	17.5	11	7.5	4	2.6	6	3.8	4	2.5
10+	7	5.1	8	5.5	4	2.6	8	5.0	0	0.0
Louisiana										
Lt -10	18	30.5	37	61.7	41	64.1	29	45.3	56	87.5
-10 - 0	23	39.0	11	18.3	9	14.1	23	35.9	4	6.3
0 - 10	8	13.6	6	10.0	4	6.3	9	14.1	1	1.6
10+	10	16.9	6	10.0	10	15.6	3	4.7	3	4.7
Mississippi										
Lt -10	32	42.7	63	79.7	51	62.2	43	52.4	78	95.1
-10 - 0	25	33.3	6	7.6	17	20.7	29	35.4	2	2.4
0 - 10	6	8.0	5	6.3	9	11.0	8	9.8	0	0.0
10+	12	16.0	5	6.3	5	6.1	2	2.4	2	2.4
North Carolina										
Lt -10	42	43.3	48	49.0	57	57.0	54	54.0	82	82.0
-10 - 0	34	35.1	34	34.7	23	23.0	32	32.0	12	12.0
0 - 10	15	15.5	9	9.2	10	10.0	9	9.0	3	3.0
10+	6	6.2	7	7.1	10	10.0	5	5.0	3	3.0
South Carolina										
Lt -10	17	42.5	26	60.5	43	93.5	37	80.4	45	97.8
-10 - 0	21	52.5	13	30.2	3	6.5	8	17.4	1	2.2
0 - 10	2	5.0	3	7.0	0	0.0	0	0.0	0	0.0
10+	0	0.0	1	2.3	0	0.0	1.	2.4	0	0.0
Texas										
Lt -10	71	46.1	59	38.3	86	55.1	91	58.3	121	77.6
-10 - 0	28	18.2	30	19.5	18	11.5	28	17.9	7	4.5
0 - 10	13	8.4	19	12.3	12	7.7	19	12.2	6	3.8
10+	42	27.3	46	29.9	40	25.6	18	11.5	22	14.1
Oklahoma										
Lt -10			44	57.9	43	55.8	54	70.1	61	79.2
-10 - 0			9	11.8	6	7.8	9	11.7	1	1.3
0 - 10			3	3.9	2	2.6	4	5.2	4	5.2
10+			20	26.3	26	33.8	10	13.0	11	14.3

TABLE 4.6

Number and Percentage of Counties in Each State Experiencing
White Net In- and Out-Migration Rates

State - rate	1900-1910 #	1900-1910 %	1910-1920 #	1910-1920 %	1920-1930 #	1920-1930 %	1930-1940 #	1930-1940 %	1940-1950 #	1940-1950 %
Alabama										
Lt -10	30	45.5	29	43.3	35	52.2	20	29.9	48	71.6
-10 - 0	22	33.3	25	37.3	20	29.9	34	50.7	6	9.0
0 - 10	7	10.6	9	13.4	9	13.4	11	16.4	7	10.4
10+	7	10.6	4	6.0	3	4.5	2	3.0	6	9.0
Arkansas										
Lt -10	26	34.7	28	37.3	49	65.3	20	26.7	54	72.0
-10 - 0	25	33.3	29	38.7	10	13.3	40	53.3	13	17.3
0 - 10	11	14.7	9	12.0	2	5.3	10	13.3	5	6.7
10+	13	17.3	9	12.0	12	16.0	5	6.7	3	4.0
Georgia										
Lt -10	73	53.3	64	43.8	109	70.3	49	30.8	105	66.0
-10 - 0	37	27.0	54	37.0	27	17.4	65	40.9	29	18.2
0 - 10	17	12.4	18	12.3	9	5.8	30	18.9	11	6.9
10+	10	7.4	10	6.8	10	6.5	15	9.4	14	8.8
Louisiana										
Lt -10	10	16.9	31	51.7	22	34.4	5	7.8	32	50.0
-10 - 0	20	33.9	11	18.3	14	21.9	18	28.1	13	20.3
0 - 10	13	22.0	7	11.7	9	14.1	28	43.8	8	12.5
10+	16	27.1	11	18.3	19	29.7	13	20.3	11	17.2
Mississippi										
Lt -10	33	44.0	42	53.2	30	36.6	6	7.3	54	65.9
-10 - 0	20	26.7	23	29.1	24	29.3	48	58.5	14	17.1
0 - 10	13	17.3	5	6.3	12	14.6	19	23.2	8	9.8
10+	9	12.0	9	11.4	16	19.5	9	11.0	6	7.3
North Carolina										
Lt -10	37	38.1	39	39.8	33	33.0	9	9.0	50	50.0
-10 - 0	36	37.1	34	34.7	35	35.0	53	53.0	30	30.0
0 - 10	19	19.6	18	18.4	19	19.0	23	28.0	12	12.0
10+	5	5.2	7	7.1	13	13.0	10	10.0	8	8.0
South Carolina										
Lt -10	12	30.0	11	25.6	20	43.5	4	8.7	18	39.1
-10 - 0	15	37.5	22	51.2	16	34.8	24	52.2	19	41.3
0 - 10	10	25.0	4	9.3	8	17.4	10	21.7	6	13.0
10+	3	7.5	6	14.0	2	4.3	8	17.4	3	6.5
Texas										
Lt -10	65	42.2	79	51.3	104	66.7	43	27.6	108	69.2
-10 - 0	26	16.9	38	24.7	20	12.8	47	30.1	23	14.7
0 - 10	14	9.1	18	11.7	15	9.6	27	17.3	6	3.8
10+	49	31.8	19	12.3	17	10.9	39	25.0	19	12.2
Oklahoma										
Lt -10			34	44.7	47	61.0	35	45.5	66	85.7
-10 - 0			11	14.5	6	7.8	16	20.8	3	3.9
0 - 10			11	14.5	13	16.9	11	14.3	2	2.6
10+			20	26.3	11	14.3	15	19.5	6	7.8

of geographical mobility and in an incessant search to find a better situation.

Several conclusions can be drawn from this discussion. Both blacks and whites tended to leave southern counties. They tended to leave counties in Texas, Oklahoma, Louisiana, and Arkansas less than counties in and Georgia and South Carolina. This trend reflected the general westward movement of blacks and whites through the first 20 years of this century. After 1930, both groups tended to leave all states. These movements reflect periods of agricultural depression (1940–1950, 1920–1930) in the face of expanding opportunities elsewhere, periods of agricultural stagnation (1930–1940) in the face of general depression, and periods of agricultural expansion (1900–1910, 1910–1920) with concomitant expansion of the rest of the economy. The major difference between white and black patterns is the fact that net out-migration rates were almost always higher for blacks than whites.

It is useful to consider other patterns of change over the 50-year span that are central to our understanding of what caused and motivated the migration patterns observed here. Particularly of interest are the patterns in the changing social relations of production, the concomitant changes in cotton production, and the introduction of machinery.

The patterns of ownership and tenantry for blacks are shown in Table 4.7. Between 1900 and 1910 there was a 38.8% increase in black ownership. These new owners were spread throughout the states of the South and reflected the expanding market and rising price of cotton. The number of tenants also increased enormously over this period (23.3%). Both ownership and tenantry grew slightly in the period 1910–1920. In the agricultural depression of the 1920s, the number of black farm owners dropped nearly 34% while black tenants increased. The depression forced a fair number of blacks to give up their land, and some probably became tenants. Through the agricultural transformation of the 1930s and 1940s, the number of black owners remained fairly constant. The number of tenants, on the other hand, dropped enormously—27.6% between 1930 and 1940 and 29% from 1940 to 1950. This displacement reflects the reorganization of southern agriculture, which was the direct result of state intervention into the collapsing southern agricultural system in the depression of the 1930s.

Patterns of ownership and tenantry among whites (presented in Table 4.8) are quite similar to those of blacks. The first decade of the century witnessed a 23% increase in white ownership and a 34.6% increase in tenantry. The decade 1910–1920 had small increases in the numbers of owners and tenants. The agricultural depression of the 1920s struck whites as heavily as blacks. While there was a reduction of roughly

TABLE 4.7
*Numbers of Black Owners and Tenants for Nine Southern States, 1900 – 1950**

State	Owners						Tenants					
	1900	1910	1920	1930	1940	1950	1900	1910	1920	1930	1940	1950
Alabama	11,123	17,082	17,202	11,417	11,776	13,269	79,901	93,309	77,874	77,820	57,651	38,026
Arkansas	9,991	14,662	15,373	9,058	8,943	8,860	34,962	48,885	56,814	68,106	47,206	28,678
Georgia	9,547	15,698	15,595	9,002	8,601	9,787	71,243	106,738	111,334	75,636	49,078	37,986
Louisiana	8,460	10,725	10,815	8,750	9,526	10,417	48,703	44,077	50,370	63,213	48,380	27,669
Mississippi	18,368	25,026	22,513	19,254	20,625	23,293	107,599	139,605	134,095	160,359	135,989	92,154
North Carolina	13,204	21,443	22,095	13,198	14,576	14,980	37,223	44,139	53,190	57,139	42,209	49,017
South Carolina	15,489	20,372	21,919	11,991	13,001	13,847	66,251	76,295	82,437	61,362	45,595	40,329
Texas	16,910	21,044	23,378	15,914	16,052	14,370	44,946	48,029	54,286	65,739	32,582	13,866
Oklahoma	10,119	11,150	9,458	6,550	4,921	4,287	2,985	9,494	9,140	14,559	7,475	3,047
Total	113,211	157,202	158,348	105,134	108,021	113,112	495,104	610,571	629,540	643,933	466,165	330,771

*Only one-half of Texas included; sample described in Appendix B.

TABLE 4.8

Numbers of White Owners and Tenants for Nine Southern States, 1900–1950[*]

State	Owners						Tenants					
	1900	1910	1920	1930	1940	1950	1900	1910	1920	1930	1940	1950
Alabama	69,923	86,847	89,887	64,757	68,497	84,480	48,973	65,017	70,395	88,545	78,573	49,587
Arkansas	74,147	91,987	97,274	63,539	78,904	84,783	46,178	58,381	62,407	84,640	69,016	39,614
Georgia	72,056	82,930	82,551	61,582	67,499	86,080	63,317	84,242	88,929	98,754	80,762	46,745
Louisiana	36,255	42,264	42,832	38,110	43,644	52,413	18,531	22,530	24,323	43,769	40,787	21,530
Mississippi	57,613	67,040	66,746	58,122	68,075	80,210	30,253	41,886	41,237	65,448	56,770	35,708
North Carolina	100,320	123,877	127,583	102,758	118,504	127,101	55,785	63,148	63,167	80,478	92,000	70,243
South Carolina	37,119	43,978	44,112	33,578	37,498	45,442	28,633	34,926	37,558	41,406	32,990	22,857
Texas	125,606	152,382	153,053	112,441	123,712	122,558	124,213	154,667	158,115	198,056	145,406	68,276
Oklahoma	50,018	74,254	83,100	47,402	50,942	59,416	44,265	95,643	87,819	110,770	90,345	41,680
Total	662,057	765,558	787,138	582,288	657,274	742,483	460,148	619,439	633,947	811,866	686,649	396,240

*Only one-half of Texas included; sample described in Appendix B.

85

200,000 owners, there was an increase of 180,000 tenants. This reflects the fact that many owners (26%) lost their land, and a fair proportion of these owners became tenants. The decades 1930–1940 and 1940–1950 saw increases in the numbers of white owners and, at the same time, white tenantry decreased dramatically.

A comparison of white and black patterns of ownership and tenantry reveals almost identical tendencies. Ownership and tenantry increased for both groups during 1900–1910 and to a lesser extent during 1910–1920. During 1920–1930, both blacks and whites lost their land and large numbers of them became tenants. The 1930s, 1940s, and 1950s show large decreases in the number of both black and white tenants. The only divergence is that black ownership from 1930–1950 remained relatively constant while white ownership increased. White owners always outnumbered black owners about five-to-one or greater; however, the vast majority of these farm owners owned less than 200 acres. Indeed, the 1910 census found that of 325 southern counties only 22,157 farms had more than five tenants. This implies that over 97% of all owner-operated farms were neither large nor plantations. Table 4.8 shows that white farm owners constituted the majority of white farmers in all decades except 1930. This suggests that the bulk of the white population was in control of its land and day-to-day activities. Blacks, on the other hand, were far less represented in the owner class. Only about 25% of all black farmers were owners.

In terms of tenant statuses, a number of studies have shown that blacks were concentrated in the lower end of the tenant distribution (U.S. Census, 1916:568–578; Goldenweiser and Truesdell, 1924:71–79;

TABLE 4.9
*Breakdown of Various Tenant Statuses by Race**

Status	Blacks		Whites	
	#	%	#	%
Cropper	79,643	48	17,935	28
Share	38,802	24	31,012	48
Cash	44,999	27	14,697	22
Unspecified	945	1	1,050	2
Total	164,389	100	64,694	100

*Data source: C. O. Brannen's data on 93 selected plantation counties in 1920.

Woofter, 1969:63 − 68, 1936:9 − 14; Brannen, 1924:36 − 38). Table 4.9 shows the breakdown of tenant status by race in 93 plantation counties (Brannen, 1924). The results show that 49% of the blacks were sharecroppers while only 25% of the whites were in this status. Whereas the bulk of white tenants were share tenants, the bulk of the blacks were sharecroppers.

These distributions suggest a number of things about the class and general socioeconomic conditions of blacks and whites. First, whites were clearly better off than blacks in general. Second, whites tended to be farm owners, and if they were tenants, they tended to be share or cash tenants and not sharecroppers. Blacks were not likely to be farm owners but were very likely to be highly concentrated in the sharecropper status. Furthermore, the majority of farm laborers tended to be black (Brannen, 1924:24 − 25). In terms of the class composition of the South, then, blacks were not only highly concentrated in the tenant farming system, but they also tended to occupy the lowest rungs in that system. While blacks may have been in the lowest positions in the tenure system hierarchy, whites often found themselves in comparably poor situations.

Given that blacks tended to occupy lesser positions, it is interesting to consider their labor mobility. Table 4.10 presents evidence which suggests that (a) sharecroppers moved more frequently than tenants; and (b) whites in similar statuses moved more frequently than blacks. High sharecropper mobility has been attributed to the eternal search for a better position (Brannen, 1924:44 − 52; Vance, 1929:151 − 154; Woofter, 1936:123 − 124). This raises two questions: (a) Why do blacks move less than whites? and (b) Is this not inconsistent with the data that suggest

TABLE 4.10
Tenants' Terms of Occupancy by Race for
*Ninety-Three Selected Counties**

Term of occupancy	White		Black	
	Croppers	Tenants	Croppers	Tenants
Under 1 year	28.4%	20.5%	19.7%	11.4%
1 year	36.8	28.0	28.9	19.8
2-4 years	25.6	30.8	35.4	34.9
5-9 years	5.9	12.4	10.5	17.8
10+ years	3.3	8.3	5.5	16.1

*Data source: C. O. Brannen's data.

greater mobility for blacks? Woofter (1936:123 – 124) argues, in answer to the first question, that blacks had less mobility within statuses because their options were unlikely to improve with geographic movement. Another explanation is that blacks may have been forced to stay on the land with coercion (Cohen, 1976). Of course, both of these factors could have been operating. These results are not inconsistent with the data presented in this chapter. Because the bulk of the whites were not sharecroppers, the majority of the white population was not experiencing high rates of geographical mobility. Because blacks were concentrated in the lower statuses, their average movement was higher than whites'.

There is certainly a relationship between the number of existing farm owners and tenants at a given time and the amounts of cotton produced and land needed to produce it. Table 4.11 shows the number of acres of cotton planted from 1899 to 1949, and Table 4.12 presents the bales of cotton produced. The pattern of acres of cotton planted suggests two things: (a) the increases in acres planted between 1899 and 1929 occur mainly in Texas, Oklahoma, Arkansas, and Mississippi, which again demonstrates the westward movement of cotton production; and (b) the increase in cotton acreage appears to be highly correlated with the increases and decreases in numbers of farm owners and tenants. The tremendous increase in the number of owners and tenants between 1900 and 1910 goes hand in hand with an increase of around 7 million acres of cotton planted. The acres remained stable from 1910 to 1920, reflecting the relative stability of the number of cotton producers. From 1919 to 1929 there was an actual increase of land planted in cotton. This reflects the dynamic that is implicit in the cotton cycle of debt discussed earlier. If one planted cotton and was in debt, the only solution was to increase the production of cotton, which increased the amount and thereby depressed the price. By 1932, this vicious circle had enveloped most farmers and there was no apparent way to end their misery. The massive decrease in acreage between 1930 and 1940 goes a long way toward explaining why the number of tenants decreased so rapidly. The major cause of this acreage decrease was government intervention. The amount of cotton produced, as shown in Table 4.12, also reflected the patterns mentioned above. Production increased between 1899 and 1929. From 1929 to 1939, an acreage reduction of 49% only produced a bale reduction of 25.5%. This is because the least productive land was taken out of production while the most productive land was still being planted.

The final indicator of social change is the growth in the number of tractors used in the South. Tractors came to the South rather late mainly because there was little capital to invest in machines prior to 1933, and labor was very cheap. The mechanization of cotton production must be viewed as the outcome of various social processes. The causal role of

TABLE 4.11

Acres of Cotton Planted, 1899–1949*

State	Acres					
	1899	1909	1919	1929	1939	1949
Alabama	3,202,135	3,730,892	2,628,160	3,566,494	1,928,680	1,851,391
Arkansas	1,641,855	1,920,458	2,553,855	3,446,485	2,056,565	2,572,610
Georgia	3,343,081	4,883,314	4,543,864	3,405,623	1,856,101	1,556,504
Louisiana	1,376,254	956,411	1,309,378	1,946,354	1,085,836	916,130
Mississippi	2,897,560	3,395,120	2,894,494	3,965,234	2,452,734	2,767,507
North Carolina	1,007,019	1,278,954	1,346,098	1,639,393	709,717	845,469
South Carolina	1,995,403	2,559,467	2,535,248	1,974,758	1,189,767	1,197,845
Texas	6,884,148	9,225,883	10,581,321	13,557,053	6,194,620	6,024,600
Oklahoma	--	1,976,935	2,707,486	4,148,267	1,671,435	1,227,911
Total	23,324,374	30,156,719	31,099,887	37,649,647	19,145,438	18,959,949

*Only one-half of Texas included.

TABLE 4.12
Bales of Cotton Produced, 1899 – 1949*

State	Bales					
	1899	1909	1919	1929	1939	1949
Alabama	1,093,697	1,129,577	715,163	1,312,028	772,511	823,910
Arkansas	705,748	781,786	869,350	1,398,455	1,351,509	1,584,306
Georgia	1,188,357	1,992,258	1,632,607	1,344,462	988,360	614,950
Louisiana	699,971	268,909	297,609	798,558	717,330	607,546
Mississippi	1,286,680	1,127,136	943,484	1,874,672	1,533,362	1,436,539
North Carolina	433,019	665,123	837,866	764,308	461,415	472,390
South Carolina	807,431	1,250,406	1,435,332	835,314	849,982	543,486
Texas	2,566,728	2,355,045	2,604,237	2,979,892	2,065,020	2,719,700
Oklahoma	- -	555,744	1,025,172	1,130,315	520,568	567,682
Total	9,337,370	10,125,984	10,360,821	12,438,005	9,260,056	9,430,507

*Only one-half of Texas included.

TABLE 4.13
Number of Tractors in Each State, 1920–1950

State	1920	1930	1940	1950
Alabama	811	4,664	7,449	37,791
Arkansas	1,822	7,066	9,415	41,415
Georgia	2,252	5,870	9,348	60,576
Louisiana	2,815	5,016	9,476	36,029
Mississippi	667	5,542	8,740	49,726
North Carolina	2,277	11,427	15,612	73,534
South Carolina	1,304	3,462	4,791	30,329
Texas	9,048	20,007	61,231	153,498
Oklahoma	6,210	25,962	45,369	93,810
Total	25,203	89,016	171,431	576,708

mechanization in displacing tenants came only after displacement due to acreage reductions had begun. Table 4.13 presents the growth in the number of tractors per state from 1920 to 1950. By 1950, machines became much more commonplace. The number of tractors more than tripled between 1920 and 1930, nearly doubled between 1930 and 1940, and increased by more than three times between 1940 and 1950. Since an enormous number of tenants were displaced between 1930 and 1940, it is clear that mechanization was not mainly responsible for that decline. One other thing to note is that mechanization began in Texas and Oklahoma and proceeded eastward.

This survey of net migration patterns and of changes in the social composition and production organization in the South represents a simplification of the key tendencies in the South. So far, this discussion has only presented the barest minimum of facts. The historical and empirical chapters ahead will lay out the causal nexus that underlies the out-migration process.

Chapter 5

The South Stumbles Along, 1900 — 1930

"It is good bye with poor white folks and niggers now," wrote one negro editor, "for the train of disenfranchisement is on the rail and will come thundering upon us like an avalanche, there is no use crying, we have got to shute the shute."

—*Huntsville Journal,* April 20, 1900
(quoted in Hackney, 1969:179)

This chapter tries to convey how the southern agricultural system worked through the period 1900 — 1930 and how the rest of the country and world impinged on that system. These changes and developments both within and outside of the South are then connected to the migration process. This consideration demonstrates how the various events and structures had direct implications for the net in- and out-migration rates of blacks and whites for counties of the South from 1900 to 1930.

The South from 1900 to 1930: Boom and Bust in the Cotton Belt

While most political activity oriented toward changing southern society had been quelled, and white domination over blacks became part of state policy, the most important factor for most southern farmers in 1900 was the price of cotton. Table 5.1 contains the average price of cotton per pound from 1890 to 1950. Cotton prices from 1890 to 1899 fluctuated between 8.59¢ and 5.73¢ per pound, on the average. Since it has been estimated that cotton cost around 8¢ per pound to produce during this period, it is clear that most farmers were losing money during most years in this decade. The decade 1900 — 1909 witnessed increases in average cotton prices with the range of prices going from 6.98¢ to 13.52¢ per

TABLE 5.1
Cotton Acreage, Production, and Price, 1890 – 1950*

	Cotton		
	Acreage harvested	Production	Price per pound
	(1,000 acres)	(1,000 bales)	cents
1950	17,843	10,014	40.07
1949	27,439	16,128	28.58
1948	22,911	14,877	30.38
1947	21,330	11,860	31.93
1946	17,584	8,640	32.64
1945	17,029	9,015	22.52
1944	19,617	12,230	20.73
1943	21,610	11,427	19.90
1942	22,602	12,817	19.05
1941	22,236	10,744	17.03
1940	23,861	12.566	9.89
1939	23,805	11,817	9.09
1938	24,248	11,943	8.60
1937	33,623	18,946	8.41
1936	29,755	12,399	12.36
1935	27,509	10,638	11.09
1934	26,866	9,636	12.36
1933	29,383	13,047	10.17
1932	35,891	13,003	6.52
1931	38,704	17,097	5.66
1930	42,444	13,932	9.46
1929	43,232	14,825	16.78
1928	42,434	14,477	17.98
1927	38,342	12,956	20.20
1926	44,608	17,978	12.49
1925	44,386	16,105	19.62
1924	39,501	13,630	22.91
1923	35,550	10,140	28.69
1922	31,361	9,755	22.88
1921	28,678	7,945	17.00
1920	34,408	13,429	15.89
1919	32,906	11,141	35.34
1918	35,038	12,018	28.88
1917	32,245	11,284	27.09
1916	33.071	11,448	17.36
1915	29,951	11,172	11.22
1914	35,615	16,112	7.35
1913	35,206	14,153	12.47
1912	32,557	13,703	11.50
1911	34,916	15,694	9.65
1910	31,508	11,609	13.96
1909	30,555	10,005	13.52
1908	31,091	13,241	9.01
1907	30,729	11,106	10.36
1906	31,404	13,274	9.58

Table 5.1 (Continued)

1905	27,753	10,576	10.78
1904	30,077	13,438	8.98
1903	27,762	9,851	10.49
1902	27,561	10,630	7.60
1901	27,050	9,508	7.03
1900	24,886	10,124	9.15
1899	24,163	9,346	6.98
1898	24,715	11,278	5.73
1897	25,131	10,899	6.68
1896	23,230	8,533	6.66
1895	19,839	7,162	7.62
1894	21,886	9,091	4.59
1893	20,256	7,493	7.00
1892	18,869	6,700	8.34
1891	21,503	9,035	7.24
1890	20,937	8,653	8.59

*SOURCE: U. S. Bureau of the Census, 1975:517-518.

pound. The decade of World War I, 1910 – 1919, witnessed an explosion in the price of cotton, and in 1919 the average price climbed to 35.42¢ per pound. There was a precipitous drop in the price of cotton from 1920 – 1929. The price decreased from 1920 to 1921, rose during 1922 – 1923, and then declined to 16.78¢ per pound in 1929.

What relevant social forces operated to expand or contract the production and consumption of cotton, and how did these forces affect production in the long run? The discussion here points out the major forces at work in each decade during the 1900 – 1930 period, and shows how these factors expanded or contracted cotton production. Such factors are linked to the changing class composition of the southern labor force. This analysis requires a consideration of the rural class structure, of the urban and industrial developments, and of the exploitation of southern resources such as iron, coal, natural gas, and petroleum. Relevant activities in the political sphere are also discussed, and the shift of political activity from the state to the federal government is considered. Finally, developments in racial relations are examined. These discussions may help us to better understand migration during the 1900 – 1930 period.

1900 – 1910

By the beginning of the twentieth century, the depression of the 1890s had ended. Manufacturing was expanding worldwide and demand for cotton increased (Street, 1957:35 – 37). From 1900 to 1910, the price of cotton increased, and it would have risen even higher had cotton production not boomed as well. The first decade of the century saw an enormous increase in both the number of tenants and farm owners (see Tables 4.7 and 4.8). Table 5.2 presents the number and percentage of counties experiencing positive growth in cotton production and of persons owning and working farms. Seventy-six percent of the counties had a growth in acres of cotton planted. Furthermore, 64.4% had an increased number of black tenants and 78.1% had an increased number of black owners. Similar patterns emerged for whites as tenantry increased in 78.7% of the counties and ownership increased in 81.9%.

TABLE 5.2
Percentage and Number of Counties with Positive and Negative Values for Selected Variables, 1900 – 1950

		1900–10		1910–20		1920–30		1930–40		1940–50	
Variable		#	%	#	%	#	%	#	%	#	%
ΔCOTTON	pos.	534	76.0	462	57.9	534	65.0	10	1.2	220	27.4
	neg.	139	24.0	336	42.1	288	35.0	794	98.8	584	72.6
ΔBALES	pos.	412	58.6	396	49.6	471	57.3	133	16.5	249	31.0
	neg.	291	41.4	402	50.4	351	42.7	671	83.5	555	69.0
ΔURBAN	pos.	472	67.1	499	62.5	466	56.7	425	52.9	756	94.0
	neg.	231	32.9	299	37.5	356	43.3	329	47.1	48	6.0
ΔTENANTSB	pos.	453	64.4	364	45.4	401	48.8	80	10.0	88	10.9
	neg.	250	35.6	434	54.6	421	51.2	724	90.0	716	89.1
ΔTENANTSW	pos.	553	78.7	439	55.0	634	77.1	190	23.6	31	3.9
	neg.	150	21.3	359	45.0	188	22.9	614	76.4	773	96.1
ΔOWNERSB	pos.	549	78.1	348	43.6	67	8.2	334	41.5	405	50.4
	neg.	154	21.9	450	56.4	755	91.8	470	58.5	399	49.6
ΔOWNERSW	pos.	576	81.9	355	55.5	56	6.8	604	75.1	604	75.1
	neg.	127	18.1	443	44.5	766	93.2	200	24.9	200	24.9
NMRB	pos.	193	27.5	178	22.3	156	19.0	112	13.9	60	7.5
	neg.	510	72.5	620	77.7	666	81.0	692	86.1	744	92.5
NMRW	pos.	216	30.7	194	24.3	201	24.5	286	35.6	140	17.4
	neg.	487	69.3	604	75.7	621	75.5	518	64.4	664	82.6

*ΔCOTTON = change over a decade in the percent of farm acres in a county in cotton; ΔBALES = percent change in bales of cotton produced over a decade; ΔURBAN = change over decade in the percent of persons living in places greater than 2,500 in a county; ΔTENANTSB, ΔTENANTSW = percent change in number of tenants over a decade in a county by race (B=blacks, W=whites); ΔOWNERSB, ΔOWNERSW = percent change in number of owners over a decade in a county by race (B=blacks, W=whites); NMRB, NMRW = net migration rate over a decade in a county by race (B=blacks, W=whites).

Expansion of cotton production occurred everywhere, but much of the growth in cotton acreage took place in Texas, Oklahoma, Mississippi, and Arkansas (see Table 4.11). Cotton production continued its westward expansion and utilized land that was previously uncultivated or was used for other purposes. With this expansion, people were moving west and were leaving the small towns in the South (not in Table 5.2 the large number of counties with urban populations experiencing negative changes). The class composition of the South was also changing. More people were entering cotton production, and this meant that more people ran the risk of being jeopardized by the agricultural credit system. The ratio of farm owners to farm tenants for blacks climbed from .24 to .27 over the period, while the ratio for whites dropped from 1.44 to 1.23. This implies that the number of black owners increased relative to black tenants while the number of white owners decreased relative to white tenants.

Northern industrialists gained control over the industrial development of the South in the late 1800s and continued to control that development into the twentieth century. The early twentieth century witnessed the consolidation of control over the marketing of cotton (Woodman, 1968). The growth in cotton farming continued to force farmers not to grow food or diversify crops, which made them more dependent on railroads and merchants to supply them with food and supplies.

Southern industry was expanding into textiles, iron and coal, aluminum mining, and oil and natural gas production (Herring, 1940; Hoover and Hatchford, 1951; Odum, 1936; Vance, 1935; Woodward, 1974:291 – 320). This industrial expansion had two major features: (a) It tended toward extractive industries thereby leaving little wealth behind; and (b) industries were almost exclusively owned and operated by northerners (Woodward, 1974:292 – 320). Textiles were manufactured in the South starting in the 1880s (Blicksilver, 1959; Street, 1957:36), and by 1910 over half of the textiles being produced in the United States were coming from the South (Street, 1957:36). Although almost all of these plants were northern owned, the South captured textile production by providing cheap labor, newer physical plants, and proximity to cotton production.

Iron, coal, and aluminum industries in the South are examples of how the North exploited southern resources to benefit itself. The extraction of oil and gas was quickly controlled by Standard Oil and Gulf Oil, which were owned by the Rockefellers and Mellons (Johnson, 1956, 1967; Woodward, 1974:303). This resulted in northern business exploiting southern natural resources without developing any indigenous industry.

For this reason, C. Vann Woodward (1974) has referred to the South during this period as a "colonial economy."

Indigenous southern industry was stifled in yet another way—the freight rate differential. Northern control of southern railroads was complete by 1900, and farmers and industrial producers were placed in the position of paying whatever freight rates were changed. Special rates made it relatively cheap to ship raw materials, but finished goods were shipped at higher rates. It became cheaper for southerners to buy their finished goods from the North than to produce these goods themselves. Capitalist expansion did not lead to a better life for most southerners (Woodward, 1974):

> Cut off from better-paying jobs, and the higher opportunities, the great majority of southerners were confined to the worn grooves of a tributary economy. Some emigrated to other sections, but the mass of them stuck to farming, mining, forestry, or some low wage industry, whether they liked it or not. The inevitable result was further intensification of the old problems of worn-out soil, cut-over timber lands, and worked-out mines [pp. 319–320].

The continued expansion of the cotton industry in the decade 1900–1910 must be seen from this perspective. With few opportunities within the South and an economy built primarily on the extraction of raw materials, it was natural that good prices for cotton and open land drew people into cotton farming. The South and southern development, then, can be seen as that of a colony. The North controlled what was produced, the cost to ship it, how high its selling price was, and determined what kinds of investments were made. Cotton farming flourished because individual producers found few opportunities to do anything else.

The decade 1900–1910 also witnessed the beginning of a major impediment to cotton farming—the invasion of boll weevils in Texas. Map 5.1 shows the extent of the boll weevil infestation from 1890 to 1921. By 1910, a large part of Texas and parts of Oklahoma, Arkansas, and Louisiana were infested by boll weevils, thereby destroying a large part of the crops. This meant that cotton farming became nearly impossible for a few years and forced people to leave the land or grow something else. Despite attempts to control the boll weevil, by the early 1920s it had spread across the entire South.

At the political level, 1900–1910 was notable for three reasons. First, Populists controlled the national Democratic party until 1901. Second, conservative elements regained control of the party and tried to renew the South—East coalition of the New South Democrats. Finally, the political struggle, insofar as it affected farmers, was no longer carried out at the state government level, but became part of national politics.

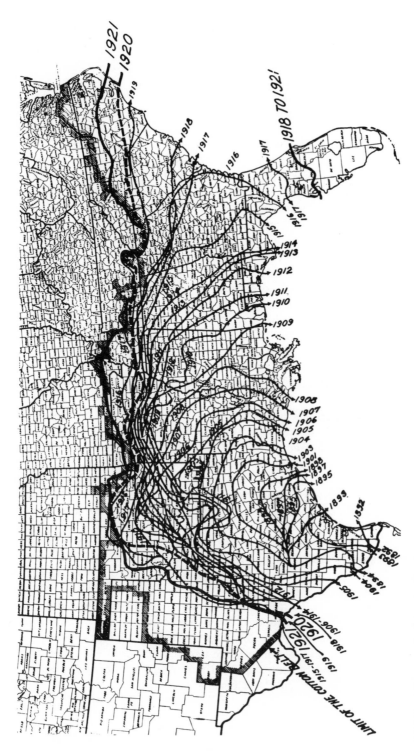

MAP 5.1. *The spread of the Mexican Cotton Boll Weevil in the United States from 1892 to 1921. (Source: U.S. Department of Agriculture, 1921.)*

The effects of fusion between southern Democrats and Populists initially had a radicalizing effect on the Democratic party (Hackney, 1969:121; Hicks, 1931:340−379; Tindall, 1967:1−32). Certain key issues of the Populists, particularly tariff reforms and the repeal of the gold standard, were taken up by the Democratic party. The Populists who were southern Democrats controlled the national party in 1896 and in 1900, and they nominated William Jennings Bryan for president. The more conservative southern Democrats regained control in the party after Bryan lost but were still unable to capture the presidency in 1904.

One movement related to populism was a movement called progressivism (Hackney, 1969:326−352; Tindall, 1967:1−32; Woodward, 1974:369−395). People who were Progressives tended to be one of two varieties: eastern, urban, elitist—oriented toward extending government services to the business community (Hays, 1957; Kolko, 1963) or western, rural, democratic—interested in enforcing competition rather than regulating monopoly, and "more interested in mechanical political reforms and legislation for social justice than in creating the conditions of business prosperity and growth [Hackney, 1969:xiii]." Both Hackney and Woodward agree that the southern Progressive tended toward the latter description. Reform at the state level occurred in the South in terms of voting primaries, railroad and oil company regulation, and the prohibition of alcohol. However, progressivism in the South affected only whites, not blacks.

Once the Populists were reabsorbed into the Democratic party, the political system became isolated from the economic system. The decade 1900−1910 was not economically bad from the farmer's point of view. However, most rural whites had been disenfranchised and political power once again was in the hands of an elite leadership. In the short run, none of the Populists' demands were met. Most of the Populist energy had been dissipated, and the social system was impervious to attempts to change things.

Because a number of events transpired in the area of racial relations, this period saw much racial strife. Jim Crow laws were passed and most blacks were forced to accept their place in the new social order. Two major movements oriented toward blacks began. Booker T. Washington argued that blacks should not struggle for political rights, but should become interested in industrial, educational, and economic opportunity. His influence was enormous and he commanded a white as well as black audience. Black society and culture began a development separate from white society, and Washington led the movement to train blacks to take their place in a segregated society.

The major opposition to this point of view came from W. E. B. DuBois and his followers who wanted to change the plight of blacks and free them from subjugation and the brutality of the lynch mob. They believed in taking aggressive action to give every black civil, social, and political rights. DuBois founded the NAACP, which initially tried to have anti-lynching laws passed by Congress. This was a precursor of the modern civil rights movement. At the turn of the century, however, it was Washington's ideas that held sway. Jim Crow legislation legalized segregation, and brutality against blacks was rampant. Washington told people that social equality of blacks was not yet possible. At this point in time, the dominant white society would tolerate little else.

1910–1920

For the cotton farmer, World War I, the continuation of the boll weevil infestation, and the election of Woodrow Wilson as president were the three major events in the 1910–1920 period. World War I produced an enormous demand for cotton and, consequently, a relatively high price. The boll weevil infestation moved into the black belt (the central South) and severely cut back cotton production. Wilson and the Progressives passed a fair amount of legislation that reflected the old demands of the Populist party. While there was little or no relief for the plight of the tenant, some solutions to long-standing problems were enacted.

In 1914, the price of cotton plunged to an all-time low for the decade. This reflected a crisis of overproduction and the onset of World War I. The enormous growth in the amount of cotton cultivated from 1900 to 1910 continued from 1910 to 1914. A number of voluntary schemes were suggested to get farmers to produce less during this period (Saloutos, 1960:236–253; Tindall, 1967:34–36). Such schemes were unsuccessful because it made little sense for an individual producer to cut back on production in the face of declining prices. If one owed money, and producing cash crops was the only way to get out of debt, one would continue producing, even in the face of falling prices. Even if one were out of debt, the only way to make money was by planting cotton, and the tendency was to increase cotton production in the face of falling prices in order to stay even. The pattern of cotton production from 1910 to 1914 reflects this perfectly. The onset of World War I caused the price of cotton to plummet because it was not initially clear how the war would affect cotton exports to Europe. The cotton markets were actually closed from August to December of 1914, and therefore, the crop was left sitting in warehouses with few buyers (Tindall, 1967:34–38; Saloutos, 1960:236–253). After December 1914, trade with all of Europe resumed until America entered the war on the side of the Allies (Tindall, 1967:38–40).

The crops of 1915 – 1922 were much smaller than those of the previous five years. The price of cotton rose enormously through these years and one wonders why American production did not increase. The explanation for this is straightforward—these were the years during which the boll weevil infestation hit the black belt counties in Mississippi, Alabama, Georgia, and South Carolina. The boll weevil infestation substantially decreased the size of the American crop. Meanwhile, in this same period, cotton production around the world was increasing in order to pick up the slack in American cotton production. In 1910, America produced 62% of the world's cotton, but by 1919, Americans accounted for only 54% of the total. Those American farmers who could grow cotton in the late 1910s were doing very well, but those who could not due to the boll weevils were being forced off the land (Scott, 1920; Woodson, 1924:169; Woofter, 1969:117 – 122).

In order to get a sense of how the boll weevil infestation differentially affected counties and races, the following evidence is considered. From Table 5.2 it is evident that 42.1% of the counties had a decline in acres of cotton during the period 1910 – 1920, while 50.4% had a decline in the bales of cotton produced. If one looks at these breakdowns by state (Tables 4.11 and 4.12), one can see that the greatest decreases in cotton acreage and production occurred in Alabama, Georgia, Mississippi. A large part of this decline was due to the boll weevil. The boll weevil infestation affected blacks and whites differentially: Over 70% of the counties in Alabama, Mississippi, and Oklahoma lost black tenants, while 62% of the counties in Georgia lost black tenants. Similar patterns held for black owners, white tenants, and white owners, but to a lesser degree. This, then, is statistical evidence that blacks were more likely to be displaced than whites due to the boll weevil infestation.

In 1912, Woodrow Wilson became the first Democrat to be elected president since the 1880s, and he depended on a coalition of southern and western states for his victory (Binkley, 1962:365 – 366; Goldman, 1966:90 – 92; Tindall, 1967:1; Woodward, 1974:470 – 474). Wilson was elected as a Progressive, and his first four years in office produced a spate of legislation that came directly from the Populist program (Benedict, 1953:138 – 173; Saloutos, 1960:213 – 235; Tindall, 1967:1 – 32). Legislation was passed that met the following needs of the cotton farmer: (a) tariffs were lowered; (b) an income tax was implemented; (c) the Federal Reserve banking system was established; (d) the Federal Trade Commission and Clayton Antitrust Acts were passed; (e) the Cotton Futures and Cotton Warehousing Acts became law; (f) the Federal Farm Loan Act provided farmers with long-term loans; and (g) the Smith – Lever and Smith – Hughes Acts gave federal grants to start the county agricultural agent and the agricultural extension systems. Although a number of these acts, in terms of practice as well as ideology, helped establish what some have called "corporate liberalism" (Kolko, 1963), they can also be seen as directly derivative from Populist demands. The lowering of tariffs was a direct blow to northern industrial interests that had been protected for years from cheaper imports. The income tax also appeared to work against the North since people there had more money and higher incomes. The Federal Reserve system was Wilson's answer to the old Populist demand for a currency system not based strictly on the gold standard (Tindall, 1967:12, 17). The Federal Trade Commission and the Clayton Antitrust Acts were important as regulations were made that prohibited "unfair trade practices" and monopolies. The Cotton Futures and Cotton Warehousing Acts established procedures and standards for cotton grading, trading, and warehousing that helped insure the farmer of not being cheated once the crop was marketed (Tindall, 1967:15; Boyle, 1935:88 – 89; Saloutos, 1960:248 – 249).

The farm credit issue was dealt with by the Federal Farm Loan Act which set up banks to make long-term loans to farmers. While this seemed like a good idea in theory, it never amounted to much (Saloutos, 1960:223). The Smith – Lever and the Smith – Hughes Acts, on the other hand, were very important to the educational needs of farmers. These acts established the county agent system and the county extension system, both of which established vocational education for the farmer. The county agent's most important function was to disseminate information on new and better methods of cultivation, and the agricultural extension system provided a better link between farmers and universities.

Most observers (Saloutos, 1960:235; Tindall, 1967:32) argue that the political accomplishments from 1912 to 1916 went a long way to improve the basic conditions of small farm owners. While this may be true, it must be noted that none of this legislation did much directly for the tenant. It did little or nothing to the credit system in the South and did not approach the issue of chronic overproduction of southern cotton. At the state government level, there was a flurry of activity. Progressives came to power throughout the South by focusing on the issues of prohibition, good government, and an anti-black, anti-elite rhetoric. However, their political programs did little to disturb the social fabric (Tindall, 1967; Hicks, 1931; Saloutos, 1960; Hunt, 1934; Hesseltine, 1936; Kirwan, 1951).

The decade 1910 – 1920 witnessed no let up in black oppression; in fact, it appeared as though segregation was only intensifying (Scott, 1920; Tindall, 1967:143 – 183; Woodson, 1924:167 – 192; Woofter, 1969:117 – 121). Wilson himself supported the continuation of segregation practices and, in the best tradition of southern paternalism, Wilson said segregation was "distinctly to the advantage of the colored people themselves" (Link, 1947:251). Under the Wilson administration, blacks became segregated within the federal government and failed to get patronage jobs usually given to them (Tindall, 1967:144). In the South, laws were passed which legislated residential segregation. In both the North and South, blacks were discriminated against and, in the South, blacks occupied the lowest statuses, enjoyed no political rights, and were oppressed by all whites through legal and extralegal means (i.e., lynchings, beatings).

The decade 1910–1920 had much urban growth and continued industrial expansion. Production of oil, natural gas, steel, textiles, armaments and furniture, as well as forestry, shipbuilding, and the growth of military bases all contributed to continued industrial growth in the South. World War I stimulated enormous growth in the American economy. While a fair amount of this development occurred in the North, the South also shared in the prosperity.

The period was relatively good for southern agriculture. While the number of tenants and owners across the South expanded slightly (see Tables 4.7 and 4.8), the price for cotton remained high after 1914. The basic problems of the boll weevil infestation and the farm credit problem, however, were not resolved during this period. Boll weevils swept across the South, displacing blacks and whites alike, although it appeared that the black belt counties were most severely affected. While money had come from Congress in an attempt to solve this problem (e.g., Seaman Knapp's experiments with controlling the boll weevil), research was not successful in halting the spread of the insect. The farm credit problem was not as pressing because the price of cotton was relatively high throughout the decade. This implied that those who could grow cotton would do so and would do fairly well. World War I had a number of effects on the South. First, people (particularly blacks) left rural areas to take jobs in towns and cities of the South and North. Second, southern industry boomed in order to supply raw materials and finished goods to the war effort. The decade also saw the continued segregation and oppression of the black population and brought about what has been called the start of the Great Migration, or as Woodson (1930) called it, the "migration of the talented tenth [p. 147]."

1920–1930

The decline in cotton production during the early 1920s eventually resulted in the transformation of southern agriculture in the 1930s. This section attempts to describe the crisis and its causes and to point to the kinds of solutions that farmers themselves suggested. While the 1920s did not see any alleviation of the crisis, ideas about what to do were debated throughout the South and the rest of the country. Here the evolution of those ideas and the interests they represented is considered.

The South of 1920 was still basically rural. In 1920, only 26.2% of the southern population lived in towns with populations greater than 2500 (Taeuber and Taeuber, 1958). The backbone of that rural economy was the production of cotton. With the boll weevil infestation and the growth of the county agent and extension systems, farmers were encouraged to diversify their crops, but this advice was rarely taken. When the price of cotton was high, people planted as much as they could. When it dropped, they continued planting in order to secure as much income as possible, and the debt cycle continued. As the price of cotton dropped, people were forced to produce more cotton. As the world market became glutted with foreign and domestic cotton, the price dropped even further. Enormous numbers of farmers lost their land and were forced to become tenants. Still, cotton production increased. The crop lien system was rapidly forcing most farmers into extreme poverty.

Before considering the political activity generated by this crisis, it is necessary to consider more closely the impoverishment of farmers (black and white) and its relation to the cotton price cycle. In 1920, the price of cotton decreased by over 50% from its price in 1919. Through the early 1920s, the price increased and peaked in 1923. From then on, the price dropped throughout the remainder of the decade. Table 5.3 shows that in 1920 there was a world carryover of 12 million bales of cotton, most of it in foreign countries. This, combined with an increase in domestic production in the face of declining demand, broke the cotton market and forced the price to plunge. The years 1921 and 1922 saw large reductions in American crop production due to bad weather and the peak of the boll weevil infestation (U.S. Department of Agriculture, 1922:1 – 3). By 1921, the entire cotton South was infested by boll weevils (see Map 5.1). The annual world carryover of cotton was reduced from 15,169,000 bales in 1921 to 6,614,000 in 1924, which is what accounted for the price increase. From 1924 on, the world and the American carryover of cotton increased, and thereafter the price decreased. Meanwhile, despite the falling prices and increasing world supply of cotton, American production increased throughout the early 1920s, peaking in 1926, and decreasing slightly thereafter (see Table 5.3). This production increase occurred simultaneously with production increases around the world, and the American share of the world market decreased slightly throughout the period.

The 1920s began an enormous proletarianization of farm owners. The number of white farm owners decreased by over 204,000 (about 25%), while the number of white tenants increased by about 177,000 (almost 29%). The number of black farm owners decreased by roughly 53,000

TABLE 5.3
World Production, Supply, and Carryover of Cotton, 1920–1950 (in Thousand Bales)*

Year beginning August	Carry-over August 1 United States	Carry-over August 1 Foreign countries	Supply World	World supply	Production United States	Production Foreign countries including China	Production World including China
1920	3,563	8,189	11,752	32,380	13,429	7,921	21,350
1921	6,534	8,635	15,169	30,342	7,945	8,025	15,970
1922	2,832	7,662	10,494	28,945	9,755	9,545	19,300
1923	2,325	5,246	7,571	26,661	10,140	9,880	20,020
1924	1,556	5,058	6,614	30,708	13,630	11,530	25,160
1925	1,610	6,338	7,948	34,691	16,105	12,135	28,240
1926	3,543	6,930	10,473	38,403	17,978	10,942	28,920
1927	3,762	8,892	12,654	35,997	12,956	11,934	24,890
1928	2,536	7,999	10,535	36,337	14,477	12,403	26,880
1929	2,312	8,229	10,541	36,792	14,825	12,035	26,860
1930	4,530	7,362	11,892	37,268	13,932	12,298	26,230
1931	6,370	8,438	14,808	41,287	17,097	10,723	27,820
1932	9,678	8,658	18,336	41,797	13,003	11,297	24,300
1933	8,165	8,951	17,116	43,182	13,047	13,873	26,920
1934	7,744	9,796	17,540	40,582	9,636	14,174	23,810
1935	7,208	7,864	15,072	41,213	10,638	16,877	27,515
1936	5,409	8,240	13,649	44,378	12,399	19,952	32,351
1937	4,499	9,196	13,695	50,440	18,946	20,059	39,005
1938	11,533	11,169	22,702	50,211	11,943	18,017	29,960
1939	13,033	8,605	21,638	48,964	11,817	17,818	29,635
1940	10,564	9,698	20,262	48,982	12,566	18,639	31,205
1941	12,166	10,001	22,167	47,783	10,744	17,161	27,905
1942	10,640	11,945	22,585	48,167	12,817	14,528	27,345
1943	10,657	12,913	23,570	48,091	11,427	14,208	25,635
1944	10,744	14,660	25,404	49,035	12,230	12,585	24,815
1945	11,164	17,500	28,700	48,100	9,015	12,110	21,125
1946	7,326	17,600	24,900	44,800	8,640	12,950	21,590
1947	2,530	15,700	18,200	42,000	11,860	13,380	25,240
1948	3,080	11,400	14,500	42,000	14,877	14,253	29,130
1949	5,287	9,500	14,800	44,600	16,128	15,147	31,275
1950	6,846	9,700	16,500	42,300	9,884	17,466	27,350

*Source: Bureau of the Census, New York Cotton Exchange, and International Cotton Advisory

(34%), and the number of black tenants increased by 14,000 (2%). These shifts show that enormous numbers of farm owners were losing their land and becoming tenants. The lack of a large increase in black tenantry was probably due to the fact that large numbers of black tenants migrated, and, therefore, the aggregate number of tenants did not rise as dramatically as the number of black owners dropped.

Most of the first 20 years of the twentieth century saw plantation owners and merchants thriving. During this period, most small farm owners and tenants went from doing fairly well to abject poverty, depending on the price of cotton and the ravages of the boll weevil. The 1920s saw plantation owners and merchants reduced to subsistence. Small farm owners went deeply into debt, and many lost their land. Those who became tenants joined other tenants who were in debt and lived near the edge of starvation (Baldwin, 1968:18 — 47; Grubbs, 1971:1 — 16; Saloutos, 1960:274 — 281; Tindall, 1967:354 — 358). In the face of this tenantization, the actual acreage planted in cotton increased during the decade (see Table 4.11), and the amount of cotton produced increased regardless of falling prices.

The 1920s produced a severe agricultural crisis that was rooted in the very set of mechanisms and social relations that allowed the southern agricultural system to exist. The causes of this crisis were the same as those of the 1880s and 1890s crises. The southern cotton farmer in the late 1890s and early 1900s was saved by the end of the worldwide depression and by an increase in the demand for cotton. The late 1920s and early 1930s did not provide such kind conditions.

Given that the situation of the 1920s was markedly similar to the situation of the 1890s, it seems reasonable to consider whether populism or some variant of it would again arise. Farm organizations in the twentieth century South and their various political programs are now considered. Given the political realities of the 1920s, one can pose the following questions:

1. What kind of programs could farm organizations come up with and who would they benefit?
2. What would the role of the black man be in these organizations?
3. What kind of political activity would farm groups undertake and where would they place pressure?
4. Would any of the evolved solutions be oriented toward reorganizing the agricultural system in the South?

In the discussion that follows, the concern is with the two largest farm organizations that evolved following the demise of the Farmers' Alliance—the Farmers' Union and the American Farm Bureau Federation. While there were a number of other farm organizations that evolved in the late nineteenth and early twentieth centuries, it was these two which had the largest memberships, the most clearcut ideologies, and the greatest impact on farm policy (Baldwin, 1968:205, 286 – 287; Ford, 1973:42 – 44; Hunt, 1934; Kile, 1948:17 – 22, 403; McConnell, 1953:36 – 55; Montgomery, 1929:76 – 77; Saloutos, 1960:212, 257 – 258; Tindall, 1967: 427 – 428).

The Farmers' Union, officially called the Farmers' Educational and Cooperative Union of America, was a direct heir to the Farmers' Alliance (Hunt, 1934:41 – 51; McConnell, 1953:36 – 43; Saloutos, 1960:184). It was founded in Rains County, Texas in 1903 by Newton Gresham, a former Allianceman (Saloutos, 1960:184 – 185). The basic goals of the Farmers' Union were quite similar to those of the Alliance. They wanted to (a) get fair prices for their product; (b) discourage credit and mortgage systems; (c) encourage farmers to cultivate using modern methods; (d) systematize methods of production and distribution; and (e) end futures trading and commodity speculation (Saloutos, 1960:186).

The Farmers' Union differed fundamentally from the Alliance in two ways. First, it held the view that farmers constituted a social class, and, therefore, farmers had interests which united them. Second, and more important, the Farmers' Union held the position that farm organizations "must have no responsibilities or commitments in the work of political parties [McConnell, 1953:39]." The Farmers' Union felt that the class interests of farmers were narrower than the general interests of political parties. Consequently, the members sought to align themselves with whoever supported them and to put pressure on whoever had power. In essence, this feature of the Farmers' Union insured the solidity and power of the Democratic party in the South. Since many of the union's issues transcended state boundaries, many of its lobbying activities took place at the federal level. While the Farmers' Union spouted the rhetoric of the Populists, it was careful never to attempt to become a political movement or party (McConnell, 1953:38 – 39). In the beginning, the Farmers' Union spread across the South, but after 1910, its activities shifted into the Midwest. By the end of World War I, midwestern membership was greater than southern membership (Crampton, 1965:56 – 58; McConnell, 1953:39; Saloutos, 1960:212).

In the first decade of the twentieth century, the major activities of the Farmers' Union were oriented toward controlling the price of cotton, and warehouses across the South were set up to store cotton until prices rose. Unfortunately, this tactic rarely succeeded since there always tended to be a fair amount of uncontrolled cotton. In 1908, an attempt was made to have members plow up 10% of their crop. This move was also not very successful because not many farmers cooperated (Saloutos, 1960:198). The idea of withholding crops and curtailing acreage, however, eventually proved to be central to American farm policy.

What the social composition of the Farmers' Union was, is difficult to ascertain. While its ideology called for control of production and marketing, the purpose was to raise the price to the producer. The producer usually tended to be a farm owner, and, as McConnell reports (1953:145 – 157), the Farmers' Union had in its membership many well-to-do farmers. It may have been primarily a middle-class farm organization in social composition, but it had a Progressive, even Populist attitude in its rhetoric.

The American Farm Bureau Federation, on the other hand, had its origins in the purely educational aspects of the county agent, the agricultural college, and the extension experimental station movements of the early twentieth century (Kile, 1948:1 – 58; McConnell, 1953:44 – 54; Campbell, 1962:1 – 13; McCune, 1956:15 – 33). To facilitate the dissemination of information, local county farm bureaus were formed during the decade 1910 – 1920. These farm bureaus began as purely educational organizations and expanded to form buying and selling cooperatives (Kile, 1948:40 – 46). Soon, state farm bureaus were organized to centralize activity and to create lobbies that would persuade legislators to allocate more money to extension activities.

In 1920, the American Farm Bureau Federation was born. Unlike the Farmers' Union, the Farm Bureau viewed itself as a nonpartisan group representing the interest of all farmers. It appealed to conservative farmers, and membership dues were $10 – $15 annually which meant only relatively wealthy farmers would join (Kile, 1948:67; McConnell, 1953:53). The organization took a stand against agrarian radicalism. Harvey J. Sconce, president of the Illinois Farm Bureau, said, "It is our duty in creating this organization to avoid any policy that will align organized farmers with the radicals of other organizations. The policy should be thoroughly American in every respect—a constructive organization instead of a destructive organization [Kile, 1948:50]." McConnell (1953:56) suggests that the Farm Bureau operated during the 1920s as a stabilizing effect and prevented radical agrarianism from reemerging. This view is somewhat naive. While the Farm Bureau appeared to have the ideology of the large-scale commercial farmer at its core, its tactics and plans did not differ significantly from the ostensibly more "radical" Farmers' Union. Although it is true that the Farm Bureau's ideology was that of an emerging capitalist agriculture (i.e., large-scale commercial crop production), its membership formed no more of an elite than did the membership of the Farmers' Union (Kile, 1948:371 – 372; McConnell, 1953:148 – 149).

The Farm Bureau was originally strongest in the Northeast, then it spread to the Midwest and finally to the South. During the 1920s the midwestern farm bureaus were the largest, and it was not until the 1930s, with the ascendancy of Edward O'Neal of Alabama (a planter) to the presidency of the Farm Bureau, that the South became important to the Farm Bureau. The Farm Bureau was interested in maintaining prices of agricultural commodities at high levels. There were disagreements within the Farm Bureau itself as to how this could be done. As a number of writers have suggested, the Farm Bureau was not the originator of ideas, but, rather, used the ideas of others. Because of its political clout, however, the Farm Bureau got results from Congress. Initially, the Farm Bureau was interested in legislation allowing cooperative ventures. Later on, the Farm Bureau supported the notion of government guaranteed prices for farm products (Campbell, 1962; Kile, 1948:203 – 244; McConnell, 1953:71 – 83).

Within the Farm Bureau there were differences of opinion regarding goals that the organization should pursue (McConnell, 1953:44 – 53). The struggle reflected regional differences as well as political differences. Initially, the eastern and southern membership wanted only to continue with the educational goals of the organization. The midwest contingent, which was the largest and best organized, wanted action that would address itself to farmers' marketing problems (i.e., low prices and high costs of selling). The midwest view predominated, and in the early 1920s, the Farm Bureau lobbied in Congress to increase farm loans and to create legislation that would legally underwrite marketing cooperatives. This legislation passed easily, and by the mid-1920s, the Farm Bureau was deeply involved in cooperative marketing and buying arrangements.

The Farmers' Union, from its origin, was also interested in marketing and buying cooperatives. The Farmers' Union supported legislative efforts to facilitate such schemes and was also involved in cooperatives by the mid-1920s. The cooperative movement really took off, and most agricultural organizations were oriented toward cooperative ventures (Montgomery, 1929:249 – 265; Saloutos, 1960:263 – 264).

Price support for various agricultural products became an important political issue from 1924 on. George Peek and his associates, Chester Davis and George Jewett, proposed a plan whereby the government would support the price of farm commodities (Benedict, 1953:207 – 238; Campbell, 1962:30 – 43; Kile, 1948:146 – 151; McConnell, 1953:61 – 64). The basic approach was that farm surpluses would be exported at world prices, while domestic prices were to be maintained at an acceptable level. The difference between the two prices would be financed by government farm tariffs. This plan was introduced into Congress in 1924 and was sponsored by Senator McNary and Representative Haugen. Its various forms came to be called the McNary—Haugen Bill.

The Farm Bureau became the staunchest advocate of this legislation in the late 1920s. The Farmers' Union also supported it because it would provide a "decent price" for the farmers' commodity. The bill passed Congress twice and was vetoed twice by a Republican president. While the McNary—Haugen Bill did not pass in the 1920s, it became the basis of the Farm Bureau's agricultural program, and the struggles of the 1920s produced price support payments in the 1930s.

The largest and most influential farm organizations had three basic programs that were supposed to solve farmers' problems—an education program, a cooperative marketing and buying program, and a government supported price program. While the ideology of the Farmers' Union and the Farm Bureau differed, their class composition and practical political programs were almost identical. The ideologies of these organizations reflected their social origins. The class interests that both groups basically represented were those of farm owners. Therefore, it was not surprising that their political programs demanded similar changes. Neither organization cared directly about the plight of the tenant, nor were activities oriented toward easing the credit burden and peonage-like state of the tenant. Neither organization was concerned about black oppression, and racist attitudes of members of the Farmers' Union prevented any real attempts to integrate blacks into the movement (Saloutos, 1960:193 —194). Since the strength of the Farm Bureau, before 1930, was in the Midwest, the black man and his plight were never a central concern of the Bureau.

Both the Farmers' Union and the Farm Bureau characterized themselves as staying out of party politics. Both organizations were deeply afraid of repeating the Populist breakdown of 1896. The Farm Bureau was against such activity. It denounced radicalism of any form and saw the farmers' interests as neither Democratic nor Republican by nature. The Farmers' Union was also careful to avoid being drawn into third party politics, and because of this political stance, both organizations showed little interest in controlling state-level politics. Instead, both concentrated on lobbying efforts in Washington.

Finally, it must be understood that neither the Farm Bureau nor the Farmers' Union were interested in a fundamental transformation of the American (or southern) agricultural system. Neither was oriented toward destruction of the crop lien or tenant systems. Rather, they were mostly interested in raising the price of their own commodities. Again, this reflects the class composition of both movements. They represented "liberal" and "conservative" farm owners, and their interests were in preserving farm ownership and the family farm concept in the face of falling prices for farmers' commodities. The key struggle became a battle over the prices of farm commodities, and the debate over the ills of agriculture became limited. The strongest opinions were those of farm owners whose concerns won out.

Outside of agriculture, the decade of the 1920s was a high growth period in America. In the South, urban centers grew, and demand for the natural resource products of the South continued to expand. Outside the South, there were numerous opportunities developing in the industries of the North. The agricultural depression in the South, combined with expanding opportunities in the cities of the South and North, gave rise to high net out-migration from rural counties of the South. Another force was entering into cotton production in the 1920s—for the first time, cotton cultivation was mechanized. While this process was just beginning, it became increasingly important over time.

The Causes of Migration, 1900 – 1930

This section serves as a connecting link between the major developments as they affected southern agriculture and some notion of the driving forces of in- and out-migration from counties of the South from 1900 to 1930. It was argued earlier that six factors structured the migration process of blacks and whites at the county level: (a) the world market and price of cotton; (b) the technical relations of production; (c) the social relations of production and exchange; (d) the state; (e) capitalist development in the South and North; and (f) other factors, such as the boll weevil infestation.

Each of these factors had a specific effect on migration during the period in question. In specific periods, different factors will have different effects. For example, mechanization could not have affected migration from 1900 to 1910 since there were no tractors in the South to displace tenants. In the period 1920 – 1930, however, some displacement could have occurred. The purpose here is to specify when and how various factors came into play (i.e., did they cause net in- or out-migration). This specification becomes even more complex because factors over the same time period could have been causing net in- and out-migration. If, for instance, tenant farming is expanding in a county, then people are being attracted to opportunities. If, on the other hand, tenantry is contracting, then people are being forced out of counties. This problem implies that one must focus on where expansion and contraction is occurring as well as on the fact that some factor is related to net migration.

The models of migration that will be presented here and in the next three chapters are limited in two ways. First, the world market and the price of cotton are not explicitly considered in these models. This is because the market and price do not vary across counties. Indirect measures of the price, however, are reflected in cotton acreage planted. In the analysis in Chapter 9, the price of cotton is explicitly considered. The second limitation is that measures of opportunities in the North are also not included. However, measures of capitalist development in the South are included. The analysis in Chapter 9 also includes measures of opportunities in the North.

The period 1900–1910 contains no shifts in either the technical relations of production or in the state's role in agriculture that would directly cause migration. Hence, no consideration is given to these factors. The social relations of production and exchange, however, should determine migration to a great degree. Since this was an era of westward cotton expansion, one would expect increases and decreases in tenantry and ownership to have affected migration. As tenantry and ownership increased, in-migration should have increased. As tenantry and ownership decreased, out-migration should have increased. Counties in Texas and Oklahoma should have experienced net in-migration as the population shifted. Increases in cotton acreage and in bales of cotton produced should also be associated with in-migration.

Capitalist development in the South should also have caused migration, and measures of urbanization and industrialization should have been related to migration. Counties with decreasing urban populations (depopulated small towns) offered migrants few opportunities and therefore experienced out-migration. One would also expect that counties with increasing industrialization would attract migrants. Large towns (populations greater than 25,000) should have grown rapidly, and counties near them could have experienced net in-migration as part of the process of urbanization. Since the agricultural system expanded in this decade, one might not expect urban counties to grow as fast as they did during the decade 1920–1930, when agriculture was depressed.

Three other factors need to be incorporated into the analysis of the 1900–1930 period. One major contributor to migration could have been repression against blacks. While repression occurred throughout the South, one can argue that differential repression caused people to move. The second factor to consider is a natural factor—the boll weevil invasion. Between 1900 and 1910, a fair amount of the western part of the South was infested. An attempt will be made to evaluate whether the affected counties tended to have out-migrants. The final factor to be considered involves population pressure. The rural South had very high birth rates, and since land was a finite quantity, it follows that a "surplus population" could have been generated very easily. In other words, there were too many people competing for too little land. If such pressure existed, one would expect out-migration.

Since the expansion of cotton in the South was basically complete by 1915, one would expect changes in ownership, tenantry, and cotton production to be less important in understanding the out-migration process from 1910 to 1920. One expects the results of capitalist development to be more highly related to in-migration in this period.

The boll weevil infestation moved into the black belt and could have forced out a large portion of the black population. A decrease in tenantry and in the amount of cotton planted could be the mechanism whereby boll weevils affected net migration. The boll weevil infestation could have caused a reduction in cotton production and, therefore, a reduction of tenants. This would then produce net out-migration as persons who were formerly tenants were forced to seek employment elsewhere. The differential repression of blacks and the population pressure on the land continued, hence, one might expect out-migration. Again, the state and the technical relations of production play no role in the migration process.

The social relations of production and exchange in the decade 1920–1930 were central to the out-migration process. As farm ownership decreased during the agricultural depression, people moved. Increases in tenantry and in land planted in cotton, on the other hand, also caused out-migration. Given the agricultural depression, one would expect the lure of urban areas and the concomitant capitalist development to be particularly strong. For the first time, the technical relations of production come into play. Mechanization in the South began during this decade with the introduction of tractors. One would expect that the mechanization of the cotton growing process led to a reduced number of farm workers, but one finds that these effects were quite small in this period. In terms of other factors, the boll weevil infestation peaked in this decade, the differential repression of blacks continued, and there was potential surplus population in the rural South.

Chapter 6

Models of the Migration Process, 1900 – 1930

This chapter will be devoted to a detailed examination of the validity of the assertions about the social relationships governing the agricultural system of the South, the changes in that system, and the net migration of blacks and whites from counties of the South. It has been argued at some length that the opportunity structure facing individuals at the point of origin is the key to understanding why they migrate. The question here is, what determines the opportunity structure? In Chapter 3 it was suggested that in the rural South from 1900 to 1950 there were six factors that structured opportunities: (a) the world market for cotton; (b) the state; (c) the social relations of production and exchange; (d) the technical relations of production; (e) capitalist development in the South and North; and (f) other factors such as the boll weevil infestation. At any given historical moment, these factors will be operating with different dynamics, and their effects on migration will be dependent on a relatively precise understanding of how they determine the opportunity structure. The preceding chapter suggested those dynamics, the opportunities they presented to persons in the South, and, hence, their pertinent effects on migration. This chapter will investigate empirically whether or not the net migration rates were responsive to the shifts and turns of the social relations in and outside the South.

The Operationalization of Relevant Factors

The discussion now turns to the operationalization of the factors that have been related to migration. The measures, their definitions, and justifications are listed below. Data sources and problems of comparability are addressed in Appendices A and B. Unless otherwise stated, the following measures appear in all models of the periods 1900–1910, 1910–1920, and 1920–1930. For the period 1900–1930, no measures are included for the price of cotton, for opportunities in the North, and for the activities of the state. The first two factors are not included because they are constant for counties across each decade, and the last factor is not measured because the state had no direct impact on migration from 1900 to 1930.

SOCIAL RELATIONS OF PRODUCTION AND EXCHANGE

It has been argued that the social relations of production and exchange governed the opportunity structure of rural southerners to a great degree. The expansion and contraction of cotton agriculture determined whether one would be a tenant or land owner. Therefore, it is most appropriate to try to construct measures that tap into the dynamics of class structure, production, and exchange in the South.

The two classes of interest in the South were farm owners and tenants. To measure the relative size of these classes and the change in them over time in a county, three measures are used:

1. *The percentage of farmers in a county who were tenants.* This is measured at the beginning of a decade, is available by race, and is used as an index that gauges when the tenant farming system penetrated a county. One expects that high levels of tenantry will be related to influxes of population, depending on whether cotton agriculture is expanding or contracting.
2. *The percentage of change in tenantry.* This variable is defined as (No. of tenants t_2 − No. of tenants t_1)/No. of tenants t_1, where t_2 is the second point in time and t_1 is the first. The measure is the percentage change in tenants over the decade and is calculated by race. A negative value on this variable indicates that tenantry was decreasing, while a positive value implies that tenantry was increasing. The change in tenantry is a crucial variable since it concerns whether or not the tenant system was expanding or contracting in a county, and it is an indicator of opportunities in tenant farming.
3. *The percentage change in owners.* This measure is calculated by race and is defined in the same way as the percentage change in

tenants. Positive and negative values of this variable imply whether or not opportunities for farm ownership were increasing or decreasing. In the 1920s, negative values of this variable suggest that farm owners were losing their farms.

The social relations of production and exchange, and their contraction and expansion, have implications that go beyond class structure. The amount of cotton produced, the farm acreage involved, and the location of that acreage, all reflect production and exchange relations. The expansion of cotton production was a function of (a) the price of cotton; (b) the crop lien mechanism; and (c) the cost of production. These factors structured opportunities because the expansion or contraction of production determined, to some degree, the number of positions available for farm owners, tenants, and laborers. Here, five measures of production and exchange are used.

1. *Percentage of farm acres in a county in cotton.* This variable is defined as (acres in cotton in a county t_1)/(total farm acres in farms t_1), where t_1 refers to the first point in time. It measures the extent to which a county was a cotton growing county. At different historical moments, cotton growing counties were more or less susceptible to net in- and out-migration.

2. *Change in cotton acreage in a county.* This variable is defined as (acres cotton in county t_2)/(total farm acres in farms t_2) − (acres cotton in county t_1)/(total farm acres in county t_1). This measure is the change in the percentage of acres of cotton in a county. A negative value implies cotton was declining as a staple, while a positive value suggests cotton was expanding. This variable is a good measure of the increase and decrease in the spread of cotton.

3. *Percentage change in bales grown in a county.* This is (bales grown in a county t_2 − bales grown in a county t_1)/(bales grown t_1). A positive value indicates an increase in cotton production, while a negative value shows that cotton production was declining. While this measure is similar in concept to the change in cotton acreage in a county, it taps into a slightly different dynamic. Increases and decreases in yields are not perfectly correlated to increases and decreases in acres.

4. *Counties in Texas.* This measure is a dummy variable that takes on the value of "1" if the county is in Texas and "0" otherwise. This measure is included because it indicates whether or not counties in Texas were increasing in population net of the other variables tapping into the growth of cotton production (which would indicate the westward movement of cotton production).

5. *Counties in Oklahoma.* This is a dummy variable for counties in Oklahoma coded similarly to the one for Texas and included for the same reason.

TECHNICAL RELATIONS OF PRODUCTION

The only time period when the technical relations of production were shifting was 1920–1930. The level (and the change in the level) of mechanization could also have caused net out-migration because opportunities declined with increased use of machines. Only one measure of mechanization is used here.

1. *Number of tractors in a county in 1929.* Tractors were the major kind of machines employed in the mechanization of cotton agriculture, and, hence, the measure captures the technical relations of production. The number of tractors in counties was unavailable in 1920, and, therefore, it is impossible to calculate the percentage increase in tractors over the decade. The measure is the level of mechanization at the end of the decade.

CAPITALIST DEVELOPMENT IN THE SOUTH

There are two aspects of capitalist development—urbanization (the growth of cities) and industrialization (the growth of the factory system). Measures of both aspects of capitalist development are offered here. As capitalist development proceeded in the United States, opportunities in cities and towns expanded. Four measures of the urbanization are considered.

1. *Percentage of those urbanized in a county.* This variable is defined as the percentage of the population living in places with a population greater than 2500 at the beginning of the decade. It is a measure of the relative urbanization of the country. A highly urbanized county should attract in-migration.
2. *Percentage change in urbanization.* This variable is defined as (percent urban in the county t_2)—(percent urban in the county t_1). It is the change in the percentage of the population living in places with a population greater than 2500 over the decade. This measure reflects the increasing (or decreasing) urbanization in a county. A positive value implies urban growth, while a negative value implies urban decline.
3. *Presence of a large city in a county.* This is a dummy variable which takes on a value of "1" if a city with a population greater than 25,000 was in the county, and a value of "0" if there was no such city. This variable attempts to capture the effect of larger urban areas on migration.
4. *Counties next to counties with large cities.* This is another dummy

variable which takes on a value of "1" if a county was next to a county with a city whose population was greater than 25,000, and "0" if not. Together, these two variables define a county's relative nearness to a large urban area. Zeros on both variables imply distance from an urban center, while "1s" on either variable imply closeness. Theoretically, one would expect counties near or with such cities to experience net in-migration.

Two measures of industrialization are offered here.

1. *Number of manufacturing establishments.* This variable is the number of manufacturing establishments in a county at the beginning of the decade and is a rough index of the level of industrialization in the county. High levels of manufacturing activity should be positively related to in-migration because manufacturing means nonagricultural job opportunities.

2. *Percentage change in manufacturing establishments.* This is defined as (No. of manufacturing establishments in the county at t_2 − No. of manufacturing establishments in the county at t_1)/No. of manufacturing establishments in the county at t_1. A positive value implies increasing industrialization, and this should be related to in-migration since it implies the existence of new job opportunities.

OTHER FACTORS

There are three other factors used in this analysis which could have caused migration.

1. *Surplus population.* This measure is defined as (rural population in a county t_2/No. farms in a county t_2)−(rural population in a county t_1/No. farms in a county t_1). This measure is considered an indicator of population pressure on the land. Since rural blacks and whites had high fertility, there was usually an excess population, and this population tended to migrate. A positive value on this variable means that there was an increase in the number of persons per farm. This should be related to out-migration. Conversely, a negative value indicates little or no population pressure on the number of farms.

2. *Differential repression of blacks.* The measure used here to capture the differential repression of blacks is whether or not a lynching occurred in a county. In counties where lynchings occurred, one could argue that blacks were more repressed. This measure is coded as a dummy variable which takes on a value of "1" if a lynching occurred in a county, and a value of "0" if no lynching occurred during the decade. Presence of a lynching should indicate greater out-migration if the measure represents differential repression and if blacks were responding to the repression.

3. *Boll weevil infestation.* Using Map 5.1, dummy variables were constructed to indicate whether or not a county was infested during that decade. For the decade 1900–1910, there is one such dummy variable coded "0" if no infestation occurred, and coded "1" if it did. For 1910–1920, there are two dummy variables. One of them takes on the value of "1" if infestation began before 1910, and the other takes on the value of "1" if it began in 1910–1920. In 1920–1930, there are two dummy variables coded exactly as they were in 1910–1920. For 1920–1930, the new infestation is represented by "0's" on both of the dummy variables. If net outmigration occurred due to the boll weevil infestation, it should be detectable.

This completes the measures description for the factors which structured migration in the South from 1900 to 1930. As stated earlier, the dependent variable in the analysis is the net migration rate by race for each county (see Appendix C for more details).

The statistical technique used in this study is a weighted least squares technique (Mosteller and Tukey, 1977:346–350; Neter and Wasserman, 1974:135–136; Theil, 1971:244–246) which is explained in some detail in Appendix D. The reason this technique was chosen is relatively simple. Use of the net migration rate can result in rates of increase that are quite high. Most of these high rates reflect the fact that the base population is very small, and the increase looks large because, proportionately, it is. Therefore, a county with a net migration of 500 and a base population of 25 has a rate of increase of 2000 per 100 people (500/25 × 100), while a net migration of 10,000 and a base population of 50,000 has a rate of increase of 20 per 100 people (10,000/50,000 × 100). Although the second county has enormous growth, it is overshadowed by the growth of the first. Upon inspection of the data, it was found that roughly 10–15 counties in each decade had rates greater than 100. These counties created large standard errors and insignificant coefficients in the regressions. Since these cases are outlyers, they are responsible for the large standard errors. One has two choices with outlyers: One can either throw them out, or one can re-weight the data to minimize their effect. Throwing them out implies believing that their measures are distorted for some unknown reason. It can be argued that this is unreasonable on the ground that the net migration rates are high because they represent large proportional changes. Therefore, here the data is re-weighted. A formal mathematical discussion and an explication of this weighting scheme appears in Appendix D.

One further technical issue should be noted here. The data used in this project were collected by a number of different agencies using various techniques. While some of the data were probably collected very carefully (for instance, data on agriculture), some were collected poorly (for instance, census data on blacks). This results in measurement error in both the independent and dependent variables. Since the magnitude and direction of such error is impossible to assess, caution should be taken in accepting all results. Such error appears to be more prevalent in data concerning blacks. The migration estimates for blacks tend to have much wider variances than those for whites, and all variables based solely on data for blacks appear to be less related to the net migration of blacks than are the same variables for whites. One could argue that this means the process of migration was different for blacks than for whites. Granted, this is probably true to some extent, but part of the observed differences could just as likely be due to measurement error.

The Model of Migration, 1900–1910

The period 1900–1910 witnessed an enormous expansion of cotton cultivation and a growth in the cities of the North and South. Migration of both blacks and whites took two forms: (a) migration to new farming opportunities in the South; and (b) migration to cities in and outside of the South to opportunities other than in agriculture. The important statistical results for understanding net migration from counties of the South are in two tables. The first three columns of Table 6.2 present the results of a regression of the various factors on the net migration rate for blacks. The first three columns of Table 6.3 present the same results for whites. These regressions are based on data for 703 counties in Alabama, Arkansas, Georgia, Louisiana, Mississippi, North Carolina, South Carolina, and the eastern half of Texas. Oklahoma is excluded from this analysis because its counties underwent numerous boundary changes in 1908, when Oklahoma became a state. Other sample characteristics are discussed in Appendices A and B. Means and standard deviations for all variables appear in Table 6.1.

The most important factor structuring the black net migration rate was the social relations of production and exchange. Five of the seven measures of this factor have statistically significant effects on the black net migration rate. Black migration was highly responsive to changes in tenantry and to the level and changes in level of cotton acreage. Blacks were migrating to places where opportunities in cotton existed and away

TABLE 6.1
Means and Standard Deviations of Various Variables, 1900–1950

Variable*	1900-10 Mean	S.D.	1910-20 Mean	S.D.	1920-30 Mean	S.D.	1930-40 Mean	S.D.	1940-50 Mean	S.D.
NMRB	-4.545	28.693	-7.571	41.356	-11.921	46.261	-8.086	16.105	-18.708	61.889
NMRW	-3.815	36.552	-10.249	7.065	-9.981	9.742	-5.214	8.301	-12.100	19.344
PAYMENTS							115.198	140.322	115.198	140.322
URBAN	.066	.139	.101	.164	.126	.178	.151	.202	.176	.195
ΔURBAN	.035	.074	.025	.064	.025	.070	.025	.062	.085	.079
COTTON	.123	.160	.134	.104	.147	.119	.173	.132	.083	.067
ΔCOTTON	.026	.113	.014	.076	.025	.079	-.090	.071	-.009	.035
TRACTORS					108.077	177.793	108.077	177.793	203.628	297.732
ΔTRACTORS							1.295	2.029	3.704	2.400
ΔSURPLUS	.253	2.842	.202	2.816	-.387	4.342	2.049	4.254	.651	10.834
ΔBALES	2.014	2.226	.658	2.286	2.357	2.581	-.251	.997	-.002	.785
MANUFACTURERS	19.994	16.244	28.494	24.036	37.844	26.775	40.721	30.345	50.350	23.668
ΔMANUFACTURERS	.229	.491	.181	.524	.160	.473	.252	.648	1.393	7.941
TENANTSB	.681	.269	.691	.277	.686	.281	.736	.245	.651	.266
TENANTSW	.394	.132	.431	.156	.430	.146	.552	.160	.496	.139
ΔTENANTSB	.270	.834	.093	.928	.415	2.547	-.288	.612	-.428	1.259
ΔTENANTSW	.518	1.617	.088	.374	.391	1.341	-.089	.478	-.352	.008
ΔOWNERSB	.466	.714	-.001	.418	-.286	.388	.083	.963	-.050	.447
ΔOWNERSW	.444	5.411	.108	.523	-.239	.405	.146	.276	.161	.274
BIG CITY	.095	.294	.094	.292	.088	.283	.088	.284	.090	.286
NEAR BIG CITY	.367	.482	.363	.481	.366	.482	.369	.483	.369	.483
LYNCHING	.350	.477	.201	.404	.266	.442				
BOLL1	.393	.489	.358	.480	.358	.478				
BOLL2			.477	.372	.477	.365				

*NMRB = net migration rate for blacks; NMRW = net migration rate for whites; PAYMENTS = agricultural payments in thousands of dollars in 1934; URBAN = percent urbanized in a county; ΔURBAN = change in the percent urbanized; COTTON = percent of farm acres in cotton; ΔCOTTON = change in percent of farm acres in cotton; TRACTORS = number of tractors in a county; ΔTRACTORS = percent change in number of tractors; ΔSURPLUS = surplus population; BALES = percent change in bales of cotton produced; MANUFACTURERS = number of manufacturing establishments; ΔMANUFACTURERS = percent change in manufacturing establishments; TENANTSB, TENANTSW = percent of farmers who were tenants by race (B=black, W=white); ΔTENANTSB, ΔTENANTSW = percent change in tenants by race; ΔOWNERSW, ΔOWNERSB = percent change in owners by race (B=black, W=white); BIG CITY = presence of a large city; NEAR BIG CITY = county next to large city; LYNCHING = occurrence of lynching in a county; BOLL1 = whether or not boll weevil infestation occurred 1910-20;

from places where opportunities were declining. There are two pieces of evidence suggesting blacks were moving west. First, high levels of tenantry implied large increases in the black net out-migration rate. Counties with high levels of black tenantry were concentrated in the states of the Southeast (Georgia, South Carolina, and Alabama), and these counties were losing more blacks than counties in the western part of the South. Second, blacks were moving into counties in Texas where new opportunities were available in the cotton fields. The class position of blacks was evident because the level and percentage change in tenantry affected the black net migration rate, while the percentage change in ownership did not.

Capitalist development was also an important factor in explaining the black net migration rate. Three of the six measures of capitalist development had statistically significant effects on the black net migration rate. Blacks were moving to counties that had growing urban populations and to counties which had large cities or cities nearby. Neither of the measures of industrialization had a statistically significant effect on the black net migration rate. These results suggest that blacks were being attracted to the expanding urban areas of the South, but not because of opportunities in manufacturing. There are two possible explanations for this. First, the effect of the industrialization variables is mediated by the urbanization variables. Second, blacks had few opportunities in manufacturing due to racist hiring practices, and changes in manufacturing did not affect the black net migration rate. Considering that other studies have shown that blacks had few industrial opportunities in the South at the turn of the century, this explanation seems fairly credible.

In terms of the "other" factors, two of the three measures were significantly related to the black net migration rate. The measure of population pressure on farmland had a very significant effect. The direction of the coefficient is negative, and this suggests that many counties that experienced population pressure on the available land were losing black residents. The differential repression, a dummy variable signifying whether or not a lynching occurred in a county, was negatively related to the black net migration rate, but did not have a statistically significant effect. This potentially suggests two things: Blacks were not moving in response to lynchings, and blacks were not moving, in the aggregate, in response to differential repression from 1900 to 1910. While the first statement seems obviously true, the second relies on our acceptance of lynching as a good measure of differential repression. Since this measure is the only one available, one must tentatively conclude that Scott's (1920) and Woodson's (1924) notions about the relation between lynching and migration are empirically unfounded. The final factor considered is the

TABLE 6.2

Results of Weighted Least Squares Regression of County Characteristics on the Net Migration Rates of Blacks for Counties in the South, 1900–1910, 1910–1920, 1920–1930

Factor	Measure[1]	1900–10			1910–20			1920–30		
		b	SE(b)	β	b	SE(b)	β	b	SE(b)	β
Social Relations of Production and Exchange	TENANTS	-121.266*	1.787	-.393	-267.025*	14.569	-.486	-214.016*	11.422	-.271
	ΔTENANTS	34.698*	2.488	.309	4.269*	.978	.106	-6.870*	.676	-.277
	ΔOWNERS	-2.024	1.673	-.008	36.494*	8.277	.133	59.385*	5.916	.288
	COTTON	132.254*	13.472	.241	159.147*	19.219	.192	188.372*	13.209	.192
	ΔCOTTON	228.812*	38.086	.218	274.381*	28.825	.130	290.360*	24.288	.315
	ΔBALES	-.083	.058	-.005	1.709	.890	.029	-.534	.381	-.022
	TEXAS	43.529*	2.944	.285	17.213	3.986	.240	6.723*	2.932	.101
	OKLAHOMA				-4.072*	.978	-.182	2.421	2.356	.034
Technical Relations	TRACTORS							-.008	.005	-.031
Capitalist Development	URBAN	.759	1.483	.001	18.873*	4.779	.144	116.445*	7.569	.397
	ΔURBAN	322.419*	5.457	.258	233.353*	23.226	.184	213.981*	42.733	.326
	BIG CITY	15.309*	.699	.098	9.083*	3.011	.056	16.895*	4.611	.141
	NEAR BIG CITY	24.043*	1.635	.112	16.304*	1.361	.216	17.047*	3.482	.163
	MANUFACTURERS	.057	.029	.019	.142	.193	.021	.143	.104	.023
	ΔMANUFACTURERS	3.022	2.868	.017	18.129*	2.241	.098	6.501	4.082	.034
Other Factors	ΔSURPLUS	-4.344*	.567	-.250	-4.977*	.298	-.267	-4.296*	.635	-.282
	LYNCHING	-1.352	.929	-.015	-3.351	2.098	-.040	-8.634	4.921	-.052
	BOLL1	-44.101*	3.943	-.231	-11.900*	8.602	-.168	6.715	4.251	.067
	BOLL2				-21.432*	7.916	-.214	9.638*	3.010	.181
	Constant	56.580			59.853			105.408		
	R²	.721			.428			.857		

* p < .05

**n = 703 in 1900–10, n = 798 in 1910–20, n = 822 in 1920–30.

[1] TENANTS = percent of farmers who were tenants; ΔTENANTS = percent change in tenants; ΔOWNERS = percent change in owners; COTTON = percent of farm acres in cotton; ΔCOTTON = change in the percent of farm acres in cotton; ΔBALES = percent change in bales produced; TEXAS, OKLAHOMA = whether or not a county was in Texas or Oklahoma; TRACTORS = number of tractors in a county; URBAN = percent urbanized; ΔURBAN = change in percent urbanized; BIG CITY = presence of a large city; NEAR BIG CITY = county next to a large city; MANUFACTURERS = number of manufacturing establishments; ΔMANUFACTURERS = percent change in manufacturing establishments; ΔSURPLUS = surplus population; LYNCHING = whether or not a lynching took place; BOLL1 = whether or not boll weevil infestation occurred in 1900–10; BOLL2 = whether or not boll weevil infestation occurred in 1910–20.

presence or absence of the boll weevil infestation in southern counties. The effect of the boll weevil on the net out-migration rate of blacks from 1900 to 1910 is large and statistically significant. Scott (1920) and Woofter (1936) had good reason to believe that the boll weevil infestation forced many blacks from the land.

The model for whites is in the first three columns of Table 6.3. The social relations of production and exchange were the major cause of the white net migration rate as six of the seven measures had statistically significant effects. White net migration was highly responsive to the expansion in cotton production. Opportunities in tenant farming and in land ownership caused whites to migrate. The expansion of cotton acreage in a county increased white in-migration, while the percentage of farm acres in cotton was negatively related to white net migration. Without knowing what the characteristics of counties with large cotton production were in 1899, these results may seem paradoxical. That is, counties devoted to cotton production tended to be plantation counties with mainly a black population. These counties tended to have few opportunities for whites, and during 1900—1910, such counties experienced white out-migration. The result concerning the change in acres of cotton reflects the continued expansion of cotton production as well as the trend whereby whites entered cotton production. Whites in the South were moving West, and counties in Texas were experiencing white in-migration. These coefficients are consistent with the speculations in Chapter 5.

Capitalist development in the South was also highly related to the white net migration rate. Five of the six variables measuring this factor had statistically significant effects. The level and change in level of urbanization implied that whites were being attracted to urbanized counties. Counties with large cities and counties next to large cities also experienced large increases in the white net migration rate. The percentage change in the number of manufacturing establishments also affected white net migration. The urbanization and industrialization of the South were drawing whites to the cities and towns of the South.

The measure of pressure on available farm land was statistically significant and implies that where such pressure existed, individuals were leaving the county. As one might expect, the presence or absence of a lynching did not affect the white net migration rate significantly. The variable was included in the model for whites in order to allow for comparisons between the models for both groups. The final variable to consider is the effect of the boll weevil infestation. This variable had a negative effect on the net migration rate of whites. This implies that from 1900 to 1910, whites were displaced from the land by the boll weevil infestation.

TABLE 6.3

Results of Weighted Least Squares Regression of County Characteristics on the
Net Migration Rates of Whites for Counties in the South, 1900–1910, 1910–1920, 1920–1930

Factor	Measure[1]	1900-10 b	SE(b)	β	1910-20 b	SE(b)	β	1920-30 b	SE(b)	β
Social Relations of Production and Exchange	TENANTS	39.580*	2.793	.125	24.204*	1.483	.242	6.293*	1.469	.146
	ΔTENANTS	19.378*	.925	.230	29.194*	1.179	.408	-2.666*	.394	-.113
	ΔOWNERS	48.632*	.939	.310	11.867*	1.163	.216	14.461*	1.340	.377
	COTTON	-12.464*	2.452	-.096	-7.795*	2.518	-.103	11.591*	2.661	.147
	ΔCOTTON	68.725*	10.884	.121	14.295*	1.513	.129	57.192*	2.726	.305
	ΔBALES	.019	.043	.000	-.287*	.089	.036	-.041*	.008	-.026
	TEXAS	9.724*	.997	.186	-1.725*	.295	-.118	-8.382*	1.161	-.202
	OKLAHOMA				-17.252*	1.193	-.258	-.372*	.118	-.019
Technical Relations	TRACTORS							.002*	.000	.027
Capitalist Development	URBAN	17.863*	4.509	.072	33.106*	2.476	.232	12.638*	1.439	.237
	ΔURBAN	33.975*	2.792	.132	113.834*	4.634	.389	86.888*	5.626	.341
	BIG CITY	20.476*	2.731	.116	5.123*	1.408	.081	11.397*	1.171	.366
	NEAR BIG CITY	6.341*	.453	.130	1.761*	.471	.118	1.064	.718	.008
	MANUFACTURERS	.051	.043	.008	.010	.020	.003	.010*	.001	.048
	ΔMANUFACTURERS	27.968*	1.660	.241	5.626*	.186	.366	.161	.081	.035
Other Factors	ΔSURPLUS	-5.654*	.208	-.144	-3.368*	.126	-.410	-1.181*	.131	-.228
	LYNCHING	.298	.563	.001	.019	.097	.001	.704	.059	.037
	BOLL1	-2.233*	.509	-.045	.340	.226	.003	-.725*	.251	-.034
	BOLL2				-1.556*	.195	-.058	-3.324*	.509	-.239
	Constant	-29.789			-21.918			-15.615		
	R²	.621			.861			.868		

*p < .05
**n = 703 in 1900-10, n = 798 in 1910-20, n = 822 in 1920-30.

The similarities and differences between the black and white processes must be viewed as a function of differential opportunities and differential social positions. Of whites, roughly 55 − 60% were owners and 45 − 50% were tenants, while blacks were roughly 20 − 25% owners and 75 − 80% tenants. Blacks were subordinate, on the whole, to white landlords. Whites, on the other hand, tended to own their own land, and if they occupied tenant statuses, they were often cash or share tenants.

The relative class positions and the underlying dynamics of those positions suggest that, in terms of the changes in agriculture, blacks and whites migrated in response to different conditions. While blacks were leaving counties with high levels of black tenantry, whites were moving into counties with high levels of white tenantry. This is consistent with the argument that blacks were leaving old areas of cotton production (and high black tenancy) for new areas. Whites, on the other hand, were still exhibiting an influx into tenantry, and, therefore, high levels of white tenantry implied new and continued opportunities. Both blacks and whites were responding to increasing tenantry by moving to where such opportunities existed. They were responding to expanding cotton cultivation, which is shown by the positive relationship between this expansion and net migration. Blacks and whites were responding differently to changes in ownership. Increasing white ownership implied white inmigration, whereas increasing black ownership suggested black outmigration. This was a result of the differences in the kinds of opportunities that existed for each group. Whites with a little money became owners on newly opened land. Blacks were unable to become owners, and when they did work newly cultivated land, they were usually tenants.

Another difference between the two groups was the effect of the boll weevil infestation. This reflects the geographic dispersion of blacks and whites as well as their class positions. From Map 5.1 it can be seen that by 1910, the boll weevil had infested much of Texas, all of Louisiana, and parts of Mississippi, Oklahoma, Arkansas, and Alabama. These areas contained many blacks who were engaged in cotton production and who were probably displaced by the boll weevil infestation. More important, many whites who owned land could switch from cotton to other crops and still survive as subsistence farmers. Blacks who were basically tenants did not have that option—without the ability to grow cotton, they had to leave the land.

The Model of Migration, 1910 − 1920

The period 1910 − 1920 had three major events that affected migration: World War I, the boll weevil invasion, and the high price of cotton from

1915 on. The war produced a fair amount of work opportunities in industries supplying the war effort, and these expanding war industries attracted people to the cities of the North and South. The boll weevil invasion continued East, and by 1920, it had affected much of the South causing many difficulties, especially for blacks. Scott (1920) and Woodson (1924) stress that the inability to grow cotton constituted a tremendous hardship, and many persons moved. The high price of cotton, which was related primarily to the needs of the war effort, made cotton production extremely profitable for those who could grow it. The sample of counties included in this analysis has been expanded to 798, with the bulk of the new counties resulting from the addition of Oklahoma to the analysis. Details on the sample and its characteristics appear in Appendices A and B.

The model of the causes of the black net migration rate in the period 1910–1920 is shown in Table 6.2. Seven of the eight measures of the social relations of production and exchange had statistically significant effects on the black net migration rate. Once again, the social relations of production and exchange played a key role in structuring the opportunities of blacks and, hence, structured the black net migration rate. The largest effect in the model is the percentage of farmers who were tenants in the county. The higher the level of black tenants, the higher the level of net out-migration. This reflects three things. First, the boll weevil caused migration by reducing the tenants' ability to earn a living. As the boll weevil infestation hit the black belt counties that had high tenantry rates, these counties tended to lose population. Second, in order to seek new farming opportunities, tenants continued to leave southeastern cotton counties that had high tenantry rates. Third, tenants continued to leave highly tenantized counties for opportunities in the cities of the North and South. Over the decade, the majority of counties experienced declines in both black tenancy and ownership, which means that out-migration ensued. In terms of cotton production, counties where production expanded experienced black in-migration, and counties where production contracted lost blacks. Blacks continued to migrate to Texas during this period, but more appeared to be leaving counties of Oklahoma than counties in the rest of the South.

The capitalist development had large effects on the net migration rate of blacks, which reflected the boom of World War I. The level of increase in urbanization implied increases in the black net migration rate. Counties with large cities and counties next to large cities also had an influx of blacks. The industrialization of the South implied that opportunities in manufacturing were attracting blacks. The war effort was expanding opportunities for blacks in the cities and towns, and blacks were moving in response to these opportunities.

The measure of surplus population had quite a significant negative effect on the net migration rate of blacks. This implies that if the change in the ratio of rural population to the number of farms is large and positive, persons left the county due to a lack of opportunities in farming. The occurrence of a lynching had a negative effect on the black migration rate, but is statistically insignificant. It seems that lynchings did not motivate blacks to move.

The final factor to consider is the effect of the boll weevil on the net black migration rate. It is apparent that the boll weevil infestation was a major cause of the black net out-migration rate. The counties that were infested from 1900 to 1910 had, on the average, an 11.9 higher net out-migration rate than uninfested counties, whereas those counties that were infested during 1910–1920 had a higher average net out-migration rate of 21.43. The infestation was a real impetus for black net out-migration.

The model of the process underlying white net migration rates is in Table 6.3. All eight of the measures that reflect the social relations of production and exchange had statistically significant effects on the white net migration rate. This factor again structured the opportunities of whites to a great degree. Counties where expansion of white ownership and tenantry were occurring experienced in-migration, whereas decreases in tenantry and ownership resulted in net out-migration. The percentage of all farm acres in cotton was negatively related to the white net migration rate, while the change in the percentage of farm acres in cotton was positively related to the white migration rate. As in the case of the white regression in 1900–1910, it seems paradoxical that counties with high levels of cotton growth in 1909 were losing population while those counties increasing cotton plantings from 1909 to 1919 were gaining population. The argument put forth earlier is still operative. Counties that used most of their total acreage to plant cotton tended to be black belt counties where few opportunities existed for whites. Counties with increasing production tended to be in newly opened lands or in places outside the boll weevil infestation. Whites tended to leave the counties of Texas and Oklahoma at high rates. One explanation for this is that Oklahoma was initially settled with many persons seeking cheap or free land in the 1890s. By 1910, many of these people were unable to make a living and therefore left.

Capitalist development in the South had large effects on the white net migration rate as five of the six measures had statistically significant effects. The level and increase in level of urbanization in a county implied high in-migration of whites. Large cities and counties next to large cities also experienced white in-migration. The industrialization of the South was drawing whites into counties where opportunities existed.

In terms of the other factors, only the presence of surplus population and, to a lesser degree, the boll weevil infestation in counties from 1910 to 1920 had a statistically significant effect on the white net migration rate. Whites were being affected by the boll weevil infestation just as blacks were. Unable to grow cotton, whites tenants were forced off the land and into other activities. However, whites were not as severely affected by the boll weevil infestation as blacks were. The effects of lynching on the net white migration rate during this time were statistically insignificant and slightly negative. Again, one would not expect these to have large effects since lynching affected only blacks.

A comparison of the black and white net migration rate models is in order. Blacks left highly tenantized counties. Furthermore, a majority of counties experienced a decline in black ownership and tenantization. This is to be contrasted with the fact that whites entered counties with high levels of white tenantry and experienced increases in ownership and tenantry in a majority of counties. The fact that 75 – 80% of black farmers were tenants suggests that much of the black net out-migration in this period was from black belt counties. What caused this black exodus from cotton farming, especially in the face of high cotton prices? The answer seems to be twofold: boll weevils and opportunities in the towns and cities of the South and North. The patterns of coefficients in the black net migration rate model suggest precisely that blacks were leaving the rural areas of the South, leaving tenant farming behind, and going to the urban areas. Since blacks tended to be tenants, they were unable to earn a living in the face of the boll weevil invasion. Black farm owners who were operating marginal land were also unable to remain in farming due to increased debt and the boll weevil infestation. With the war years, there was an economic boom, and blacks gravitated to the cities and towns where jobs existed.

Whites, on the other hand, were also affected by war, boll weevils, and the high price of cotton. But because of their differential social positions, they were migrating in response to slightly different factors. The historical process by which whites were becoming tenantized continued. The majority of southern counties experienced increases in white tenantry and ownership. The boll weevil infestation was not as severe for white farmers because the majority of them were farm owners, and in the face of insect infestation, they remained on their land and grew other crops. Urban areas and the growth of industrialization appeared to be strong for both whites and blacks. Even so, the war probably presented more opportunities for whites than for blacks since blacks were not allowed to hold certain positions.

One other fact should be noted. The decade of 1910—1920 marked the first period when enormous new cotton lands were not being planted. That is, by 1910 or so, cotton was being grown in Texas, Oklahoma, Louisiana, and Arkansas in about as many places as it could be grown. While there was acreage expansion in the next decade, cotton cultivation had finished spreading throughout the South. This resulted in a stabilization in the number of persons engaged in cotton production. From 1920 on, the number of cotton farmers decreased even though acreage cultivation climbed in the 1920s. In essence, then, the decade 1910—1920 meant a closing off of opportunities in cotton farming. The flow of black tenants seeking new positions in the western half of the South needed redirection. For blacks and whites alike, opportunities were becoming circumscribed, and the major option became rural-to-urban migration. This, then, is a third factor, along with boll weevils and job opportunities in the cities, that shaped black and white migration from the land.

The Model of Migration, 1920—1930

The central focus of the decade 1920—1930 was the agricultural depression, which was caused by low prices and cotton overproduction. This depression led to the gradual downfall of all cotton farmers whether they were tenants, small farm owners, or large plantation owners. Since this agricultural depression and its causes have been discussed quite thoroughly, it is now of interest to see how the depression affected the net migration rate of blacks and whites. The central feature of this decade was the rapid decrease in both white and black ownership, which reflected a loss of land due to indebtedness. White tenantry increased greatly while black tenantry increased slightly. This occurred while cotton acreage expanded. This social process was caused by the crop lien system in interaction with the supply and demand for cotton. It is within these macrosocial changes that one seeks the causes of black and white migration.

Table 6.2 also presents the model of black migration rates from 1920 to 1930. The social relations of production and exchange had the largest impact on the black net migration rate. Six of the eight measures had statistically significant effects. Counties with high levels of tenantry had large amounts of black net out-migration. Counties where tenantry was increasing also had net out-migration. This is consistent with the idea that in counties where the depression was severe and where blacks were becoming tenantized, out-migration was occurring. The percentage change in black owners had a large, positive, statistically significant effect on the net migration rate of blacks. However, 91.8% of the counties experienced a loss of black farmers. This means that for most counties, the percentage change in owners was negative. Therefore, in most counties, net out-migration was occurring (a negative percentage multiplied by a positive parameter means a negative addition to the net migration rate). This, again, supports the argument that the loss of land by farm owners forced people off the land, and those who lost their farms tended to migrate.

If acreage in cotton production either increased or was at a high level over the decade, this implied net in-migration for blacks. Sixty-five percent of the counties had cotton acreage increases, which implied net in-migration into counties that were: (a) already cotton producers and (b) increasing cotton production. The effects are net effects, and they reflect the fact that increased cotton production was causing in-migration of blacks even though the percentage of black tenants and the percentage change in black ownership both imply net out-movement. These net effects demonstrate that even in an agricultural depression, increases in cash crop cotton cultivation implied increases in the black net migration rate. The Texas dummy variable showed that blacks tended to move into counties of Texas at a high (statistically significant) rate net of the other variables in the model. The Oklahoma dummy variable showed that blacks were moving into counties of Oklahoma at a positive yet statistically insignificant rate.

For the first time in the analysis, the technical relations of production come into play. The measure of mechanization is the number of tractors in a county in 1929. This variable had a negative, statistically insignificant effect on the black net migration rate. Therefore, in the period 1920 – 1930, tractors were not displacing blacks from the land. This finding is consistent with the argument made previously that out-migration was not related to mechanization from 1920 – 1930.

Four of the six measures of capitalist development had statistically significant effects on the black net migration rate. The results suggest that the urbanization of blacks in the South was a cause of black in-migration. Blacks were going to the towns and cities of the South during this period to (a) escape the collapsing rural farm system; and (b) find opportunities. Counties near large urban centers (population greater than 25,000) and counties with large urban centers experienced net in-migration of blacks. Neither the level nor the percentage change in manufacturing was significantly related to the black net migration rate. This suggests that the level and growth of manufacturing were not strongly related to black net in-migration.

Two of the three "other" factors had statistically significant effects on the black net migration rate. The measure of surplus population had a statistically significant effect on net migration, which suggests that population pressure caused persons to move. The dummy variable that signifies whether or not a county had a lynching during 1920–1930 had a negative, statistically insignificant effect on the black net migration rate. While the coefficient is not small, its standard error is also large. One can conclude only that the effect lynching had on black net out-migration was highly variable across counties.

The final factor to consider is the boll weevil infestation. Counties first infested from 1900 to 1910 experienced net in-migration of blacks, whereas counties first infested after 1920 did not, but this is not statistically significant. Counties first infested from 1910 to 1920, however, experienced a statistically significant increase in black net in-migration, whereas counties infested after 1920 did not. These results suggest that counties infested after 1920 experienced more out-migration due to boll weevils than did counties first infested from 1900–1910 and 1910–1920. This difference is greatest between counties first infested in 1910–1920 and those first infested after 1920.

The model of migration for whites from 1920 to 1930 is in Table 6.3. All eight of the variables measuring the social relations of production and exchange had statistically significant effects on the white net migration rate. This means that the agricultural depression struck whites as hard as it did blacks. Enormous numbers of farm owners lost their land and became tenants. As the decade progressed, more and more whites became impoverished. For that reason, the measures which reveal class structure are particularly interesting. The percentage of white farmers who were tenants had a positive, statistically significant effect on the white net migration rate. This suggests that counties with high levels of white tenantry had net in-migration. The percentage change in tenants had a negative, statistically significant effect on the white net migration rate. While this effect is not large, it implies that increases in white tenantry meant white net out-migration. Since 77.1% of the counties showed increases in white tenantry, most counties had out-migration of whites even though white tenantry increased. As suspected, white tenantry expanded from 1920 to 1930 because owners lost their land and people were becoming impoverished. The percentage change in white ownership from 1920 to 1930 had the largest effect in the model. For most of the counties, white ownership decreased and was accompanied by white net out-migration. Again, a positive parameter value multiplied by a negative variable value produces a negative addition to the white net migration rate. This variable offers evidence that many whites lost their land and left the counties to seek opportunities elsewhere.

The two dummy variables (reflecting whether a county was in Texas or Oklahoma) had negative, statistically significant effects on the white net migration rate. This means that whites were not moving West during this decade because they tended, on the average, to move out of counties in Texas and Oklahoma. This is plausible, for many whites were cotton farmers in Oklahoma and Texas. Since these were the fastest growing areas of production from 1900 to 1920, the agricultural depression hit them hardest and forced whites out of counties in these states.

The technical relations of production came into play in this decade. However, tractors were not displacing whites. Indeed, this variable had a positive, statistically significant effect on the white net migration rate. This could have resulted from the fact that individuals needed to be brought in to operate and tend the machines.

Four of the six measures of capitalist development had statistically significant effects on the white net migration rate. Both the percentage of the population urbanized in 1920 and the change in the percentage urbanized from 1920 to 1930 had positive, statistically significant effects on the white net migration rate. Whites were also being attracted to counties with large cities. The level of manufacturing in a county in 1920 was positively and significantly related to the net migration rate of whites. While this effect was small, it implied that counties with a large number of manufacturing establishments were attracting white in-migrants, net of the urbanization of such counties. The percentage change in manufacturing establishments had a positive, statistically insignificant effect on the white net migration rate. These results suggest that whites were moving to the urban areas of the South. This was due to two factors: (a) the push out of agriculture; and (b) increased opportunities in cities and towns because of the relative prosperity of the 1920s.

Two of the three other factors had statistically significant effects on the white net migration rate. Positive population pressure implied increases in the white net out-migration rate, while negative population pressure meant white net in-migration. The dummy variable for whether or not a lynching occurred in a county had, of course, a positive, statistically insignificant effect on the white migration rate. The final factor to consider is the effect of the boll weevil invasion on the white net migration rate. Both dummy variables had statistically significant effects on white migration. This means that counties infested before 1920 were having net out-migration of whites, whereas counties infested after 1920 were not. As the boll weevil invasion completed its sweep across the South in the early 1920s, the displacement of farmers continued.

A comparison of the causal patterns of black and white net migration rates is now appropriate. From 1920 to 1930, the proportion of black farm owners dropped from 20 to 15%, while the proportion of white farm owners dropped from 55 to 42%. Both black and white farm owners were suffering equally from the depression since the percentage decrease in farm ownership for both blacks and whites was about 25%. Still, by 1930, 85% of black farmers were tenants while 57% of white farmers were tenants. Tenants tended to be more impoverished than owners, and at least 85% of rural blacks were very poor, if not starving. From 1920 to 1930, there was shift in the class distribution of whites whereby a majority became tenants, implying real impoverishment for many whites. The level of rural poverty in 1930, if viewed from this perspective, was staggering.

Since blacks started out in a worse position, it is not surprising that the percentage changes in both tenantry and ownership were highly related to the black net out-migration rate. For whites, the most serious problem was losing land, for the majority of them were landowners in 1920. The tenantization (the increase in the percentage of whites who were tenants) of whites and the decline in white ownership were the forces pushing whites off the land. The differential class positions in 1920 meant that the forces displacing whites from the land were of a different character than those displacing blacks. Both blacks and whites were suffering from the crisis of cotton overproduction and from the crop lien which enabled them to produce cotton. The net out-migration rates, however, reflect the fact that most blacks tended to be tenants faced with few alternatives, while a large proportion of whites tended to be landowners who, upon losing their land, were forced to become tenants or to migrate.

Finally, the effects of mechanization on migration are considered. There is little association between the number of tractors in a county in 1930 and the black net migration rate. There is a small, positive association between the number of tractors and the white net migration rate. This could be due to the fact that tractors were introduced in Texas and Oklahoma first, and their introduction required persons to drive and repair them. Machine care and handling was thought to be work appropriate for whites and meant that there was a need for whites to handle the machines initially. Before 1930, however, there was no displacement of blacks or whites by machines.

Summary

This chapter has shown that the migration of blacks and whites in the South can only be understood in terms of the developments which took place in the social relations of the South. Specific factors structured the net migration rates in precisely the ways that were anticipated in the preceding chapter. The most important factor has proven to be the social relations of production and exchange in agriculture. The dynamics of cash crop agriculture interacting with an emerging urban culture produced the net migrations of blacks and whites.

The period 1900–1930 was a period of stability in the agricultural system. The fundamental social relations of landlord/tenant, merchant/small farm owner, and blacks/whites remained in place. The result was an expansion of cotton production from 1900 to 1910, an era of relative prosperity from 1910 to 1920, and an agricultural depression from 1920 to 1930. The migration of blacks and whites reflected these changes and, as well, reflected the relative class position of blacks and whites and the changing opportunities in towns and cities.

Chapter 7

Transformation of Southern Agriculture and the Creation of a Surplus Farm Population

"I let 'em all go. In '34 I had I reckon four renters and I didn't make anything. I bought tractors on the money the government give me and got shet o' my renters. You'll find it everywhere all over the country thataway. I did everything the government said—except keep my renters. The renters have been having it this way ever since the government come in. They've got their choice—California or WPA."
—A landlord, Texas, 1937 (quoted from Lange and Taylor, 1969:63).

While the period 1900 — 1930 saw no fundamental change in the social relations of production in the South, the period 1930 — 1950 began the upheaval that destroyed the need for the crop lien system, prepared the way for the destruction of the tenant farming system, and began the mechanization of cotton production. The transformation that took place resulted from the relatively class-conscious efforts of large farm owners to secure government intervention in their behalf during the depression of the 1930s. The Agricultural Adjustment Administration's program beginning in 1933 provided large farm owners in the South with the capital to buy machines, and the owners were then able to displace their tenants. It seems that a dominant class fraction, in its own interest, precipitated state action. Such action resulted in the transformation of southern agriculture from a labor-intensive tenant system to a mechanized, capitalist agriculture. The major effect of this transformation was the outmigration of black and white tenants.

1930 — 1940

The agricultural depression of the 1920s only intensified in the early 1930s. To get a sense of the magnitude of the cotton production crisis, it is necessary to consider the price of cotton, the demand for cotton, and the carryover of cotton. From Table 5.1 one can see that the price of cotton dropped from 17.98¢ per pound in 1928 to 5.66¢ per pound in 1931. This drop was due to a number of factors. First, the world demand for cotton declined precipitously from 1928 (nearly 26 million bales) to 1931 (around 22 million bales) because of the worldwide depression. From Table 5.3 it can be seen that the world carryover in cotton increased from 10.5 million bales in 1928 to over 18.3 million in 1932. American cotton accounted for the bulk of this as the American cotton carryover increased by 7.1 million bales during those four years.

These figures starkly demonstrate the overproduction crisis that affected American cotton farmers. In the face of a dropping demand, a gigantic cotton carryover in the world at large, and a plunge in price, cotton was still being produced at high levels. By 1933, most farmers, including most planters, were deeply in debt to merchants, banks, or, in the case of tenants, landlords. The debt cycle went even further up the line since planters owed banks, and merchants owed manufacturers and banks. Because merchants, planters, and small farm owners were unable to pay off manufacturers and banks, these institutions were also in trouble. The entire credit system was in crisis, and until 1933, people did the only thing they could do in the face of falling prices—plant more cotton. The credit crisis and the overproduction crisis were linked; together, they threatened to bankrupt the entire South.

In Chapter 5 it was argued that in the 1920s, American farm policy was being shaped by the Farm Bureau and the Farmers' Union. The scope of the debate centered on the price of farm commodities. The crop lien system and the poverty of tenant farmers were not salient issues. The crisis of the early 1930s can be characterized very easily from these organizations' point of view: production was too high and prices were too low. Neither cooperative marketing nor an attempt to have farmers voluntarily reduce crop acreage could increase cotton prices and solve farmers' problems. Given the organizations' purposes, along with the seemingly insoluble problems of the 1920s, it is easy to see why any farm policy in the 1930s would be oriented toward raising crop prices and cutting production.

After the McNary—Haugen Bill (which would have created crop price supports) was vetoed for a second time in 1928, a political compromise was struck. The Federal Farm Board was set up (by the Hoover Administration) to aid cooperative organizations in holding on to crop surpluses in order to manipulate prices in both the domestic and foreign markets (Benedict and Stine, 1956:8—10; McConnell, 1953:63—65; Nourse et al., 1937:8). This act was significant since it accepted the premise that the federal government had to play a major role in solving the surplus problem. The difficulty was that the Farm Board was unable to act on the central problem—overproduction. The early 1930s saw the notion of production control on the political agenda more and more.

By 1932, the situation for farmers in the South and in the rest of the country was becoming critical. In the Midwest, members of the Farmers' Union and a related organization, the Farmers' Holiday Movement, demanded government reimbursement for the cost of production and a cessation of mortgage foreclosures (Campbell, 1962:60 — 63; Crampton, 1965:139 — 140). Their program did not call for cuts in production; rather, they wanted the government to pay them the difference between the market price and the price of production (i.e., parity). The problem of surplus production was very serious, and in 1932, there was nearly a whole year's supply of cotton in the world that was unsold. Worse yet, it appeared that one of the largest crops in history was being planted.

The Agricultural Adjustment Act of 1933 was the solution to the emergency. This act represented a permanent change in the government's attitude toward farm production and toward the prices of commodities. From this time on, the government intervened in and regulated the production process and insured "stable" prices. The basic provisions of the Agricultural Adjustment Act were relatively simple. The government paid farmers subsidies to cut down on the amount of acreage planted (Nourse *et al.*, 1937:78 — 114; Richard, 1936:30 — 42), and bought surpluses already on the market in order to stabilize the price. Thus, farm income was raised in two ways: (a) direct government subsidy payments to farmers; and (b) commodity prices increased, therefore farm income increased.

The basic support for the legislation came from the Farm Bureau and, to a lesser degree, the Farmers' Union. While there is some historical uncertainty as to precisely the role that farm organizations played in the legislative struggle (see Benedict, 1953:339 — 340; Campbell, 1962:44 — 67; Ford, 1973:38; McConnell, 1953:72 — 75), it is clear that the "domestic allotment" plan embodied in the Agricultural Adjustment Act met with the approval of most of these organizations. The Farm Bureau, in particular, played a key role. It accomplished two major feats under the guidance of Ed O'Neal, a southerner and planter who was the Farm Bureau president throughout the 1930s. First, the Farm Bureau brought about a sectional alliance between the Midwest and the South. In 1932, O'Neal undertook the task of presenting a unified front of agricultural organizations that were in support of legislation embodying principles like those contained in the Agricultural Adjustment Act (McConnell, 1953:71 — 72; Campbell, 1962:44 — 84). Second, the Farm Bureau provided the Department of Agriculture and its Secretary, Henry Wallace, with strong political support by convincing local farmers of the efficacy of farm policy and by pressing Congress at the national level (Campbell, 1962:56 – 57).

The struggle for control over the Agricultural Adjustment Administration (AAA) was complex. Paying farmers subsidies in order for them not to produce did not necessarily mean that only farm owners benefited. Indeed, the farm owner who had tenants was supposed to share his subsidies with his tenants. The plantation owner's ability to keep the entire subsidy payment and remove the tenants was the result of a political struggle within the AAA over who would control the subsidies and how they would be distributed.

Since the crop of 1933 was already planted when the AAA came into existence, it was necessary for a plow-up of cropland to occur in order for cotton farmers to get subsidy payments (Nourse *et al.*, 1937:95 – 96; Richards, 1936:38). It is, at this point, important to consider the dynamics of the administration of the subsidy programs. The central issue here is the distribution of the benefits. From the very beginning, there was tension in the AAA between the rather conservative Department of Agriculture forces, who saw the Agricultural Adjustment Act as strictly a measure to raise prices, and the liberal New Dealers, who were concerned with rural poverty and wanted to insure that tenants received their share of subsidy benefits (Conrad, 1965:105 – 119; Grubbs, 1971:31). The head of the AAA for most of its early period was Chester Davis, a conservative who believed that the AAA was not "an effort to deal with deep-seated social problems" and that the AAA would not "undertake to dictate the usual and normal relationships and tenure arrangements in the South [Grubbs, 1971:36]." It was Davis who stood in the way of attempts to monitor the plantation owners' payment of subsidies to tenants and to keep tenants on the land in the face of acreage reduction.

The basic administrative mechanisms were the county farm extension service and the county agent system (Grubbs, 1971:36 – 38; Nourse *et al.*, 1937:51 – 54; Richards, 1936:67 – 81). These educational services attracted the support of the wealthier farmers in an area. The county agent in the South was occasionally a planter. The basic mechanism by which contracts were signed and enforced and by which subsidies were paid was the county agent system, which by its very nature was biased toward the interests of the large farm owners. The farm owner was entitled to a subsidy for part of his land and was paid for the "usual" amount of crop grown. If the owner had cash tenants (i.e., renters), the tenants were entitled to the entire subsidy. The landowner was not supposed to change the tenants' statuses, nor was he supposed to reduce the number of tenants (Nourse *et al.*, 1937:340 – 349; Richards, 1936:135 – 146). In the case of a rental agreement, the renter was sent the subsidy check. In the cases of share tenants and sharecroppers, the farm owner was supposed to split the check according to each one's share. The tenant could express grievances to a local committee made up of the county agent and respected members of the community (in the South, this usually meant planters).

Given this kind of organization and the possibility of denying tenants' rights, it is not surprising that reports of abuse of tenant rights were widespread (Conrad, 1965:64—82; Grubbs, 1971:30—61; Myrdal, 1944:269). In Arkansas, the Southern Tenant Farmers' Union was formed in 1934 with the goal of preventing the spread of these injustices (Grubbs, 1971:29). Certain members of the AAA were also alarmed at the possibility of landlord domination. This group attempted to help the tenants by investigating whether landlords were keeping a disproportionate share of the income and whether tenants were being displaced or being forced to become wage hands. These investigations, in particular the Myers report, strongly indicated that tenants were being either denied payments, forced off the land, or forced to become wage laborers (Conrad, 1965:177—186; Grubbs, 1971:54; Nourse *et al.*, 1937:347—348). The issue came to a head in 1935, when Chester Davis demanded a purge of the liberals in the AAA who tried to enforce a rule that would force landlords to keep their tenants. Davis went to Secretary Wallace and threatened to quit if the liberals were not forced to resign, and Wallace supported Davis for political reasons. Roosevelt depended upon cotton-state spokesmen for support, particularly Senators Robinson (Arkansas) and Harris (Mississippi). Alienating such spokesmen by alienating planters was not politically feasible. Also, Davis and his supporters controlled the structures of the AAA and the Department of Agriculture. In view of this, Wallace had little choice but to accept Davis's demands. Thus, control was in the hands of county agricultural agents, which meant that planters could do what they pleased. Perhaps Rupert Vance summed it up best (in Grubbs, 1971):

> The greatest efficiency of the southern planters consists of securing government subsidy to uphold a system that might otherwise break down of its own weakness. . . . With one hand the cotton landlord takes agricultural subsidies and rental benefits from his government, with the other he pushes his tenants on relief . . . in the South when the government salvages the landlord it creates almost as great a problem of displaced and dispossessed tenants whose only hope is further demands on the federal treasury [p. 26].

The hopes of tenants were later satisfied in a partial way by the creation of the Farm Securities Administration. While the tenants' difficulties would be dealt with by other means, one thing was clear: From 1935 on, the Department of Agriculture and the farm policy debate were clearly oriented to the needs of commercial producers (Baldwin, 1968:86; McConnell, 1953: 173−181). The Farm Bureau's view that farmers are businessmen and the concept of the family farmer became the dominant ideologies of the Department of Agriculture.

The transformation of southern agriculture had begun. With subsidy payments, landowners no longer needed tenants. Tenants who remained often became wage laborers. The infusion of capital into the South allowed southern farmers to buy machines, and the influx of tractors into cotton production during the late 1930s and the 1940s was related to the growth of capital in the South.

The agricultural policies of the 1930s were extensions of earlier attempts to raise the prices of agricultural commodities. The development of agricultural policy had its roots in the Populist revolt. The Department of Agriculture began as an organization that was basically oriented toward agricultural education and the regulation of agricultural commodities marketing. These "passive" activities helped shape what was possible in agricultural policy and who it would aid. Various kinds of price supports were finally implemented only after years of political struggle. The whole notion of price supports defined a community of interests, that is, producers of cash crops. This struggle resulted in a policy oriented toward the natural constituency of a Department of Agriculture that had developed and nurtured commercial farming (i.e., large commercial farmers). Not surprisingly, the farm organization with the largest input into the policy process (the Farm Bureau) had the ideology and rhetoric most consistent with the Department of Agriculture. Indeed, the Farm Bureau's roots were so intermingled with the Department of Agriculture's that they became difficult to separate.

The view that mechanization occurred in the South in order to make production more efficient is an oversimplification. Mechanization did occur in the South because it was more efficient (in the sense that profits were higher); however, mechanization could not have occurred if social conditions had not been right. The federal government provided the catalyst whereby the infusion of capital and the control of production allowed the transformation of southern agriculture to proceed. When intervention comes into the accumulation of capital in agriculture, it comes first and foremost in the interests of farm owners, particularly those producing commercially.

There are two residual issues to take up in this section: (a) the effects of acreage restriction on the production of cotton; and (b) the decline in tenantry. Table 5.1 shows the steady decrease in cotton acreage planted from 1930 to 1939. Production of cotton, however, remained relatively constant. This implies that while a fair amount of land was retired from cotton growth, production did not decrease; therefore, productivity in cotton growing increased. There are two major explanations for this phenomenon. First, marginally productive land was being removed from production. Second, land that was cultivated was more intensively cultivated with the use of machines and more fertilizers. Tables 4.7 and 4.8 show an enormous displacement of black and white tenants. The statistical patterns, then, are consistent with the basic argument. Acreage reduction resulted in tenant displacement, while the productivity of acreage still in production increased. Subsidy payments were used to make the land that was still in production even more productive by using more machines and fertilizers to increase output.

These processes resulted in the destruction of crop lien and tenant farming systems. With additional capital, planters were able to mechanize their field operations. Farmers were more willing to invest in machines, knowing that the federal government would support the price of cotton and, therefore, would help avoid further overproduction crises.

1940 – 1950

Two major features of the 1940s are relevant—the continuation of farm programs and World War II. The reorganization of southern farming and the government control of production continued through the 1940s. Reductions in cotton acreage continued, while cotton yields remained constant. Tenants were displaced, and the only government programs oriented toward helping tenants were destroyed by conservative commercial farmers through the influence of the Farm Bureau. Mechanization, meanwhile, proceeded quite rapidly. World War II provided opportunities in the cities and towns of the South and North for a displaced rural population. As the decade proceeded, there was an acceleration of movement off the land. In this part of the chapter, the following topics are treated: (a) a general discussion of cotton prices, acreage, production, and mechanization; (b) a consideration of cotton programs from 1936 to 1950; (c) a look at the Farm Securities Administration and its demise; (d) the pace and meaning of mechanization; and (e) the war and the opportunities it brought.

From Table 5.1, it can be seen that the price of cotton rose from 9.89¢ per pound in 1940 to 40.07¢ per pound in 1950. The price increase throughout the decade was rather constant with three major exceptions—1940 – 1941, 1945 – 1946, and 1949 – 1950. At the first juncture,

the price increased when less cotton was grown and prewar demand intensified. The price jump between 1945 and 1946 reflected the
decrease in the amount of cotton produced. The sharp increase in price
in 1950 reflected a relatively strong world market. By 1940, the United
States was no longer producing the majority of the world's cotton. America's share hovered between 30 and 40% of the world's production. Most
of the decline in market share was due to the increase in production
around the world. Cash crop production was cheaper in India, Egypt,
and Brazil, and these countries were increasing production and selling in
foreign markets that were formerly controlled by United States' producers. Tables 4.7 and 4.8 show decreases in white and black tenantry. These
massive changes show that from 1930 to 1950, black tenantry decreased
313,158, or 48.6%, and white tenantry decreased 415,626, or 51.2%. Black
ownership increased about 8%, while white ownership grew by 27%. Massive numbers of blacks and whites were being displaced by the acreage
restrictions. As cotton lost its stranglehold on a large number of persons,
mechanization proceeded. Table 4.13 shows that between 1940 and 1950,
the number of tractors on southern farms tripled. The number of people
in cotton production continued to decrease, while the cotton business
continued to evolve into an agribusiness of large commercial farms and
plantations that used wage labor instead of sharecroppers.

In 1936, the Supreme Court declared the major provisions of the Agricultural Adjustment Act of 1933 unconstitutional. A new bill was quickly
passed that sidestepped the objections of the Supreme Court and was
supported vigorously by the major farm organizations, particularly the
Farm Bureau (Benedict, 1953:249; McConnell, 1953:78 – 81). The major
features of the new act were twofold. First, payments to farmers were to
come from federal revenues instead of from processing taxes. Second, the
act was couched in terms of "soil conservation." Farmers were to be paid
to shift from soil-depleting crops (i.e., cash crops like cotton, corn, wheat,
and tobacco) to soil-conserving crops (like hay and legumes [Benedict,
1953:350]). Most researchers agree that the major function of this legislation was to decrease cash crop production in such a way as not to run
afoul of the Supreme Court (Benedict, 1953:35; Kile, 1948:236 – 246;
McConnell, 1953:78 – 81). In the South, this act produced its intended
effect since the production of hay and other forage crops increased dramatically from 1935 to 1940 (Vance, 1945:186 – 187).

The Agricultural Adjustment Act of 1938 represented the culmination
of the efforts of the Farm Bureau to pass its basic legislative program (Kile,
1948:236 – 237; McConnell, 1953:79). This legislation was a permanent
government tool for adjusting agricultural production and for maintaining agricultural income (Benedict, 1953:375). Four major mechanisms

were available to control production: (a) the payments begun under the conditions of the 1936 Act; (b) quotas levied on production, which penalized persons for growing too much; (c) loans available to allow farmers to hold onto their crops if the price dropped too low (Benedict, 1953:378); and (d) parity payments made by the Secretary of Agriculture (i.e., farmers could be paid the difference between the cost of production and the market price). The major effect of this legislation was to continue the limitation on the amount of cotton grown, to encourage the production of alternative crops, and, most importantly, to guarantee income to cotton producers who were increasingly utilizing wage laborers rather than tenants on large land holdings.

It is of some interest to consider how these various mechanisms worked to stabilize price and to control production throughout the 1940s. The war years were quite good for cotton production. Prices were high even though the immediate effect of the war was to require more foodstuffs and decreased emphasis on cotton (Benedict and Stine, 1956:26). From Table 5.1, it can be noted that cotton acreage dropped during World War II. However, the cotton carryover during the war increased in the United States as prices continued to climb. This reflected the fact that the Commodity Credit Corporation bought cotton at parity, and, therefore, farmers were guaranteed an income and a market for their product (Benedict and Stine, 1956:29–30). Under pressure of the war, then, cotton production was stable while cotton acreage decreased. From 1945 to 1948, there were no controls on production. In 1949, overproduction again threatened price stability, and once again, controls came into action. From 1949 to 1950, acreage allotments were decreased, and the Commodity Credit Corporation became active in buying up cotton.

The Southern Tenant Farmers' Union and the Roosevelt Administration attempted to alleviate the rural poverty that the AAA programs aggravated. In 1932, Roosevelt came to power with the message that he was committed to solving the problem of rural poverty (Baldwin, 1968:48). His first response was an attempt to raise prices of farm commodities through the AAA. This attempt only made the plight of the tenant farmer more desperate. In opposition to the AAA, the Southern Tenant Farmers' Union (STFU) was formed in Tyronza, Arkansas, in 1934 (Baldwin, 1968:80; Grubbs, 1971:27–29). The STFU was formed by two socialists, H. L. Mitchell and Clay East, who wanted to organize tenants to fight for their share of AAA payments and to force landlords to keep them on the land. These immediate practical goals only formed the backdrop of the Union's attempt to organize all farm workers. The STFU also did something that no farm organization had tried since the 1890s—it recruited blacks. While whites and blacks were organized into different locals at first, all were part of the same union, and within a short period of time, racial differences were put aside (Grubbs, 1971:68−70).

From 1934 to 1936, the STFU fought and lost, but kept on organizing. The Supreme Court of Arkansas ruled against the STFU's attempt to make landlords split AAA payments. STFU members and organizers were harassed, beaten, and arrested by county sheriffs and deputies under the urging of landlords. Their one successful action, which occurred in the fall of 1935, was a strike against landlords for higher wages and an increased share of the crop (Grubbs, 1971:86−88). After the defeat of the AAA liberals, the government demonstrated massive indifference to the situations of tenants. This attitude continued until 1936, when the STFU and others got Roosevelt to form the President's Commission on Farm Tenancy. The Commission was composed of liberals who were sympathetic to the tenants' plight. The Farm Securities Administration (FSA) was the legislative outcome of the Commission's report (Baldwin, 1968:167−169; Grubbs, 1971:136−161). The tenant's basic problem was seen as that of landlessness; that is, the problem with tenants was that they were not landowners. It was thought that if tenants could be made landowners, they would shy away from radicalism (as Henry Wallace, Secretary of Agriculture, expressed it [Baldwin, 1968:88−89]).

The basic programs of the FSA were oriented toward providing tenants with land. Blacks were highly discriminated against and were greatly underrepresented in the land-buying schemes (Baldwin, 1968:196−198). The FSA provided loans to low-income families for farmland, homes, machines, and other services, as well as providing relief to persons in need. This relief took the form of a cash payment. Finally, the FSA organized cooperative farms, where members worked on land bought with loans from the government and shared the income. By the early 1940s, the FSA had helped over 700,000 people, had over 19,000 employees, and had loaned out over $170 million (Baldwin, 1968:398).

In the early 1940s, the Farm Bureau led the attack on the FSA. Kile (1948), in his "official" history of the Farm Bureau say, "The AFBF received much credit for stepping out boldly and scotching this bureaucratic machine which in its post-depression years was apparently doing its best to give a government-controlled socialist, if not collectivistic, trend to American agriculture [p. 264]." The success of the Farm Bureau to destroy the FSA was due to a combination of factors (Baldwin, 1968:411; McConnell, 1953:173−181). First, as McConnell (1953:177) argues, the Farm Bureau was most interested in protecting the county agent system, which was being undermined by the FSA. Second, cotton growers, represented by the National Cotton Council, thought that the FSA was forcing wage increases by giving rural inhabitants alternatives to working in the cotton fields. Third, as Baldwin (1968:411) suggests, the mood of Congress was such that the FSA programs were seen as outrageous experiments and, as such, were vulnerable to backlash. Finally, with the coming of the war, the New Deal programs seemed unnecessary and lost their earlier appeal. The decline of the FSA meant that the only programs supporting tenants and sharecroppers ended. Opportunities to become landowners lessened, and the middle and late 1940s witnessed no further relief for tenants.

The existence of the FSA did have real results. The increase in white farm owners from 1930 to 1950 was, at least to a small degree, a result of FSA efforts. Baldwin's (1968:196—198) data shows that blacks were systematically underrepresented as clients of the FSA. The New Deal efforts to help tenants did not often reach those who needed it most. By 1941, the Southern Tenant Farmer's Union was also in decline as internal politics and joining the Congress of Industrial Organizations (CIO) destroyed it (Grubbs, 1971:162—192). Government programs oriented toward tenant farmers took an unnecessarily narrow view of tenants' problems. Instead of seeking to prevent continued tenant displacement, Roosevelt's liberal administration sought to turn a small minority of southern tenants into farmowners. For the rest, it offered only relief. Even these minimalist strategies eventually gave way when challenged by the Farm Bureau. The 1940s made the options of the tenant farmer very obvious: They were vulnerable to being forced off the land, and only the cities of the North and South offered opportunities to escape poverty and starvation.

The issue of mechanization is a complex one, and, here, it is important to make two points: (a) how mechanization proceeded in cotton, and the pace of mechanization in the 1930s and 1940s; and (b) the relation between mechanization and migration. There were really two stages in the mechanization of cotton production—the introduction of tractors and the introduction of cotton pickers (Day, 1967; Ford, 1973:28—29; Fulmer, 1950:60—82; Street, 1957:91—134). In the first stage, tractors aided the farmer in tilling the soil, in planting the crop, and in plant cultivation. Tractors came into use in Texas and Oklahoma first because the larger farm operations could more easily utilize the machines. The second phase of mechanization did not begin until the late 1940s (Street, 1957:132—134). At this time, the first mechanical cotton pickers were introduced and, for the first time, the need for an enormous amount of labor at harvest time was reduced.

Of great concern here is the pace of mechanization, its relation to the AAA, and the demise of tenant farming. Before 1930, there were few tractors in the South (see Table 4.13). Mechanization did not proceed rapidly in the South since labor was cheap and credit to buy machines was scarce. With the AAA, farm incomes rose and rose, especially for plantation owners (Nourse *et al.*, 1937:287 − 323). The plantation owners were able to buy tractors to cultivate their land more efficiently (Ford, 1973:55 − 57; Street, 1957:160). Street (1957) and McKibben and Griffen (1938) suggest that the immense growth in tractors in the South in the 1930s occurred mainly between 1935 and 1940. Initially, mechanization followed the decline of tenancy (Fite, 1950) and continued to do so through 1945. The enormous growth in the use of tractors in the 1940s was not the cause of the out-migration or displacement of tenants. Rather, it was the government's subsidizing of agribusiness that displaced tenants and caused out-migration. Government assistance to large farm owners produced a reduction in acreage. Farm owners invested in tractors and reduced their need for tenants and laborers. At the first stage of displacement, tenants became laborers and remained in the rural nonfarm population.

Even as mechanization increased and subsidies continued, there was still a need for farm laborers to harvest the crop. The introduction of cotton pickers in the late 1940s made the rural nonfarm population a total surplus population and left them no choice but to migrate. Some argue that mechanization forced blacks and whites out of the rural areas of the South, but such a view is somewhat shortsighted as it tends to see only the migrations that occurred after the cotton picker was introduced. The mechanical cotton picker was the last link in the transformation of southern cotton farming. The process of that transformation began with state intervention into production in the 1930s, which initially forced tenants off the land and provided the capital for the mechanization of agricultural production. Tractors and continued subsidies worked to complete the agricultural transformation. However, even through the late 1940s, most cotton was picked by hand. The introduction of the mechanical cotton picker only completed the transformation of southern cotton farming. The 1940s witnessed the continued destruction of tenant farming as well as an enormous increase in the use of tractors.

While the tenant farming system was disappearing through the 1940s, the cities and towns of the North and South were booming with war industries. The South was the major training ground for America's soldiers, and before the war ended, armaments, planes, and ships were being produced in substantial quantities in the South. Textile factories, refineries, and steel mills were booming (Tindall, 1967:687 − 731). Of course, similar opportunities existed in the North, and many blacks and whites moved out of the South to find work. After the war, there was a recession, but by 1948, the recession ended and opportunities continued to open up in the industries of the North and South.

One other factor should be mentioned. The decade 1940 – 1950 was also the beginning of the decline of the South's dominant position in the production of American cotton. By 1950, large amounts of cotton were being produced in Arizona and California. Cotton in the West was produced at a lower cost because the land required less fertilizer and operations were more mechanized. Some acreage reduction in the South during the period 1940 – 1950 was probably due to this competition. This took some business away from southern producers.

The Causes of Migration, 1930 – 1950

It was argued earlier that in any given period, there are six factors that structured the process of migration at the county level: (a) the world market and the price of cotton; (b) the technical relations of production; (c) the social relations of production and exchange; (d) the state; (e) capitalist development in the South and North; and (f) other factors, such as the boll weevil infestation. The goal here is to precisely relate these factors and their operations to the migration of blacks and whites in the 1930 – 1950 period. The price of cotton and capitalist development in the North are again left out of this analysis and will be considered in Chapter 9.

1930 – 1940

For the first time, activities of the state need to be incorporated into the model as a factor that will explain black and white migration. The central argument of this chapter has been that plantation owners were able to secure subsidy payments from the federal government, and these payments brought capital to the South and caused the demise of the crop lien and tenant farming systems. In their place rose a mechanized, cash crop agricultural system. The need for agricultural labor was substantially reduced; therefore, government subsidy payments to counties of the South should have caused a large amount of black and white out-migration. Since more blacks were tenants, these subsidies ought to imply higher rates of black out-migration. The social relations of production and exchange were transformed in this period by these subsidy payments, and one would expect these factors to also have a large impact on migration. Because cotton acreage and tenantry decreased, one should find high levels of out-migration for blacks and whites, but again, particularly for blacks. One aspect of the social relations of production during the 1930s should have caused in-migration, particularly for whites: during the depression, a large number of people became subsistence farmers who owned their own land, and where this occurred, one would expect in-migration.

The effects of capitalist development on migration during the 1930s was probably small since the depression lasted most of the decade and there were few opportunities in the cities and towns. One might expect some movement into the towns and cities because when individuals were forced off the farms, they went into the towns and cities rather than starve in the countryside.

The technical relations of production shifted as the agricultural system was transformed. Tractors became commonplace throughout the South. It has been argued in this study that mechanization resulted from subsidy payments and from the reorganization of southern class relations. One might expect that mechanization caused some out-migration in the 1930s, but it was not a major cause of out-migration at that time. From the economist's point of view, it was the major cause of out-migration. To assess who is right is an empirical question.

In terms of other factors, only a measure of population pressure is included in this decade. The boll weevil infestation had ended and there is no available measure of the differential repression of blacks in this period.

1940 – 1950

The period 1940 – 1950 was basically a continuation of the previous decade. The state continued to subsidize agricultural production, and, hence, the transformation of southern agriculture proceeded. Out-migration was still being caused by subsidy payments. The social relations of production and exchange were also still being transformed, and the results were fewer opportunities for tenant farming and more out-migration. The technical relations of production continued to develop and resulted in a more highly mechanized agricultural system. In the period 1940 – 1950, this could have caused out-migration. Again, one would expect these factors to affect blacks more than whites. One would also expect changes in white farm ownership to be highly associated with net in-migration, whereas changes in black farm ownership should be only minimally related to net in-migration.

Southern capitalist development should be strongly related to net in-migration for both blacks and whites. As the war economy boomed and the need for agricultural labor continued to decline, both groups were probably attracted to industrial and urban areas. Large cities and nearby counties were, in all probability, growing due to the war boom.

Finally, the only "other" factor considered for this time period is the effect of population pressure on the land. Where such pressure existed, out-migration probably occurred.

Chapter 8

Models of the Migration Process, 1930 — 1950

The era 1930 — 1950 began the transformation of the social relations of production that were essentially operative throughout much of the South from 1867. In the main, this transformation was brought about by two forces: (a) the perennial up-and-down cycle of cotton production and the debt structure of the South (i.e., the crop lien system); and (b) federal government intervention, which provided production stabilization through subsidy payments and other mechanisms. In Chapter 7, it was noted that one result of this transformation was the further impoverishment of tenant farmers and the beginning of their displacement. When landlords reduced cotton acreage, they had little use for tenants, and tenants were forced off the land. Landlords began to cultivate smaller tracts of land more intensely and used subsidy money to buy tractors, which forced more people off the land. From 1933 to 1950, any potential crisis of overproduction was met by government support through either the purchase of surplus cotton or direct payment to farmers (for taking land out of production). None of this helped tenant farmers, who found themselves shut out of this new, commercial cash crop farming.

The logic behind the models in this chapter is identical to that of the models in Chapter 6. The process of net migration from counties of the South is viewed as the outcome of various social processes reflected in the social and economic compositions of each county. Variables that embody aspects of relevant social processes are measured, and models that show the relation of the variables to the net migration rates of blacks and whites are presented. Then, the patterns of the variables' parameters are interpreted in the context of the underlying social and historical processes. Different factors can have entirely different implications, depending on what is considered to be the social process generating the effects. For example, the variable "change in the percentage of all farmers who were tenants" is a measure of the expansion of the cotton system in 1900 – 1910. In 1930 – 1940, this same variable mainly reflects the destruction of tenant farming that resulted when agricultural payments reduced cotton acreage. The meaning of the parameter of this variable (regardless of whether its sign is positive or negative) is contingent upon what the social and historical context was. The precise strategy is to measure the net migration rates of blacks and whites in the 804 sample counties for both decades. Then, a variant of weighted least squares regression is run, using the net migration rates as the dependent variables and using the social and economic characteristics of the counties as independent variables.

This set of analyses suffers from a problem of causal ordering. In the previous analysis, each of the independent variables exercised net independent effects on the dependent variable. None of the variables were seen as "working through one another." The logic was that A, B, and C all affect D. In the 1930 – 1940 and 1940 – 1950 analyses, one could argue that agricultural payments caused cotton acreage reduction, which further reduced the need for tenants, which then implied net out-migration. In this case, A causes B, which results in C, and this results in D. One could argue that what is needed is a structural equation model that would embody this causal ordering. This kind of model implies, however, the need to place the other variables in the equation somewhere in the causal chain. Since it is not apparent where these variables belong in such a causal ordering, the following strategy is used. All of the variables are treated as though they have equal effects on the net migration rate. This results in the estimation of the net effect for each dependent variable. The interpretation of these net effects will, however, embody the notions that acreage and tenant reductions were occurring, in part, due to government payments to landlords.

Operationalization of Relevant Factors

The discussion now turns to the measurement of factors relevant to explaining the net migration rates of blacks and whites from 1930 to 1950. The world market, the price of cotton, and the opportunity structure in the North are not factors relevant to this analysis. Chapter 9 presents an attempt to include measures of these factors. Data sources and problems of data comparability are addressed in Appendices A and B. The following measures appear in all models for both periods. The means and variances of the variables appear in Table 6.1.

SOCIAL RELATIONS OF PRODUCTION AND EXCHANGE

In this period, the social relations underlying southern agriculture were transformed. As a result, tenants were forced off land and cotton acreage was curtailed. The measures of the social relations of production and exchange, therefore, reflect the crumbling rural opportunity structure. There are six measures of the social relations of agriculture: (a) the percentage of farmers who were tenants; (b) the percentage change in the number of tenants and owners by race; (c) the percentage of all farm acres in cotton; (d) the change in the percentage of all farm acres in cotton; (e) the percentage change in bales of cotton produced; and (f) variables signifying whether or not a county was in Texas or Oklahoma. These variables were all defined in Chapter 6. Therefore, no details on the definitions or the justifications for the measures are offered here.

TECHNICAL RELATIONS OF PRODUCTION

From 1930 to 1950, mechanization in southern agriculture began. The main form of machine utilized was the tractor, and the measures used here reflect this. There are two measures considered here.

1. *Number of tractors in the county at the beginning of the decade.* This measures the level of mechanization in a county at the beginning of a decade. One would expect highly mechanized counties to be experiencing net out-migration.

2. *Percentage change in tractors.* This variable is defined as (No. of tractors in a county t_2—No. of tractors in a county t_1)/number of tractors in a county t_1, where t_1 and t_2 refer to the beginning and the end of the decade. This measure is the percentage increase in tractors in a county over the decade and reflects the changing level of mechanization. This variable should be negatively related to net migration because increases in mechanization should cause net out-migration.

STATE INTERVENTION

For the first time, state intervention had a direct effect on the opportunity structure of rural inhabitants. Agricultural subsidy payments caused acreage reduction and gave plantation owners capital to mechanize. Both of these results sharply reduced the need for tenants and, therefore, caused out-migration. Two measures of state intervention are used.

1. *Agricultural payments.* This variable is the dollar amount (in thousands of dollars) that counties received in agricultural payments in 1934. This measure is used in both the 1930–1940 and 1940–1950 analyses as the measure of government subsidy payments. One might initially feel hesitant about using only one year's subsidy payments for both decades, but this is a good measure because subsidy payments were based on past production. Those counties receiving large payments were large cotton producing counties, and they continued to receive large payments. Measures from other years at the county level were not available, and, therefore, this is the only measure possible.

2. *The effect of interaction between agricultural payments and the percentage change in the number of tractors.* This interaction can be interpreted in the following way if it has a statistically significant effect: Counties with agricultural payments and large percentage increases in tractors experienced higher rates of net migration. One way to interpret this is that counties with agricultural payments mechanized more rapidly and lost population more rapidly than counties without agricultural payments. This is indirect evidence that the agricultural payments were being used to buy tractors and that people were being forced off the land at higher rates.

CAPITALIST DEVELOPMENT

Six measures of capitalist development are used here: (a) the percentage of people urbanized in a county; (b) the change in the percentage urbanized; (c) the presence of a large city; (d) the nearness of a county to a large city; (e) the number of manufacturing establishments in a county; and (f) the percent change in manufacturing establishments. These measures reflect urbanization and industrialization and are coded precisely (as they were in Chapter 6).

OTHER FACTORS

The only other factor included in this analysis is whether a county had a surplus population. This measure is the same as the measure used in Chapter 6.

Models of Migration, 1930 — 1940

The models of the net migration rates of blacks and whites from 1930 to 1940 are now presented. The results of a weighted least squares regression of county characteristics on the net migration of blacks are in the first six columns of Table 8.1. There are two major factors structuring opportunities in the South and, hence, structuring black migration rates: (a) the depression; and (b) the intervention of the state to aid large landholders. To understand how these operated, consider the first three columns of Table 8.1. In terms of explaining the black net migration rate, one of the most important factors is state intervention. The second largest effect in the model is the agricultural payments measure. Counties receiving government subsidy payments at high levels lost black population at a higher rate than counties with no payments. This effect is very much in line with the theoretical and historical argument.

Subsidy payments affected the way in which the social relations of production and exchange were related to the migration of blacks. Seven of the eight measures of social relations had statistically significant effects on the black net migration rate. Counties with a large number of black tenants lost the black population at relatively high rates, reflecting the rapid decline in the need for tenant labor. Over the decade, the percentage change in black tenants and the percentage changes in black owners had statistically significant positive effects on the black net migration rate. However, 90% of the counties had decreases in black tenantry and 58.5% of the counties had decreases in black ownership. For a vast majority of the counties, then, decreases in black tenantry and ownership meant loss of black population. Black tenants were forced to move when acreage reductions in cotton as well as the depression closed off opportunities. Black owners lost their land because they were in debt, and many were forced off through foreclosures.

Both the percentage of farm acres in cotton and the change in the percentage of farm acres in cotton had statistically significant effects on the black net migration rate. The percentage of acres in cotton in 1929 was negatively related to the black net migration rate, while the change in the percentage of acres in cotton from 1929 to 1939 had a positive, statistically significant effect on the black net migration rate. Since 98.8% of the counties decreased cotton production, cotton acreage reduction must have caused increases in net black out-migration. This effect clearly reflects what cotton acreage reductions did to black tenants — it made them migrate. In sum, the transformation of the social relations of southern agriculture caused the out-migration of blacks to a large degree.

TABLE 8.1

Results of Weighted Least Squares Regression of County Characteristics on the
Net Migration Rates of Blacks for Counties in the South, 1930–1940, 1940–1950 (N = 804)

| Factor | Measure[1] | 1930-1940 | | | | | | 1940-1950 | | | | | |
| | | Without Interaction | | | With Interaction | | | Without Interaction | | | With Interaction | | |
		b	SE(b)	β	b	SE(b)	β	b	SE(b)	β	b	SE(b)	β
Social Relations of Production and Exchange	TENANTS	-72.162*	2.676	-.444	-69.725*	2.523	-.412	-45.949*	1.159	-.450	-46.226*	1.359	-.491
	ΔTENANTS	1.174*	.199	.125	1.851*	.287	.140	.319	.563	.012	.293	.256	.011
	ΔOWNERS	3.654*	.674	.054	3.625*	.621	.065	.604	.447	.026	.464	.324	.025
	COTTON	-131.396*	12.958	-.297	-113.640*	12.765	-.242	-33.365*	1.269	-.305	-42.537*	2.836	-.314
	ΔCOTTON	125.698*	19.105	-.188	100.517*	14.954	.181	36.258*	1.555	.258	28.410*	1.993	.208
	ΔBALES	-.746	.549	-.040	-.472	.384	-.029	3.889*	1.134	.172	4.224*	.876	.252
	TEXAS	-2.207*	.292	-.041	-3.186*	.316	-.088	-5.398*	1.148	-.167	-5.371*	.687	-.166
	OKLAHOMA	-14.927*	1.352	-.296	-14.652*	1.382	-.245	-28.078*	4.214	-.241	-28.015*	1.252	-.272
Capitalist Development	URBAN	18.820*	1.306	.418	18.736*	1.362	.409	58.168*	1.276	.485	60.023	1.886	.378
	ΔURBAN	6.103*	2.301	.012	5.113*	1.866	.010	44.992*	2.893	.374	46.365	2.532	.278
	BIG CITY	5.583*	1.141	.254	5.521*	1.213	.238	-1.709*	.646	-.010	-2.540*	.649	-.135
	NEAR BIG CITY	12.075*	1.229	.282	12.136*	1.156	.247	.216*	.080	.022	.084	.036	.002
	MANUFACTURERS	.049*	.012	.086	.049*	.008	.109	.007	.006	.017	.006	.007	.027
	ΔMANUFACTURERS	2.532*	.765	.122	2.475*	.776	.140	.057	.038	.006	.064	.112	.013
Other Factor	ΔSURPLUS	-.572*	.085	-.168	-.639*	.043	-.142	.109	.444	.002	.180	.114	.004
Technical Relations of Production	TRACTORS	-.009*	.001	-.079	-.006*	.001	-.028	.013	.021	.003	.009	.014	.002
	ΔTRACTORS	-.653	.408	-.023	-.975*	.264	-.151	-.209*	.081	-.151	-.315*	.094	-.181
State Intervention	PAYMENTS	-.035*	.0008	-.435	-.0397*	.001	-.312	-.0226*	.0008	-.351	-.009*	.0004	-.302
Interaction	PAYMENTS X ΔTRACTORS				-.0068*	.0004	-.190				-.0047	.0001	-.318
	Constant	31.153			30.461			-4.921			-5.766		
	R²	.859			.878			.866			.872		

*p < .05

[1] TENANTS = percent of farmers who were tenants; ΔTENANTS = percent change in tenants; ΔOWNERS = percent change in owners; COTTON = percent of farm acres in cotton; ΔCOTTON = change in percent of cotton acreage; ΔBALES = percent change in bales; TEXAS, OKLAHOMA = whether or not a county was in Texas or Oklahoma; URBAN = percent urbanized; ΔURBAN = change in percent urbanized; BIG CITY = whether or not a large city was present; NEAR BIG CITY = whether or not county was next to a large city; MANUFACTURERS = number of manufacturing establishments; ΔMANUFACTURERS = percent change in manufacturing establishments; ΔSURPLUS = surplus population; TRACTORS = number of tractors in a county; ΔTRACTORS = percent change in tractors; PAYMENTS = agriculture payments in thousands of dollars in 1934.

The technical relations of production were shifting during this period, and one might expect that mechanization could have caused some black out-migration. In 1930, the number of tractors in a county had a negative, statistically significant effect on the black net migration rate, while the percentage change in the number of tractors had a negative, but statistically insignificant effect on the black net migration rate. While the mechanization of cotton is related to black out-migration in 1930 −1940, it is not as important a cause as agricultural subsidy payments and cotton acreage reductions.

All six of the measures of capitalist development had statistically significant effects on the black net migration rate. Blacks moved to counties already urbanized and, to a lesser degree, to counties increasing in urbanization. Since the era 1930 − 1940 was one of widespread depression, black in-migration was associated with the level of urbanization rather than the level of change in urbanization. As opportunities decreased in rural areas, blacks moved to cities and towns. Dummy variables that reflect whether counties contained or were next to large cities (population greater than 25,000) had positive, statistically significant effects on the black net migration rate. Both measures of industrialization had statistically significant, positive effects on the black net migration rate, indicating that counties with a large or an increasing number of manufacturing establishments attracted black population.

The measure of surplus population has a small but statistically significant, negative effect on black net migration. Since 91.8% of the counties had positive values on this variable, which means that there was population pressure on the land, one can argue that some black migration was due to the competition of too many persons over too little land.

A more detailed consideration of the relationship between subsidy payments, percentage change in the number of tractors, and migration is in order. It has been suggested that landlords used their subsidy payments to buy machines, thereby forcing tenants out. While the direct evidence for this is slim, the following model is introduced to give credibility to this assertion. The second three columns of Table 8.1 present the results of a weighted least squares regression exactly like that of the first three columns. The only difference is the inclusion of an interaction between the level of agricultural payments in a county and the percentage change in the number of tractors in the county from 1930 to 1940. Here, the concern is only with the interaction; therefore, no discussion of any of the other coefficients is presented. The interaction is statistically significant, and it implies that increases in agricultural payments or increases in the number of tractors meant a further decrease in the black net migration rate. That is, counties with increases in mechanization and nonzero levels of subsidy payments experienced higher levels of black net out-migration due to an interaction. While this does not show that agricultural payments were used to buy tractors, it is indirect evidence linking subsidy payments and growth in mechanization to increased rates of black net out-migration. Plantation counties with agricultural subsidies and increases in mechanization experienced more black out-migration than counties without agricultural subsidies. Black out-migration was intensified by the presence of both factors.

The model for the white net migration rate is in Table 8.2. The transformation of southern agriculture affected whites in much the same way it affected blacks. State intervention, through the mechanism of agricultural payments, had the largest effect on the white net migration rate. This effect suggests that whites were forced out of counties as a result of government intervention in cotton production. Six of the eight measures of the social relations of production and exchange had statistically significant effects on the net migration rate of whites. The direction of the coefficients suggests very clearly that acreage reduction and tenant displacement were major causes of white out-migration. The percentage of whites who were tenants in a county had a negative, statistically significant effect on the white net migration rate, and this implies that counties with high levels of white tenantization lost population as a result of the lack of farming opportunities in such areas. The percentage of change in white tenantry had a positive, statistically significant effect on the white net migration rate. White tenantry decreased in 76.4% of the counties. Thus, for the majority of counties, declines in tenantry meant white out-migration. In 1929, the percentage of farm acres in cotton was negatively, statistically significantly related to the white net migration rate. Counties with high cotton acreage in 1929 lost population as compared to counties with no (or low) cotton acreage. The percentage change in cotton acreage had a positive, statistically significant effect on the white net migration rate, and since 98.8% of the counties had reductions in cotton acreage, most counties experienced white net out-migration. Taken together, these results quite clearly imply that the transformation of southern agriculture caused a fair amount of white net out-migration.

The percentage of change in white owners from 1930 to 1940 had a positive, statistically significant effect on the white migration rate. White ownership increased in 75.1% of the counties. There are two explanations for this effect. First, during the Depression, many persons left cities and towns, returned to the land, and took up subsistence farming. Part of the increase in the expansion of white farm ownership was the result of this movement. Second, from 1937 on, the Farm Securities Administration gave loans that enabled a small number of people to become farm owners. Most of the increase in farm ownership was due to the former cause.

TABLE 8.2

Results of Weighted Least Squares Regression of County Characteristics on the Net Migration Rates of Whites for Counties in the South, 1930–1940, 1940–1950 (N =804)

Factor	Measure[1]	1930–1940						1940–1950					
		Without Interaction			With Interaction			Without Interaction			With Interaction		
		b	SE(b)	β	b	SE(b)	β	b	SE(b)	β	b	SE(b)	β
Social Relations of Production and Exchange	TENANTS	-22.168*	1.350	-.090	-22.643*	1.264	-.156	-25.200*	2.385	-.190	-24.818*	2.454	-.157
	ΔTENANTS	2.123*	.206	.072	1.264*	.252	.050	.821	.573	.008	1.290*	.877	.009
	ΔOWNERS	18.497*	2.165	.174	18.065*	1.898	.142	11.272*	2.363	.131	10.787*	2.212	.048
	COTTON	22.286*	3.112	-.220	-20.008*	2.498	-.236	-7.187*	1.040	.037	-10.769*	1.706	-.020
	ΔCOTTON	8.609*	2.064	.103	6.821*	2.165	.088	74.238*	11.508	.159	71.453*	11.660	.169
	ΔBALES	-.149	.151	-.003	-.361	.258	-.031	-.108	.082	-.003	-.142	.113	-.001
	TEXAS	3.896*	.424	.161	5.253*	.813	.154	-4.488*	.860	-.155	-4.594*	.865	-.128
	OKLAHOMA	.168	.240	.000	.429	.307	.302	-12.625*	1.154	-.231	-12.385*	1.197	-.168
Capitalist Development	URBAN	22.141*	2.302	.267	22.175*	2.205	.298	36.040*	1.182	.494	36.315*	1.423	.371
	ΔURBAN	60.821*	4.842	.281	59.630*	4.441	.272	66.890*	2.701	.336	67.070*	1.946	.333
	BIG CITY	.994	.527	.001	.743	.415	.004	16.233*	1.173	.283	15.854*	1.286	.283
	NEAR BIG CITY	3.361*	.447	.235	3.251*	.469	.208	1.882*	.322	.075	1.849	.402	.017
	MANUFACTURERS	.006	.004	.007	-.006	.003	.004	.028*	.005	.080	.026*	.002	.040
	ΔMANUFACTURERS	.043	.025	.003	.051	.041	.013	.069	.090	.010	.064	.092	.009
Other Factor	ΔSURPLUS	-1.603*	.332	-.083	-1.508*	.296	-.056	-.168	.020	-.024	-.176	.025	-.027
Technical Relations of Production	TRACTORS	-.003*	.0003	-.132	-.006*	.001	-.137	.010	.020	.017	.009	.008	.033
	ΔTRACTORS	-.245*	.087	-.069	-.273*	.039	-.045	-.066*	.002	-.035	-.029	.015	-.007
State Intervention	PAYMENTS	-.0325*	.0005	-.367	-.0236*	.0007	-.397	-.0204*	.005	-.181	-.0167*	.0011	-.133
Interaction	PAYMENTS X TRACTORS				-.0072*	.0003	-.220				-.002*	.0002	-.034
	Constant	-5.850			-6.216			-11.621			-11.647		
	R²	.938			.945			.944			.951		

*p <.05

The shift in the technical relations of production caused some white out-migration since both measures of mechanization had negative, statistically significant effects on the white net migration rate. Both the number of tractors in a county (in 1930) and the percentage change in the number of tractors had negative effects on the white net migration rate. While mechanization appears to have caused some white out-migration, much more was caused by agricultural subsidy payments and the transformation of the social relations of production and exchange.

Capitalist development in the South had relatively small effects on the net migration rate of whites. This probably reflected the effects of the Depression. Only three of the six measures of capitalist development had statistically significant effects on the white net migration rate. The percentage and the change in the percentage of urbanized populations had positive, statistically significant effects on the white net migration rate. Counties next to large cities experienced increases in the white net migration rate. Neither measure of industrialization affected the white net migration rate, and this is evidence that the depression presented few opportunities for whites in the cities. There was a statistically significant effect of surplus population. Where population pressure existed, counties experienced white net out-migration.

It is of interest to further disentangle the relationship between agricultural subsidies, the percentage increase in the use of tractors, and the net migration rate of whites from counties of the South. In order to examine this relationship more closely, a model of migration is presented in the second three columns of Table 8.2. These columns show the results of a weighted least squares regression of the white net migration rate on the same variables as the first three columns, except for the inclusion of an interaction between the level of agricultural subsidies and the percentage increase in tractors. The interaction between the level of agricultural payments and the percentage increase in tractors has a negative, statistically significant effect on the white net migration rate. This interaction implies that the levels of both variables interact to produce even higher levels of out-migration. Counties that received agricultural payments and that mechanized quite rapidly experienced higher rates of white net out-migration than would be expected under an additive, linear model. While this evidence does not directly suggest that subsidies were being used to buy tractors, it does suggest that the white net out-migration rate was being intensified in counties where high levels of agricultural subsidies and large increases in mechanization occurred.

The era 1930 – 1940 was a period of tremendous transition in southern agriculture. The social relations of production and exchange began transforming when the federal government agreed to stabilize the price of agricultural commodities. The acreage reductions brought about by the AAA subsidy payments forced tenants off the land and gave capital to landlords and other potentially large commercial producers, which they invested in machinery, thereby reducing the need for tenants even further. These forces created a rural surplus population, which had few choices but migration. The regression analyses provide clearcut support for this version of the causes of the migrations during the 1930–1940 period.

In 1930, 42% of whites were farm owners, while only 14% of blacks were farm owners. This immediately suggests that blacks were much more vulnerable to the transition from a tenant plantation system to a highly mechanized capitalist agribusiness. Of the 749,000 black farmers in 1930, only 574,000 remained by 1940. The decrease in the number of black tenants accounted for almost all of that change. For whites, the numbers suggest a different story. While white tenantry decreased 125,000 (15%), white ownership increased 74,000 (12%). There were 1.39 million white farmers in 1930 and 1.34 million in 1940, a decrease of less than 4%. It is clear that blacks and whites occupied different positions in the rural class structure. Blacks were highly tenantized and had been from 1870 onwards. The percentage of blacks who owned land peaked around 1920 and from then on declined. This percentage was never more than 20%. On the other hand, a majority of whites had, until 1930, been farm owners. The dip in white ownership during 1920–1930 reflects the severity of the agricultural depression more than any other factor. The Depression of the 1930s, therefore, had two kinds of effects on white migration in rural areas and one effect on black migration. For whites, there were two kinds of rural movements: (a) a large number of whites were displaced as a result of the AAA and cotton acreage reductions; and (b) whites left cities and towns to become subsistence farmers. For blacks, displacement occurred due to the AAA's acreage reductions and subsidy payments. Blacks had little capital and could not afford to become subsistence farmers. They had no choice but to migrate.

The rural black population, therefore, had two options in the face of both the Depression and the transition in southern agriculture. First, they could go to small towns (in the South) and become part-time laborers who picked cotton in the fall and subsisted off part-time work the rest of the year. Second, they could migrate to the cities and large towns of the South and North. Whites, on the other hand, had a third choice. They could buy a small piece of land and attempt subsistence farming. Many whites left the cities and towns (where there was little work) and became small farm owners.

To conclude, in the decade 1930–1940, blacks and whites had different options as a result of the Depression. The transition to capitalist agriculture and varying class positions structured each group's options. Both black and white tenant farmers were displaced by the AAA's acreage reductions and subsidy payments. In counties with nonzero levels of subsidies and concomitant increasing levels of mechanization, tenants of both races were displaced at even higher rates. Those blacks and whites who were affected by the destruction of the tenant system had only two options—become part-time wage labor or migrate. Blacks suffered more from this displacement since they were more vulnerable to it. Whites who were not tenants and who came from the cities and towns of the South became small farm owners. They worked these farms with their families, and their major goal was subsistence. Since the rural areas offered few work options, blacks and whites were attracted to the cities and towns of the South.

The Model of Migration, 1940 – 1950

The decade 1940 – 1950 brought an intensification of the forces of change through the agricultural South. This intensification was accompanied by World War II, which introduced new opportunities into the cities and towns of the South and North. Because agricultural conditions continued to deteriorate while opportunities abounded in the war industries, black and white migration out of the rural South increased. In Chapter 4, it was shown that 1940 – 1950 had the highest levels of net migration (and net migration rates) of any of the periods under study. It is under the rubric of these forces that models of the black and white net migration rates from counties of the South for this period are presented.

From 1940 to 1950, the effects of subsidy payments and the transformation of the social relations of production and exchange continued to have large effects on the black net migration rate and the effects of state intervention continued to cause black net out-migration (see Table 8.1). The percentage of black farmers who were tenants in 1940 had a negative, statistically significant effect on the black net migration rate. This effect was the second largest in the model, and it suggests that counties with large black tenant populations were losing blacks at a high rate. Neither the "percent change in black tenants" nor the "percent change in black owners" had statistically significant effects on the net migration rates of blacks. One could argue that it was not the percentage change in black tenantry that drove blacks out, but that the limitation of opportunities for blacks who were tenants is what forced black migration to increase. Changes in black ownership were also not highly related to the black net migration rate. There are two reasons for this. First, most blacks were tenants; therefore, changes in ownership would not have had that great an effect on black net migration. Second, the major force operative in this period was the agricultural transformation, and changes in black ownership were pretty much unrelated to this.

All three of the variables measuring levels of and changes in cotton cultivation and production had statistically significant effects on the black net migration rate. These variables reveal part of the causal process in southern commercial crop production. In the 1940s, there was continued cotton acreage reduction and continued declines in southern cotton production. These reductions were accompanied by a more intense cultivation of the land that was in production. Blacks, who for over 70 years cultivated the crops as sharecroppers, were no longer needed. The number of farm acres in cotton in 1939 had a negative, statistically significant effect on the black net migration rate. Change in the percentage of acres in cotton and in the percentage change in bales produced both had positive, statistically significant effects on the black net migration rate. Since 72.6% of the counties experienced acreage declines and 69% had declines in bales produced, most counties had increases in black net out-migration. The continuing transformation of southern agriculture caused black out-migration to a significant degree in the 1940—1950 period.

The shift in the technical relations of production came into play in an interesting way. The number of tractors in a county in 1940 did not affect the black net migration rate, but the percentage change in tractors did. This pattern must be viewed in the context of the earlier model. From 1930 to 1940 the strongest causes of black migration were the measures of the transformation of southern agriculture. Earlier, it was argued that mechanization was a result of that transformation and, therefore, did not function as a cause of migration from 1930 to 1940. The data bear this out. However, by 1940, mechanization became a cause of net out-migration of blacks because the initial transition from tenant to commercial agriculture was well on its way. All of the unstandardized coefficients on the transformation variables, except for the percentage change in bales, were smaller in 1940—1950 than in 1930—1940. The 1940s mechanization, then, which was caused by the transformation of southern agriculture, became a cause of out-migration in its own right.

Four of the six measures of the capitalist development in the South had statistically significant effects on the net migration rate of blacks. Both the percentage of persons urbanized and the change in the percentage of persons urbanized had large positive, statistically significant effects on the black net migration rate. This reflects the continued deterioration of opportunities for blacks in rural areas, as well as the enormous growth of opportunities due to the war in the cities and towns of the South (and for that matter, the North).

The two dummy variables, measuring (a) whether or not a county contained a city with 25,000 or more population; (b) was next to a county with such a city; or (c) was not near a county with a large city, both had statistically significant effects. Counties with large cities had a black in-migration rate that was less than counties without a large city. At first glance this might seem odd. However, it should be noted that this variable is net of the percentage and the change in the percentage urbanized in the county. As such, it does not mean that blacks did not go to counties with large cities; rather, it implies that a heavily urbanized county had slightly less black in-migration than would otherwise be expected. One interesting theoretical implication is that blacks were going to cities and towns that were not large (i.e., population greater than 25,000), in the first step of a two or three-step migration. This is purely speculation, however. Neither the number of manufacturing establishments nor the percentage change in manufacturing establishments had statistically significant effects on the black net migration rate. One implication that can be drawn from this is that blacks were migrating to cities or towns regardless of the possibility for employment in manufacturing.

The measure of population pressure on the land had a positive, statistically insignificant effect on the black net migration rate. This suggests that too many persons trying to make a living from too few farms is not a good explanation of the black net migration rate during 1940 – 1950.

In order to further understand the relation between agricultural subsidy payments, changes in mechanization, and the black net migration rate, a model was run and appears in the last three columns of Table 8.1. This model is identical to the model just described, except for the inclusion of an interaction term (i.e., the level of agricultural subsidy payments multiplied by the percentage change in tractors from 1940 to 1950 for any given county). This model measures whether black net migration increases when amounts of subsidy payments change and when there is a percentage increase in tractors. The results of this analysis show that the interaction had a negative, statistically significant effect on the black net migration rate. This implies that in plantation counties, increases in subsidies and in the number of tractors caused still higher levels of black net out-migration. Again, while this is not proof that subsidy payments were being used to buy tractors, one can argue that the presence of subsidy payments did intensify the displacement effects of mechanization.

The model of white migration for 1940 – 1950 is in Table 8.2. There were three major forces affecting the white migration rate in this decade: (a) the continued decline of cotton agriculture; (b) urban and industrial growth spurred by the war; and (c) the continued increase in the number of non-cotton-producing farm owners. It is within these social and historical processes that the net migration of whites is explicable. Agricultural subsidy payments still had an effect on the white net migration rate, and the transformation of the social relations of production and exchange also narrowed the opportunity structure of whites, causing white net out-migration. The percentage of white farmers who were tenants had a negative, statistically significant effect on the white net migration rate. The percentage change in the number of white tenants did not have a statistically significant effect on the white net migration rate. This suggests that while white tenants were declining in numbers, this was not the "cause" of migration. The change in the percentage of farm acres in cotton from 1939 to 1949 exerted a positive, statistically significant effect on the white net migration rate, while the percentage of farm acres in cotton in 1939 had a negative, statistically significant effect on the white net migration rate. Since 72.6% of the counties had a negative change in the acres of farm land in cotton from 1940 – 1950, the majority of counties experienced increases in the net out-migration rate of whites as cotton acres decreased. It can be concluded that the continued presence and decline in cotton acreage were operating to force whites off the land.

The percentage change in white owners had a positive, statistically significant effect on the white net migration rate. Since 75.1% of the counties in the study had increases in white farm ownership from 1940 to 1950, most of the counties experienced net in-migration of whites as farm ownership grew. Most of these new farm owners owned small tracts of land. Many were probably truck and dairy farmers who sold their products in the cities and towns. This growth of farm owners was perhaps one positive result of the AAA programs. Most of these farmers were not growing cotton, and a diversification in crops grown in the South was finally taking place.

The changing technical relations of production had very small effects on the white net migration rate. The number of tractors in a county in 1940 had a slightly positive, statistically insignificant effect on the white net migration rate. The percentage change in tractors from 1940 to 1950 had a negative, statistically significant effect on the white net migration rate. This effect is quite small; therefore, mechanization was not a major cause of net out-migration.

The effects of capitalist development on the net migration rate of whites were quite strong. Five of the six measures had statistically significant effects. The largest effect in the model was the percentage of southerners living in places with a population greater than 2500 in 1940. The second largest effect in the model was the change in the percentage urbanized over the decade. Some of this effect, again, was probably due to the lack of opportunities in the countryside. However, most of this effect reflects the boom the South experienced as a result of the war. Counties with large cities (population greater than 25,000) had a white net migration rate that was significantly higher than counties without large cities. Counties next to large cities also had a statistically significantly higher white net migration rate than counties not near such cities. Independent of the effects of the level of and change in level of urbanization, whites were moving into counties with or near large cities. The number of manufacturing establishments in a county in 1940 had a positive, statistically significant effect on the white net migration rate, while the percentage increase in manufacturing had a statistically insignificant effect. These findings imply that counties with already established manufacturing units were attracting white in-migration, while the changing levels of manufacturing were not affecting in-migration.

The measure of population pressure on the land had a negative, statistically insignificant effect on the white net migration rate. This might mean that lack of farming opportunities was not a cause of white net migration.

To assess more closely the relationship between agricultural payments, percentage increases in the number of tractors, and the white net migration rate, the following analysis is presented in the last three columns of Table 8.2. This analysis is a weighted least squares regression identical to the one just described, except for the addition of a variable that interacts the percentage increase in the number of tractors with the agricultural subsidy payments in 1934. From Table 8.2 it can be seen that the interaction between agricultural payments and the percentage increase in tractors had a negative, statistically significant effect on the white net migration rate. Counties with some level of subsidies and large increases in the number of tractors produced still higher levels of white net out-migration. Again, this is not proof that subsidy payments were used to buy tractors, but it can be argued that presence of agricultural subsidies intensified the displacement effects of mechanization.

The regression analyses starkly demonstrate the class composition of blacks and whites. Of the six largest effects on the black migration rate from 1940 to 1950, four were measures of the changes sweeping the tenant farming system. Blacks, who made up a good deal of the tenant population, suffered the effects of displacement more often than whites. These same variables had large net effects on whites. However, whites who were part of the tenant system often had more capital than blacks; therefore, whites had the advantage of being able to become either subsistence, dairy, or truck farm owners. This clearly demonstrates the differential opportunities for whites. Finally, while both blacks and whites were attracted to urban areas, the white net migration rate was affected to a slightly greater extent by urbanization and industrialization. Both blacks and whites were moving to the cities and towns of the South as a result of (a) being forced off the land; and (b) the growth of the southern economy that was fueled by World War II.

Conclusions

Chapter 7 argued that the net migrations from rural counties of the South were structured by the collapse of the cotton farming system and by the federal government's intervention into the production of cotton. It was suggested that the definition of the problem, and the eventual solution was shaped by farm organizations representing the interests of farm owners and by commercial farmers interacting with the U.S. Department of Agriculture and Congress. It was argued that the implementation of acreage reductions, subsidy payments, and the control of the price of cotton, all worked to the advantage of the farm owner and commercial producer. Tenants, both black and white, were forced off the land as cotton acreage was curtailed and as farm machinery was brought in, which further intensified production on land still planted in cotton.

The regression analyses of this chapter provide clearcut evidence that this process worked precisely in the way just described. Black and white tenants were victims of the federal government's actions to save farm owners and commercial producers. The empirical evidence for this is strong and unequivocal. The introduction of tractors did not force black and white tenants off the land. It was mainly acreage reductions in cotton and the presence of agricultural subsidies which allowed the mechanization to proceed. Since the 1930s was an era of depression, cities and towns offered few opportunities to blacks and whites displaced from the land. The 1940s and World War II changed that, and both blacks and whites streamed into towns and cities of the North and South to escape the decay and decline of the rural areas. A number of whites who could get capital became farm owners who produced for local markets. Many blacks left the rural areas altogether and sought opportunities in towns and cities.

After 1950, those blacks and whites who stayed in rural areas continued to find few opportunities in agriculture. In the early 1950s, mechanical cotton pickers were introduced throughout the South. People who lived in the rural areas of the South and were part-time agricultural laborers (who mainly picked cotton) found their opportunities destroyed.

The transition from the tenant farming system (based on crop liens) to a fully mechanized large-scale capitalist agriculture (that had prices and production regulated by the Department of Agriculture) was completed. By the mid-1950s, the so-called Great Migrations of blacks into northern central cities was underway. This migration was the result of 25 years of political action which, in essence, destroyed the way of life of millions of blacks and whites. While some have argued that blacks went to northern cities looking for opportunities, they ignore the fact that many had no choice. Staying in the rural South meant severe poverty. Leaving for the North implied the possibility of survival.

The method and theory of this study have pointed to the differential processes of black and white net migration from counties of the South. The empirical analyses have provided evidence for the validity of the assertions made. The black and white net migration rates from counties of the South clearly reflect the differential class positions of blacks and whites, the dynamics of southern agriculture, and the federal government's intervention that eventually resulted in the transformation of southern agriculture.

Chapter 9

Net Migration of Blacks and Whites, 1900 – 1950

This chapter will attempt to assess the effects of the pull of opportunities in the North and the changing price of cotton on the net migration rates of blacks and whites from the counties of the South. One criticism that can be made of this study is that these key factors, which could have affected the net migration rates of blacks and whites, were left out of the models. Indeed, the theoretical model posed in Chapter 3 included both of these factors as causes of migration. It is important, then, to explicitly incorporate these factors into a model of migration. Vickery (1977) concludes that the major cause of black migration out of the South was wage rate differentials. In the analyses done here, no measures of wages or opportunities in the North are in the models, and to the degree that these things are important, the model is potentially misspecified. Clearly, it could be argued that one of the most important rival theories of the one advocated here (that which purports to explain migration out of the counties of the South) is not assessed in the models of the migration process presented here.

The major reason such measures have not been used is methodological. Since the models of migration have been models of each decade separately, it is difficult to include measures of wage rate or income differences between areas in the South and areas in the North. The key problem is that it is not clear which point of destination in the North is relevant. For instance, it is known that blacks in the eastern part of the South tended to go to the Northeast, while blacks in the western part of the South tended to go to the upper Midwest. But many blacks from South Carolina ended up in Chicago, and, similarly, blacks from Texas found their way to New York. Perhaps the best potential solution is to try to construct county wage rates. If one could assess where persons in a given county of origin ended up, and one could measure wages in the county of destination, then this would be a good measure of the pull of the north. This strategy is difficult for two reasons. The fact that a majority or plurality of people from a given place ended up in a given place would then require us to assign a wage rate to the county of origin. This would be very problemmatic, for it means that one would be using an income or a wage rate for an entire county that applied only to a subportion of that county. Further, estimating wage rates at the county level with any accuracy back to 1900 would require an enormous leap of faith, for there is literally no data.

One could argue that it is not any specific destination that is important, but only the fact that the level and change in level of income is higher in the North than the South. This presents impossible difficulties because for any given decade the value on variables that measure opportunities in the North are constants. Thus, in the decade 1900 – 1910, the growth of opportunities outside the South would be constant in each part of the South. Of course, it is very difficult to predict a change in a dependent variable with a constant. Despite these difficulties, however, it does seem important to incorporate some measures of pull from the North into the model.

The price of cotton and the changes in that price are also important measures that have been left out of the analyses. Such measures reflect complex theoretical processes such as (a) the amount of cotton produced in the South, in the rest of the United States, and the rest of the world; (b) the carryover of cotton from previous years in the United States and around the world; (c) the demand for cotton products; and (d) the ability to use substitute products for cotton. The price of cotton determined whether or not an individual producer made money or went into debt. One would expect that the price of cotton and its increase or decrease over a period would be related to the net migration rates of blacks and whites.

Measures of cotton prices have been excluded from the study, for the most part, because the price of cotton at the beginning of any given decade, and its change over that decade, are also constants for all counties. The price that a farmer received in any given county depended on the quality of the crop, its distance to a large market, and the cost of transporting the crop. The differences in prices received, while they varied from county to county and farmer to farmer, were nearly the same across the South at all points in time. If the average price of cotton was high, most cotton farmers received a high price. If the price was low, most received a low price. Even if one believed the price across counties varied significantly, it would be impossible to get data on the average price received by farmers in any given county over the decade.

There appear to be theoretical reasons for including variables like opportunities in the North and cotton prices into the models of net migration, but the methodological problems appear insurmountable in the decade-by-decade analysis. In order to assess the relative effects of these factors, it is necessary to adopt a different analytic strategy. To facilitate the presentation of this strategy, the following are considered: (a) the measurement of these factors; (b) the logic of the analysis; (c) the advantages and shortcomings of the technique; and (d) a suggestion as to the credibility of the model.

Four measures were chosen to assess the amount of opportunities in the North and the changes in cotton prices. To measure the level of opportunities in the North at the beginning of each decade, the income per capita for the northeastern United States in 1957 dollars is used (Perloff et al., 1960). To measure the change in the level of opportunities, the percentage change in income per capita for the northeastern U.S. in 1957 dollars from the beginning to the end of the decade is used. These measures have been chosen because they represent relative income differences. If opportunities expand, one would expect income per capita to rise. If blacks and whites respond to high or rising income per capita (or wages or opportunities), these measures should have a negative effect on the net migration rates of blacks and whites. The measures of cotton prices are the average price in cents per pound for cotton in the first year of the decade, and the percentage change in the average price for cotton over the decade. These are straightforward measurements of cotton prices.

Given the way they are defined, these variables imply the same value for every county in each decade. Table 9.1 presents the values these measures take. Because of the implicit limitations of these measures, it is opportune to consider the logic of the analysis. Basically, the five panels, with counties as units of analysis, are stacked to form a single data set. In this way, opportunities in the North and the price of cotton are constant within decades, but variable across decades. The basic statistical tool remains weighted least squares regression. Appendix E contains a more thorough justification of this approach and also discusses some potential pitfalls.

The first objection to this model is whether or not a single measure of

TABLE 9.1
Assorted Variables and Their Changes over Time

Variable	1900	1910	1920	1930	1940	1950
COTTON PRICE[1]	.096	.151	.339	.135	.104	.362
Δ COTTON PRICE[2]	--	.572	124.5	-.616	-.230	248.
INCOME PER CAPITA[3]	570.2	671.35	772.5	912.9	965.8	1255.2
Δ INCOME PER CAPITA[2]	--	.1774	.1507	.1817	.0579	.2996

[1]Cotton price in cents per pound.

[2]Percent change; reflects $(t_2 - t_1)/t_1$, where t_1 = first time point, t_2 = second time point

[3]Income per capita in Northeast U. S. in 1957 dollars.

*Source: Cotton prices from Street (1957); Income per capita from Perloff et al. (1960).

opportunities in the North successfully captures the opportunity structure of the rural resident. The issue here is whether or not the average level and percentage change in income per capita in the Northeast is a good proxy for the opportunity structure of the North (i.e., for blacks in South Carolina and whites in southern Texas). This specification suffers because obstacles to migration differed across the South, because distances between points varied, and because the proper reference point for migration from any given place in the South is unclear. Examples of the first two difficulties are the money one needed to travel and how near one was to a large northern city. An example of the latter is the documented fact that blacks on the eastern seaboard tended to go to New York, Philadelphia, and Boston, while those in Mississippi, Alabama, Arkansas, and Louisiana tended to go to Chicago, Cleveland, and Detroit.

The measures used here are adequate since they represent the fact that northern development increased at different rates in different decades. The zero-order correlation between percentage change in income per capita in the Northeast and the upper Midwest is .96. This implies that the measures did not obscure the relation between the increase in income per capita and destination. The arguments about distances and obstacles are more difficult to respond to and, to the extent that they are not measured, the model is misspecified. These variables are difficult to quantify since it is unclear what constitutes obstacles and distances to an undefinable object. That is, since one does not know where people went, it is hard to quantify the distances and hardships suffered to get there.

The second objection to this approach is perhaps more serious. One basic assumption of this model is that the effects of variables present across all decades are assumed to have a constant effect from 1900 to 1950. This project has proceeded on the assumption that not only do these parameters differ across decades, but the meaning of each parameter also differs across decades. Given this, to produce a model that averages these effects and attempts to interpret each variable as having a single effect over time is, at the very least, unrealistic. One who is oriented toward data analysis will suggest that an analysis of covariance approach be tried. Unfortunately, such an approach has two drawbacks. First, to use such an approach would require the inclusion of dummy variables representing decades. From analyses already performed, it was discovered that these dummy variables are multicollinear with the measures of cotton prices and pulls from the North; therefore, this strategy will not succeed. Second, such a model would be enormously complex and would be difficult to explain and present. Instead, an oversimplified model is chosen. While this model does injustice to the social and historical processes underlying the process of net migration, it is estimable and relatively straightforward.

Given the rather serious shortcomings of this analysis, the question arises: "Why bother with this model in the first place?" It is reasonable to estimate this model for two reasons. First and foremost, it is important to attempt to answer potential critics as to the possible misspecification of the decade-by-decade models. Perhaps the major theoretical and historical point of this project is that the large movement of blacks and whites out of the South from 1930 on was not the result of forces such as wage rate differentials or mechanization. Rural poverty in the South after 1935 was not caused by tractors or inefficient farm operations. Rather, the transformation of southern agriculture, and the impoverishment of hundreds of thousands of blacks and whites, was the direct result of political activity generated by the New Deal, which was oriented toward saving the large farm owners, the landlords, and the commercial farmers. The movement of the black and white population after 1935 was, on the whole, a response to these forces. The final push out of the rural areas (which was precipitated by the mechanical cotton picker) could only have been operative under these conditions. The point here is to demonstrate the size of the relative pull of the North and to argue that the pull itself was only operative as the result of the changes in the social organization of the South. For this reason alone, it is important to get some sense of the size of these effects.

Second, it is of some value to interpret the results of such a model, even if it is only a heuristic device. While the specification of the model may be in error, the usefulness of the model justifies it. It can be argued that the model presents a baseline that demonstrates how strongly the levels and percentage changes in cotton prices and income per capita in the Northeast affected the net migration rates of blacks and whites. These variables' effects are net of the counties' social compositions and, thus, offer us a feel for the general size and directions of the more intangible effects. While these models do not adequately mirror the complexities of the social reality as it has been described, they do offer some sense of the relative importance of the factors that have been discussed.

Finally, the theoretical argument made in Chapter 3 specifies the inclusion of these factors, and without them, the theoretical model underlying this project has not been adequately tested.

From an epistemological point of view, then, the models in this chapter are inadequate representations of the social reality as it has been portrayed. However, they are useful because they provide us with some solid evidence on which to evaluate the assertions of economists and other social scientists who tend to have different views of the process of net migration of blacks and whites from the counties of the South than the one presented here.

Factors and Their Measures in the Model of Migration, 1900 – 1950

Measures of all six factors, which, theoretically, were expected to structure the net migration rate of blacks and whites in Chapter 3, are available for the model used here. Most of these measures have been defined and justified before; therefore, no theoretical discussion is necessary.

THE WORLD MARKET AND THE PRICE OF COTTON

Two measures of the price of cotton are used.

1. *Cotton price.* This variable is the average price of cotton per pound in the first census year of the decade. Within decades, it is a constant and the values of this variable are in Table 9.1.
2. *Percentage change in cotton price.* This variable is the percent change in the price per pound of cotton from the beginning to the end of the decade. A positive value means an increase in the price of cotton and a negative value implies a decrease.

THE SOCIAL RELATIONS OF PRODUCTION AND EXCHANGE

There are six measures of the social relations of production and exchange: (a) the percentage of farmers who were tenants at the beginning of the decade; (b) the percentage change in tenants over the decade; (c) the percentage change in owners over the decade; (d) the percentage of farm acres in cotton at the beginning of the decade; (e) the change in the percentage of farm acres in cotton over the decade; and (f) the percentage changes in bales produced over the decade. The measures were defined and justified in Chapter 6.

THE TECHNICAL RELATIONS OF PRODUCTION

Because tractors came to the South rather late, it is necessary to incorporate three measures of mechanization.

1. *The number of tractors in a county in 1929.* For all decades except 1920 – 1930, this measure takes on a value of zero. For the decade 1920 – 1930, this measure is the number of tractors in a county in 1929.
2. *The number of tractors in a county at the beginning of a decade.* This measure takes on a value of zero for all decades except 1930 – 1940 and 1940 – 1950. For these decades, this variable measures the level of mechanization at the beginning of the decade.
3. *The percentage change in number of tractors over a decade.* For all decades except 1930 – 1940 and 1940 – 1950, this measure takes on a value of zero. For these decades, this variable measures the percentage change in the use of machines.

CAPITALIST DEVELOPMENT

There are six measures of capitalist development in the South and two measures in the North. The six measures in the South are (a) the percentage urbanized at the beginning of the decade; (b) the change in percentage urbanized; (c) whether or not a county contains a large city; (d) whether or not a county is next to a large city, (e) the number of manufacturing establishments in a county at the beginning of the decade; and (f) the percentage change in manufacturing over the decade. These measures were defined and justified in Chapter 6.

The two measures of development in the North are (a) income per capita in the Northeast at the beginning of the decade in 1957 dollars; and (b) the percentage change in income per capita in the Northeast. Both of these measures have also been justified in this chapter.

STATE INTERVENTION

State intervention into agriculture came in the form of agricultural subsidy payments. Since these payments began in 1933, all counties in decades prior to 1930 – 1940 are scored zero. For the periods 1930 – 1940 and 1940 – 1950, this measure is the subsidy payments allotted in 1933 in thousands of dollars.

OTHER FACTORS

There are three other factors included in this analysis. They have been justified theoretically in Chapter 6; the relevant variable codings are presented here.

1. *Surplus population.* This measure is defined as (rural population in a county t_2/number of farms in a county t_2) – (rural population in a county t_1/number of farms in a county t_1). This measure is considered an indicator of population pressure on the land.

2. *Whether or not a lynching occurred.* For the decades 1930–1940 and 1940–1950, this variable takes on the value of zero for all counties. For earlier decades, the variable takes on a value of one if a lynching occurred in that county in that decade and a value of zero otherwise.

3. *Boll weevil infestation.* Three dummy variables are used to indicate when the boll weevil infeston first occurred: (a) counties first infested in 1900–1910 were coded one, and all other counties were coded zero; (b) same as above, except the relevant decade is 1910–1920; and (c) same as above, except the relevant decade is 1920–1930. All counties in the 1930–1940 and 1940–1950 decades were coded zero on all three dummy variables.

The Model of Migration, 1900–1950

The major theoretical purpose of looking at the model of migration as it has been constructed is to assess the aggregate effect of factors that transcend local conditions on the net migration rates of blacks and whites from counties of the South.

The model, with the results of a weighted least-squares regression, using the black net migration rate as the dependent variable appears in the first three columns of Table 9.2. This model is based on the pooled data and includes 3931 counties from 1900 to 1950. The first factor to consider is the price of cotton. Both the cotton price at the beginning of the decade and the percentage change in this price over the decade had positive, statistically significant effects on the net migration rate of blacks. On the average, counties experienced net in-migration of blacks as the level of cotton prices increased. The same was true if the percentage change in the cotton price was positive. When this change was negative, however, net out-migration of blacks occurred. It should be noted that while these effects are statistically significant, this factor has a relatively small effect in the model.

The social relations of production and exchange measures were most strongly related to the net migration rate of blacks. The percentage of black farmers who were tenants at the beginning of the decade had the largest effect in the model because counties with high levels of tenantry experienced large increases in the black out-migration rate. Both the percentage change in black tenants and the percentage change in black owners had statistically significant effects on the black net migration rate. Counties with an increase in the number of tenants or owners had black net in-migration, while counties with a decrease in the number of tenants or owners had black net out-migration. The percentage of farm acres in cotton in the year before a given census year and the change in that percentage over the decade both had enormous statistically significant effects on the black net migration rate. Blacks were attracted to counties with large and increasing cotton acreage. Counties with decreasing acreage had negative shifts in their black net migration rates. These results imply that the social relations governing agriculture at the county level were most important in explaining the black net migration rate.

Two of the three variables related to the technical relations of production had statistically significant effects on the black net migration rate. The number of tractors in 1930 had a slightly positive statistically insignificant effect on net migration in the decade 1920 – 1930. The number of tractors present in the county at the beginning of the decade and the percentage change in the number of tractors over the decade both had negative, statistically significant effects on the black net migration rate. Since these variables only pertained to 1930 – 1940 and 1940 – 1950, these effects occurred for counties only during these periods. Both effects imply shifts in the black net out-migration rate as mechanization increased.

The capitalist development in the South and North affected the net migration rate of blacks. The capitalist development in the South, however, was a more important cause of black out-migration than the capitalist development in the North. Five of the six variables concerned with urbanization and industrialization in the South and both of the variables relating to income per capita in the Northeast had statistically significant effects on the black net migration rate. Both the percentage of southerners living in counties with a population greater than 2500 and the change in that percentage over the decade had positive, statistically significant effects on the black net migration rate. The level and changing level of urbanization in southern counties implied net in-migration of blacks for many counties. Throughout the period 1900 – 1950, blacks were attracted to counties with large cities and next to large cities. The number of manufacturing establishments in a county had a positive,

Table 9.2

*Results of Weighted Least Squares Regression on Pooled Data, 1900 – 1950:
Dependent Variable Is Net Migration Rate[a]*

Factor	Measure	Blacks			Whites		
		b	SE(b)	β	b	SE(b)	β
Price of Cotton	COTTON PRICE	2.710*	1.002	.084	.185*	.064	.093
	COTTON PRICE	8.379*	2.354	.175	1.556*	.223	.191
Social Relations of Production and Exchange	TENANTS	-224.701*	12.703	-.538	-10.245*	1.155	-.167
	ΔTENANTS	5.259*	1.226	.121	5.849*	.357	.178
	ΔOWNERS	20.615*	2.632	.219	14.254*	.551	.541
	COTTON	238.543*	12.329	.494	17.215	1.122	.241
	ΔCOTTON	292.726*	30.628	.385	39.086*	2.176	.228
	ΔBALES	-.273	.203	-.204	-.006	.005	-.003
Technical Relations of Production	TRACTORS-1920	.099	.303	.003	-.002	.028	.002
	TRACTORS	-.081*	.010	-.062	-.003	.042	.000
	ΔTRACTORS	-.114*	.299	-.203	-.070*	.003	-.060
Capitalist Development The South	URBAN	107.458*	14.995	.241	23.435*	.534	.506
	ΔURBAN	141.973*	10.621	.283	80.312*	2.182	.370
	BIG CITY	24.888*	2.407	.282	9.173*	.449	.258
	NEAR BIG CITY	15.097*	1.175	.413	1.555*	.155	.131
	MANUFACTURERS	.353	.526	.004	.013	.025	.021
	ΔMANUFACTURERS	2.691*	1.033	.021	.507*	.199	.015

		-.007*	.001	-.066	-.005*	.001	-.089
Capitalist Development The North	INCOME PER CAPITA	-.007*	.001	-.066	-.005*	.001	-.089
	Δ INCOME PER CAPITA	-9.407*	3.442	-.059	-16.027*	2.795	-.157
State Intervention	PAYMENTS	-.011*	.001	-.382	-.017*	.001	-.248
Other Factors	ΔSURPLUS	-1.846*	.305	-.189	-.674*	.056	-.133
	LYNCHING	-.889	.530	-.023	-.952	.854	-.011
	BOLLA	-22.462*	6.632	-.114	-.893*	.066	-.082
	BOLLB	-6.908*	1.928	-.082	-1.633*	.623	-.046
	BOLLC	.796	.852	.014	.241	.161	.021
	Constant	236.301			-7.819		
	R^2	.986			.966		
	N =	3931			3931		

*$p < .05$

[1] COTTON PRICE = price of cotton; Δ COTTON PRICE = percent change in the price of cotton; TENANTS = percent of farmers who were tenants; ΔTENANTS = percent change in tenants; ΔOWNERS = percent change in owners; COTTON = percent of farm acres in cotton; ΔCOTTON = change in the percent of farm acres in cotton; ΔBALES = percent change in bales; TRACTORS-1920 = number of tractors in a county for 1920-30 decade; TRACTORS = number of tractors; ΔTRACTORS = percent change in tractors; URBAN = percent urbanized; ΔURBAN = change in the percent urbanized; BIG CITY = presence of large city; NEAR BIG CITY = county next to large city; MANUFACTURERS = number of manufacturing establishments; ΔMANUFACTURERS = percent change in manufacturing; INCOME PER CAPITA = income per capita in Northeast; Δ INCOME PER CAPITA = percent change in income per capita; PAYMENTS = agricultural payments; LYNCHING = whether or not a lynching occurred; BOLLA = boll weevil infestation, 1900-1910; BOLLB = boll weevil infestation, 1910-1920; BOLLC = boll weevil infestation, 1920-1930.

181

statistically insignificant effect on the black net migration rate. However, the percentage change in manufacturing establishments had a positive, statistically significant effect on the black net migration rate. Counties with expanding manufacturing establishments attracted blacks, while those with shrinking manufacturing lost them.

Both the income per capita in the Northeast at the beginning of the decade and the percentage change in income per capita over the decade had negative, statistically significant effects. As northeastern income per capita increased both in level and percentage change, the black net out-migration rate for counties of the South increased. This increase is in the proper direction; as the North expanded, the black net out-migration rate increased if blacks responded to the pull of the North. It should be noted that although these effects are statistically significant, they are not large. These parameters offer clearcut evidence that the major cause of the black net migration rate was not opportunities in the North.

State intervention through the use of agricultural payments had one of the largest effects on the model's measure of the black net migration rate. The level of agricultural subsidies in 1934 had a negative, statistically significant effect on the black net migration rate. For the decades in which it appears and for the counties for which it is important, it meant large increases in the black net out-migration rate.

Two of the three other factors had statistically significant effects on the black net migration rate. The measure of surplus population was related to the black net migration rate in a way that suggests increased population pressure on farm land caused black out-migration. The dummy variable that represented whether or not a county had a lynching in the decades 1900 – 1930 had a negative, statistically insignificant effect on the black net migration rate. This evidence suggests that black migration was probably not in response to lynchings or differential repression across the South. Two of the three dummy variables signifying whether or not a county was first infested by boll weevils in a particular decade had statistically significant, negative effects on the black net migration rate. Counties first infested in 1900 – 1910 and 1910 – 1920 had statistically significant increases in their black net out-migration rates in relation to counties not infested in those decades and all other decades. Those counties first infested after 1920 had a statistically insignificant, positive effect on the black net migration rate.

The second three columns of Table 9.2 present a model of the causes of the net migration rate of whites from 1900 to 1950. The price of cotton had statistically significant effects on the white net migration rate. This means that when cotton prices were high or rising, there was white net in-migration. When cotton prices decreased, there were white net out-migration rates. While these effects are statistically significant, they are not large. The social relations of production and exchange of southern agriculture played a major role in explaining the net migration rate of whites. The percentage of white farmers who were tenants at the beginning of the decade had a negative, statistically significant effect on the white net migration rate. Both the percentage change in the number of whites who were farm owners and the percentage change in the number of white tenants had positive, statistically significant effects on the white net migration rate. The percentage change in white farm owners had the largest effect in the white net migration rate model. For counties where white ownership or tenantry increased, the white net in-migration rate increased. For those counties where white tenantry and ownership decreased, the white net out-migration rate increased. The percentage of farm acres in cotton in the year before the census year and the change in that percentage over the decade had positive, statistically significant effects on the white net migration rate. Whites were attracted to counties with high levels of cotton acreage and increasing acreage, while they left counties with decreasing acreage.

Only one of the three measures of mechanization had a statistically significant effect on the white net migration rate. The percentage change in the number of tractors in counties had a negative, statistically significant effect on the white net migration rate. While the presence of tractors in counties did not cause increases in the white net out-migration rate, the percentage increase in the number of tractors did. This effect was small, and one can conclude that the technical relations of production were not causing much white out-migration.

Capitalist development in the South and North did cause migration of whites. Of the six variables pertaining to the urbanization and industrialization of the South, five had statistically significant effects on the net migration rate of whites. Both the percentage of persons living in places with a population greater than 2500 at the beginning of the decade and the change in that percentage over the decade had positive, statistically significant effects on the white net migration rate. The level of urbanization and increases in urbanization implied positive shifts in the white net migration rate. Whites moved to counties with and next to large cities net of the level (and change in level) of urbanization in such counties. The number of manufacturing establishments had a positive, statistically insignificant effect on the white net migration rate. The percentage change of manufacturing establishments over the decade, however, had a positive, statistically significant effect on the white net migration rate. Whites were attracted to counties with increasing opportunities in manufacturing, and they left counties where the growth of manufacturing was negative.

Income per capita in the Northeast at the beginning of the decade and the percentage change in that measure over the decade both had negative, statistically significant effects on the white net migration rate. This means that as the level and the percentage change in the level of income per capita in the Northeast rose, the white net out-migration rate increased. The North exerted a relatively clearcut pull effect on whites from counties of the South. However, the relative sizes of these effects suggest that the North's pull effect was not large when compared to some of the other factors in the model.

State intervention into production through subsidy payments also affected the white net migration rate. The level of agricultural subsidy payments in 1934 had a negative, statistically significant effect on the white net migration. Since this variable was only present in counties from 1930 on, those counties receiving nonzero levels of subsidies had shifts in the white net out-migration rate relative to counties with no subsidies in all decades.

Two of the three other factors had statistically significant effects on the white net migration rate. The effects of population pressure on the land had a statistically significant effect on the white net migration rate. Counties with increases in the ratio of rural population to farms over the decade were having increases in the white net out-migration rate because population pressure existed. Counties with decreases in this ratio experienced increases in the net white in-migration rate since opportunities existed in farming. The dummy variable indicating whether or not a lynching occurred in a county in the decades 1900 – 1930 had a negative, statistically insignificant effect on the white net migration rate. However, one would not expect white migration to be responsive to differential black repression. Two of the three dummy variables which describe the decade in which a county was first infested with boll weevils had statistically significant effects on the white net migration rate. If a county was first infested in 1900 – 1910 or 1910 – 1920, it had a white net out-migration rate that was significantly higher than counties not infested in those periods and counties in other decades. If the infestation first occurred after 1920, there was a statistically insignificant effect on the white net migration rate.

In order to compare the differential effects of various variables on blacks and whites, it is necessary to restate the differential class composition of blacks and whites over time. Since blacks were always between 75 and 90% tenants, and since they tended to be in the lowest status positions among tenants (i.e., sharecroppers), their migration was vulnerable to the fluctuations of the cotton system. While whites were also involved in cotton growing, only 40 −60% of them were tenants. As such, their migration was caused by a number of different factors. Most blacks had to move to where they could be tenant farmers or do some kind of labor in a city or town. Since whites had more capital and were not stigmatized by race, their movement reflected (a) opportunities in farm ownership; (b) opportunities as tenants; or (c) opportunities in cities and towns in a variety of positions.

The analysis of the process of migration from 1900 to 1950 reveals precisely these kinds of patterns. For blacks, the level of tenantry and the percentage and change in percentage of farm acres in cotton in a county were extremely important causes of net migration. These factors imply opportunities in tenant farming, and black migration reflects these factors. For whites, on the other hand, the percentage change in ownership was the most important indicator of agricultural change. While tenantry and cotton acreage affected white net migration, changes in white ownership had the largest effect on the white net migration rate. The black migration rate was also more strongly affected by the boll weevil invasion than the white net migration rate. This indicates that blacks were more vulnerable to the infestation than whites because they tended to be tenants and were unable to control what they could produce in the face of the boll weevil infestation. Both blacks and whites were attracted to the urbanizing areas of the South and also moved to counties with or near large cities. Furthermore, the transformation of southern cotton agriculture as reflected in both the percentage change in mechanization and agricultural subsidies in 1934 caused increases in the black and white net out-migration rates.

The level and percentage of change in cotton prices and income per capita in the Northeast all had statistically significant effects on the black and white net migration rates. However, for both blacks and whites, these effects were not all that large. This means that while the pull of the North was operative from 1900 to 1950, it was by no means the major cause of the black and white net migrations from counties of the South. It is clear that the differential class positions of blacks and whites and the opportunities those positions implied, along with the ups and downs of the cotton-based economy and the transformation of that economy beginning in 1933, played the greatest roles in determining the net migration rates of blacks and whites.

Before concluding this chapter, one methodological note is in order. One might not be too surprised by the fact that the pull of the North was not one of the strongest effects in the model because it has less variation than inter- and intracounty variables. Variables such as "percent urbanized" have more variation across counties than a variable like "income per capita" in the Northeast. It seems likely that variables such as "percent urbanized" should have larger effects merely because they vary more. The major argument here is that however people in counties of the South conceptualized opportunities in the North, such opportunities were probably less varied and certainly less relevant to migration decisions than conditions in the area in which the potential migrant lived. Proximate conditions structured opportunities, whereas conditions in the North and changes therein were far less certain and far less differentiated in the migrant's mind. The strategy of this analysis reflects this and forms what could be considered an accurate representation of people's cognitive maps.

Conclusions

This chapter is an attempt to measure how the six sets of factors operated to structure the opportunities of blacks and whites in the South and North from 1900 to 1950. There are five major conclusions to be drawn from this analysis:

1. The theoretical model has great utility.
2. Proximate causes structured migration more than distal causes.
3. Opportunities in the North and the wage rate differential are inadequate as explanations of black and white migration during 1900–1950.
4. Mechanization was a minor cause of black and white migration during 1900–1950.
5. The social relations of production and exchange and their dynamics (including state intervention), the relative class positions of blacks and whites, and capitalist development in the South were the major causes of the opportunity structure in the South and, hence, the major causes of migration.

The social–historical approach of this project has been vindicated by the empirical results. Migration is most sensitive to the conditions from where the potential migrant originates. In the case of black and white net out-migration from counties of the South during 1900 to 1950, it is clear that the developments in cotton agriculture and in urbanization of the South were the major causes of net migration. The pull of opportunities in the North was a result of the decline and transformation of southern cotton agriculture. With the social and historical background and the statistical models presented here, it should be obvious that the out-migrations of blacks and whites were not mere flights to take advantage of higher wages. Rather, the migrations were dictated by an agricultural system that was drifting in and out of crisis and by the political activity of the state, which transformed that system. The migrations reflected the differential class positions of blacks and whites; that is, because blacks were concentrated in a more vulnerable part of the class structure, they suffered disproportionately and their migration patterns reflect an attempt to escape this suffering. The analysis ends where it began—the migration of blacks and whites from counties of the South during 1900 – 1950 was not caused by mechanization or higher wages in the North. Migration was the direct consequence of historical and structural social relationships, of the development of those relationships in and outside of the South, and of contradictions inherent in those relationships. The analyses—social, historical, and statistical—reflect this.

Chapter 10

Conclusions and Reflections

Initially, this study began by suggesting two major themes: pro-letarianization and development. In this chapter, it is of some interest to return to these themes and attempt to shed some light on them in terms of the results presented here. In some sense, this study is a natural history of one part of American society over one period of time. The migration of blacks and whites from the South in this century is perhaps the key social process to understand when attempting to generate a view of the South, of its relation to the North, and of its social and economic development over a good part of this century. Having done this, it is of some value to try to understand why all of this is relevant to American history and American development. The return to the themes of pro-letarianization and development is a natural step.

The history of American development bears marked similarities to the underdevelopment in the Third World today. From a world-system perspective, the United States was once in the periphery (i.e., a colony) and subject to domination by a core nation, Great Britain. The British exploited the American colonies for agricultural products and natural resources. The American Revolution and its aftermath presented a classic case of how a nation moved from the underdeveloped periphery to the developed core. The United States closed its borders and raised tariffs on foreign goods in order to become a goods producer rather than just a natural resource supplier. The roots of capitalist development in the

United States were in the North and in particular, the northeastern United States. Here, a nascent capitalist class was forming after the Revolutionary War. That class, in order to gain control of American development, had to defeat the two groups that had other interests: the southern planters and the small farm owners.

Tariffs and slavery were the critical issues that faced the American state during the Civil War. The agricultural South was dominated by the planter class, which basically produced cotton through the use of slave labor and sold it to British mills. In the first part of the nineteenth century, British industry was so efficient that it was cheaper to ship raw cotton to Britain and have it return to the United States as cloth than to produce the same cloth in the United States. To protect U.S. industry, tariffs were introduced. These tariffs did little to aid the South and indeed made the price of finished cloth higher. The political struggles before the Civil War reflected these regional differences in economic strategies. As has been argued by others, the Civil War was, in essence, the second American Revolution. The complete domination of the American continent by an indigenous American state required the closing off of the British colony on the American continent (i.e., the South). The Civil War established the political rule of the northern capitalists and insured that the South remained within control of American capitalist interests and not British capitalist interests. Within the national borders of the United States, the South became a northern colony, and as a colony, it experienced what is now recognized as underdevelopment.

This underdevelopment proceeded first on a political level and only later on an economic level. The North came to dominate the South by supplying credit to grow cotton, by shipping cotton, by shipping food and finished goods, and by controlling the cotton markets. The planters reemerged as leaders in the South, but their political position was limited. They were forced to take a subordinate position in the American economic system. They were allowed to control the South politically, but only as a region subordinate to the North. The northern industrialists did not develop southern industries. Rather, they used the South to supply themselves with natural resources such as coal, iron, timber and with cash crops such as cotton, tobacco, and sugar. The control over the South was exercised through capital markets (i.e., loans) on the one hand and markets for commodities on the other. The South was much like one of today's Third World countries that depends on one or two crops or minerals for its livelihood. For a long time, then, the northern industrialists did not need external colonies or markets; the northern core had its southern (and western) periphery.

The Populist revolt was the only sustained attempt to undercut northern control over the rural areas. The radical farm movements began as a response to the increasing encroachment of railroads, merchants, and industrial markets. Small farm owners were helpless in the face of merchants, banks, and railroads, who controlled credit, the movement of crops to market, and the prices of their commodities. The Populist revolt in the South placed the planters in a particularly vulnerable position. While planters were benefitting from the tenant farming system and the crop lien mechanisms on the whole, they were being threatened politically and economically by the small farm owners. The destruction of populism and the rise of racism secured the planters' position and, at the same time, gave the North relatively free reign to continue their exploitation of the South. It is ironic that the planters, who 40 years earlier fought a war against northern capitalist interests, came to preserve those interests in their instrumental role in defeating populism. The planters and merchants in the South could be thought of as a colonial bourgeoisie (comprador class) whose interests were clearly linked to those of the colonizing power and who used political power to maintain those interests.

Given this structure of power and interests, one needs to ask why the underdevelopment changed. Why were the tenants turned out and forced to become an urban proletariat? The answers to these questions are intimately tied to the depression and the world market for cotton. The Populist defeat preserved the southern tenant system for 30 years, even though many people suffered severe poverty. The crisis brought on by the Depression was a general crisis in the accumulation of capital. It is no exaggeration to say that the depression brought the entire world's economic system to the brink of destruction. In the face of severe unemployment and glutted world commodity markets, prices remained low. The entire society, South and North, was threatened by bankruptcy. Major realignments of the underlying social relations that governed production were required to bring the society out of depression and to solve the chronic crises of overproduction caused by industrialist free markets. The state was the only agent which had the relative autonomy to produce such sweeping changes. The general crises inherent in capitalist production brought forth a more aggressive federal government that began active interventions into markets in order to raise prices and stimulate demand. From 1933 on, a new era of state—capitalist class relations began.

The state intervention into agriculture produced two immediate results: (a) it provided farmers with capital; and (b) it supported commodity prices. These moves accelerated the concentration of farm land and placed it in fewer and fewer hands. With the capital provided by the acreage reductions, the larger farm owners could afford to invest in machines and, hence, maintain and expand their incomes. The small farm owners did not get large enough benefits and many of them went bankrupt. In the South, the general effect was to destroy tenant farming and the crop lien mechanism. The underdevelopment of the South was preserved in the sense that the South still depended on northern machines and northern markets for their raw materials. The rural population, however, became a surplus population, and as has been shown, were forced to migrate. Today, the South remains an underdeveloped country. Instead of natural resource exploitation, however, the South has become a haven for industries seeking low wages, no organized labor, low taxes, and few environmental restrictions. The South's role in this stage of industrialism is similar to Taiwan's, South Korea's, or Mexico's. The underdevelopment continues today (albeit at a higher level of income for workers).

All in all, then, it is evident that U.S. development was not a smooth, uncomplicated process whereby people moved from the rural areas to the cities for higher wages. Indeed, the history of American development, in part, is the story of how northern business interests defeated the southern planters, exploited the South and West, and defeated the Populist movement, which had a Jeffersonian vision of America's future. The exploitation of the American continent required the underdevelopment of that continent by one self-serving region.

The proletarianization of the Southern population resulted from the shift in the social relations governing agriculture. Blacks and whites were forced from the rural areas to the cities. The result of this transformation has been the creation of a permanent underclass in the cities of the South, North, and Midwest. This condition continues today.

Data Sources

This appendix lists the various sources for the data used in this project. Unless otherwise indicated, the data were collected at the county level. Here the data concepts and sources are given, and the years for which the data are available are listed. The citations to data sources are abbreviated and are defined at the end of this appendix.

1. *Census forward survival rates by race, sex, and age.* These rates refer to standards for the entire population and are available for 1900 – 1910, 1910 – 1920, 1920 – 1930, 1930 – 1940, 1940 – 1950. Source: Lee, Miller, Brainerd, and Easterlin, 1964:17 – 23.

2. *Number of males and females by race.* Available for each year 1900, 1910, 1920, 1930, 1940, and 1950. Source: ICPSR, 1974.

3. *Number of males and females by race, 10 years of age and older.* Available for 1910, 1920, and 1930 from ICPSR, 1974. Years 1940 and 1950 are available from Gardner and Cohen, 1971.

4. *Number of persons living in places with a population greater than 2500.* Available for each year 1900, 1910, 1920, 1930, 1940, 1950. Source: ICPSR, 1974.

5. *Age structure by race by sex at county level.* Available for 1930, 1940, 1950. Source: Gardner and Cohen, 1971.

6. *Age structure by race, sex, and urban–rural for each state.* Available for 1900, 1910, 1920, 1930, 1940. Sources: U.S. Bureau of the Census: 1900—Vol. II, Part II, Table 2 (1902a); 1910—Vol. II, Table 8 for each state (1913a); 1920 and 1930—1930 Census, Vol. III, Table 3 for each state (1932a); 1940—Vol. II, Table 7 for each state (1943a).

7. *Number of manufacturing establishments.* Available for 1900, 1920, 1930, 1940. Source: ICPSR (1974). 1947 source: U.S. Bureau of the Census, Census of Manufacturers, 1947, Vol. III, Table 2 for each state (1950). 1954 source: U.S. Bureau of the Census, Census of Manufacturers, 1954, Vol. III, Table 3 for each state (1957).

8. *Number of farm owners and tenants by race.* Available for 1900, 1910, 1920. Source: ICPSR (1974). Sources for 1930, 1940, 1950: U.S. Bureau of the Census, Census of Agriculture: 1930—Vol. II, Part II, County Table 1 for each state (1932b); 1940—Vol. II, County Table 2 for each state (1942); 1950—Vol. I, County Table 2a for each state (1952b).

9. *Number of farms.* Available for 1900, 1910, 1920, 1930, 1940, 1950. Source: ICPSR (1974).

10. *Number of acres and bales of cotton.* Available for 1899, 1909, 1919, 1929, 1939, 1949. Sources: U.S. Bureau of the Census: 1900—Vol. VI, Part II, Table 10:430 — 436 (1902b); 1910—Vol. VI, Table 4 for each state (1913b); 1920—Vol. VI, Part 2, Table IV for each state (1922); 1930— Census of Agriculture, Vol. II, Part 2, Table V for each state (1932b); 1940— Census of Agriculture, Vol. I, County Table VII for each state (1942); 1950— Census of Agriculture, Vol. I, County Table V for each state (1952b).

11. *Number of tractors.* Available for 1930, 1940, 1950. Sources: U.S. Bureau of the Census, Census of Agriculture: 1930—Vol. II, Part II, County Table XII for each state (1932b); 1940— Vol. I, County Table X for each state (1942); 1950—Vol. I, County Table III for each state (1952b).

12. *Boll weevil infestation.* Data on the dispersion of boll weevil are available from 1892 to 1921. Source: U.S. Department of Agriculture, 1922.

13. *Data on lynchings available by county by year, 1889 – 1918.* Source: NAACP, 1969.

14. *Agricultural subsidy payments.* Data available for 1933 and 1934 at county level. Source: Agricultural Adjustment Administration (1935), Exhibit 12, "Rental and benefit payments through Dec. 31, 1934—by states and counties," pp. 358 – 435.

15. *Total acres in farms.* Available for 1899, 1909, 1919, 1929, 1939, 1949. Source: ICPSR (1974).

16. *Cities with population greater than 25,000.* Available 1900, 1910, 1920, 1930, 1940, 1950. Sources: U.S. Bureau of the Census, 1900 and 1910—in 1910 Census, Vol. II, Table 2 for each state (1913a); 1920 and 1930—in 1930 Census, Vol. 3, Table 15 for each state (1932a); 1940 and 1950—in 1950 Census, Vol. II, Table 10 for each state (1952a).

17. *Cotton prices.* Source: U.S. Bureau of the Census, Historical Statistics of the U.S., 1975, Table K550-563, pp. 517 – 518.

18. *Per capita income in the Northeast.* Source: Perloff *et al.*, 1960:Table 198, p. 591.

The following are full citations to items abbreviated above.

Agricultural Adjustment Administration (AAA)

1935   "Agricultural adjustment in 1934," a report of administration of the Agricultural Adjustment Act from Feb. 15, 1934 to Dec. 31, 1934; U.S. Department of Agriculture, Agricultural Adjustment Administration, Washington, D.C.: U.S. Government Printing Office.

Gardner, John, and William Cohen

1971   "County-Level Demographic Characteristics of the Population of the United States, 1930 – 1950." (Machine readable data file.) Produced by ICPSR (ed.), Chicago, Illinois: Center for Urban Studies. Distributed by ICPSR, Ann Arbor, Michigan. In one data file (3111 logical records) and accompanying documentation.

Inter-university Consortium for Political and Social Research (ICPSR)

1974   U.S. Bureau of the Census. County Level Census Data 1900 – 1950. (Machine readable data file.) Produced and distributed by Inter-university Consortium for Political and Social Research, Ann Arbor, Michigan. In six data files (approximately 19,000 logical records) and accompanying documentation.

Lee, Everett, Ann Miller, Carol Brainerd, and Richard Easterlin

1957   "Population Redistribution and Economic Growth in the United States, 1870 – 1950," Vol. 1. Methodological Considerations and Reference Tables. Philadelphia: American Philosophical Society.

NAACP
1969   *Thirty Years of Lynching, 1889 – 1918.* New York: Negro Universities Press.
Perloff, Harvey S., Edgar Dunn, Jr., Eric Lampard and Richard Muth
1960   *Regions, Resources and Economic Growth.* Lincoln: University of Nebraska Press.
U.S. Bureau of the Census
1902a   12th Census of the United States, Census of Population, Vol. II. Washington, D.C.: U.S. Government Printing Office.
1902b   12th Census of the United States, Census of Agriculture, Vol. VI, Part 2. Washington, D.C.: U.S. Government Printing Office.
1913a   13th Census of the United States, Census of Population, Vol. II. Washington, D.C.: U.S. Government Printing Office.
1913b   13th Census of the United States, Census of Agriculture, Vol. VI. Washington, D.C.: U.S. Government Printing Office.
1922   14th Census of the United States, Census of Agriculture, Vol. VI, Part 2. Washington, D.C.: U.S. Government Printing Office.
1932a   15th Census of the United States, Census of Population, Vol. III. Washington, D.C.: U.S. Government Printing Office.
1932b   15th Census of the United States, Census of Agriculture, Vol. II, Part 2. Washington, D.C.: U.S. Government Printing Office.
1942   16th Census of the United States, Census of Agriculture, Vol. I. Washington, D.C.: U.S. Government Printing Office.
1943   16th Census of the United States, Census of Population, Vol. II. Washington, D.C.: U.S. Government Printing Office.
1950   1947 Census of Manufacturers, Vol. III. Washington, D.C.: U.S. Government Printing Office.
1952a   17th Census of the United States, Census of Population, Vol. II. Washington, D.C.: U.S. Government Printing Office.
1952b   17th Census of the United States, Census of Agriculture, Vol. I. Washington, D.C.: U.S. Government Printing Office.
1957   1954 Census of Manufacturers, Vol. III. Washington, D.C.: U.S. Government Printing Office.
1975   Historical Statistics of the United States, Colonial Times to 1970. Washington, D.C.: U.S. Government Printing Office.
U.S. Department of Agriculture
1922   "Dispersion of the boll weevil in 1921." U.S. Department of Agriculture circular 210. Washington, D.C.: U.S. Government Printing Office.

Data Structure, Coding, and Comparability

This appendix has three purposes: (a) a discussion of the data structure and its implications for the selection of counties in the sample; (b) a detailed presentation of the coding of various variables; and (c) a critical look at the comparability of various measures across time.

The data structure of this project has important ramifications for the selection of counties included in the analysis. Since the major variable in this study is a net migration rate, it is important to consider what this measure necessarily implies about a data file. The most important feature to consider is that a net migration rate pertains to a change over a period of time. Here, census decades are used, and net migration rates of blacks and whites are computed for 1900—1910, 1910—1920, 1920—1930, 1930—1940, and 1940—1950. The other important feature is that the rates are measured for counties. This presents one basic difficulty—county boundaries change over time and increases or decreases in a county's population are potentially due to such boundary changes. In order to get around this problem two strategies were adopted: (a) a county was not included into any given decade's analyses unless it existed at both census points in time; (b) a county was not included into the analyses if a boundary shift caused a reduction or increase of more than 10% in an area over the census decade. These strategies mean that a number of counties in a number of states are not represented in the analyses. A decade-by-decade account of the sample is now given that describes how many counties are in the sample, which counties in which states are excluded, and other pertinent information.

1. *1900–1910*. There are 703 counties in this analysis. The following counties are excluded from the following states: Alabama—Houston, Henry; Georgia—Ben Hill, Crisp, Grady, Jeff Davis, Jenkins, Tift, Toombs, Turner; Louisiana—La Salle, Catahoula; Mississippi—Franklin, Forrest, George, Jefferson Davis, Lamar; North Carolina—Lee, Chatham, Moore; South Carolina: Calhoun, Dillon, Lee. None of Oklahoma's counties are in the sample from 1900 to 1910 since statehood brought about large-scale redrawing of county boundaries. The counties in Texas that are included in the analysis are shown in Map B.1.

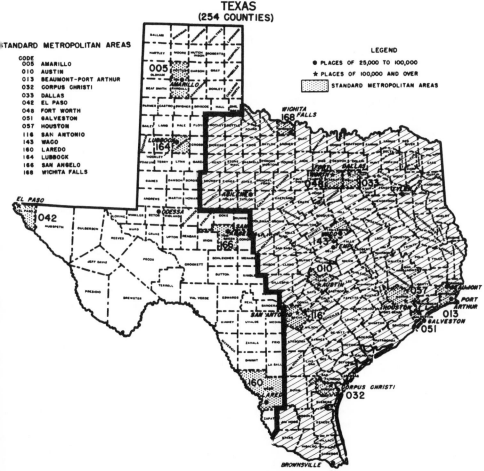

MAP B.1. *Boundary of counties in Texas used in the analysis. Counties in the shaded area in the analysis.* (*Source: U.S. Bureau of the Census, 1950.*)

2. *1910 – 1920*. There are 799 counties in this analysis. The following counties are excluded from the analysis: Georgia—Atkinson, Bacon, Barrow, Bleckley, Candler, Cook, Evans, Treutlen, Wheeler; Louisiana—Allen, Beuregard, Evangeline, Jefferson Davis; Mississippi—Humphrey, Stone, Walthall; North Carolina—Avery, Hoke; South Carolina— Allendale, Jasper, McCormick; Oklahoma—Cotton, Comanche; Texas—Brooks, Culberson, Hudspeth, Jim Hogg, Jim Wells, Kleberg, Real, Willacy.

3. *1920 – 1930*. There are 824 counties in this analysis. Counties excluded are: Georgia—Brantley, Lamar, Lanier, Long, Peach, Seminole.

4. *1930 – 1940*. There are 826 counties in this analysis. None of the counties in the states involved are missing because of substantial boundary changes. However, the analysis contains only 804 counties since 22 are excluded due to missing data. Campbell, Milton, and Fulton counties in Georgia are combined during this decade. The data from 1930 is summed over these three counties and Fulton county remains in the analysis.

5. *1940 – 1950*. There are 826 counties in this analysis. None of the counties in the states involved are missing because of substantial boundary changes. The analysis contains only 804 counties since 22 are excluded due to missing data.

In this section, each variable used in the analyses is discussed. After considering how the variable is constructed in each decade, some comments are made on the comparability of each variable across decades. The concern here is with the actual construction of variables and not with their theoretical relevance.

1. TENANTS. This variable is the percentage of all farmers in a county who were tenants at the initial census point in time. In all of the decades, this measure is calculated by race. This variable is constructed from 1900, 1910, and 1920 census data that has been put on computer tape by ICSPR. Total farmers by race in a county is computed by summing the number of tenants and farm owners. The percentage is computed by dividing the number of tenants by this estimate of total number of farmers. In 1930 and 1940, the data were hand-coded and keypunched by the author. The variable coding is consistent over time.

2. ΔTENANTS. This variable is the percentage change in the number of tenants in a county over a decade by race. For 1900, 1910, and 1920, the data on number of tenants by race come from ICSPR. For 1930, 1940, and 1950, the data were hand-coded and keypunched by the author. The variable is computed by the following formula (tenants t_2 – tenants t_1)/tenants t_1, where t_2 and t_1 are the end and beginning points of the decade. The measures are computed from a similar kind of data in a similar kind of way across time.

3. ΔOWNERS. This variable is the percentage change in the number of farm owners in a county over a decade by race. Its coding and data sources are exactly like those for TENANTS.

4. COTTON. This variable is the percentage of all farm acres in a county that were planted in cotton at the first decade point (t_1). The number of farm acres in a county is available from ICPSR for each year before the census year. The number of farm acres in a county includes all land on farms, including uncultivated land. The number of acres in each county planted in cotton is available in the various censuses and was hand-coded and key punched by the author. The variable COTTON is the number of acres in cotton divided by the total farm acres in a county. It is consistently coded across decades.

5. ΔCOTTON. This variable is the change in the percentage of all farm acres in a county that were planted in cotton over a decade. Its sources are identical to COTTON. The variable

is computed by the following formula: COTTON t_2 − COTTON t_1. The coding is consistent across decades.

6. SURPLUS. This variable is the change in the ratio of the total rural population over the total number of farms over a decade. The total rural population of a county is calculated in the following way. First, for each decade, the total population is computed by summing the number of white men and women and the number of black men and women. For each census point, these data are available from ICPSR. Then the number of persons who lived in places with populations larger than 2500 is subtracted from the total population. This number also comes from ICPSR. This difference is considered to be the rural population. One could argue that this is not really a good measure of the rural population because some persons living in places with less than 2500 persons still live in towns. While this argument has some merit, the measure of rural population used here is consistent over time and, therefore, offers a yardstick (although perhaps an arbitrary one) to get a sense of how large the rural population was. The total number of farms in a county is available from ICPSR. This measure counts any tract of land over 3 acres that has farm crops growing. Thus, tenant plots are counted as separate farms as are small subsistence farms. Again, the measure is consistent over time. The measure, SURPOP is formally computed as follows: [total farms t_2/(total population t_2 − urban population t_2)] − [total farms t_1/(total population t_1 − urban population t_1)]. Its coding is based on similar concepts over time.

7. ΔBALES. This variable is the percentage change over time in the number of bales of cotton produced in a county. The number of bales of cotton in a county reflects the amount produced in the year before the census and was coded and keypunched by the author. The precise variable coding is (bales t_2 − bales t_1)/bales t_1. This measure is consistently coded over time.

8. URBAN. This variable is the percentage of the population who lived in places with populations greater than 2500 at the first census point. The denominator is constructed by summing the number of white men and women and the number of black men and women. The components of this total population measure come from ICPSR. The number of persons who lived in places with populations greater than 2500 is also available from ICPSR. Again, one could argue that 2500 is an arbitrary number to choose in deciding if a population is urban. It is counterargued here that the key issue is to choose a level of "urban" that is consistent. In this analysis, the level that qualifies as urban is 2500, and it is consistent because the measure is the same over each decade.

9. ΔURBAN. This variable is the change in the percentage of the population who lived in places with greater than 2500 persons over the decade. Its data sources are identical to URBAN and its coding is URBAN t_2 − URBAN t_1. The measure is consistent over time.

10. BIG CITY. This is a dummy variable that takes on a value of "0" if a county does not contain a city with a population greater than 25,000 and a value "1" if it does. The data for this variable come from the various censuses and were coded and keypunched by the author. The level of population was chosen rather arbitrarily. If a lower level had been chosen, many more cities would have been included and that would not have been consistent with the concept of a "large city." If a higher level had been chosen, that would have eliminated most cities. The variable refers to the initial decade point and the coding is consistent across decades.

11. NEAR BIG CITY. This is a dummy variable that takes on the value of "0" if a county is not next to a county with a city with a population greater than 25,000 and takes on a "1" if it is. The data sources are identical to BIG CITY and the coding is consistent across time.

12. MANUFACTURERS. This variable is the number of manufacturing establishments in a county at the beginning of a census decade. For the decades 1900, 1910, 1930, and 1940,

the data are available from ICPSR. The data are not available at the county level for 1920. In order to obtain data for 1920, the number of manufacturing establishments in 1910 and 1930 were summed and divided by two. The estimate of manufacturing establishments in a county in 1920 is based on the assumption that manufacturing growth was constant from 1910 to 1930. While this assumption is probably not true, it does give an estimate of manufacturing establishments in 1920. This assumption, however, could introduce potential bias into this variable in this decade.

13. ΔMANUFACTURERS. This variable is defined as the percent change in the number of manufacturing establishments over the decade. It is defined as (MANUFACTURERS t_2 − MANUFACTURERS t_1)/MANUFACTURERS t_1. This variable is potentially problematic in three of the five decades. In decades 1910 − 1920 and 1920 − 1930, it presents difficulties since the estimate of manufacturing establishments in 1920 is potentially flawed. In the decade 1940 − 1950, the measure presents difficulties because the estimate of manufacturing establishments in 1950 was obtained in the following way. From 1947 on, the Census of Manufacturers was not taken in the census year. The number of manufacturing establishments in a county in 1950 was estimated by summing the number of establishments in 1947 and 1954 and dividing by two. The assumption here is that growth in manufacturing was relatively constant over the period. If this assumption is not true, then the measure is potentially flawed.

14. TEXAS and OKLAHOMA. These are dummy variables that take on a value of "0" if the county was not in Texas or Oklahoma and a value of "1" if it was. These variables were coded consistently across decades.

15. BOLL1 and BOLL2. These are dummy variables that take on a value of "0" if the county was not first infested by boll weevils in the relevant decade and a value of "1" if it was. These assignments were based on the data in Map 5.1. If a county was partially infested in any given decade, it was coded "1" for the first decade in which it was infested. There is no comparability problem for this variable.

16. LYNCHING. This is a dummy variable coded "0" if no lynching occurred in a county during the decade and coded a "1" if a lynching occurred. This variable has difficulties since the data it is based on is seriously flawed for two reasons. First it is not clear whether the lynchings recorded were all of the lynchings that occurred or were even a representative sample of them. Indeed, there is evidence that the data used here are not a good sample. Second, the county that is reported to be the place of the lynching may not have been the place where the "crime" originated. That is, many persons tried to escape their potential lynching and some were caught in nearby counties.

17. TRACTORS—1920. This variable is the number of tractors in a county in 1930. It is only used in the 1920 − 1930 decade as a rough measure of the level of mechanization in a county.

18. TRACTORS. This variable is the number of tractors in a county at the beginning of a decade. It is used only in the 1930 − 1940 and 1940 − 1950 decades. The measure is comparable across decades and is based on data hand-coded and keypunched by the author.

19. ΔTRACTORS. This variable is the percentage change in the number of tractors in a county over a decade and is formally defined as (TRACTORS t_2 − TRACTORS t_1)/TRACTORS t_1. The source of the data is comparable over time and the variable appears only in 1930 − 1940 and 1940 − 1950.

20. PAYMENTS. This variable is the agricultural payment made in a county in 1934 in thousands of dollars. It is only used in the 1930 − 1940 and 1940 − 1950 analyses and was hand-coded and keypunched by the author.

21. PAYMENTS × TRACTORS. This variable is an interaction that results from the prod-

uct of $\triangle$TRACTORS and PAYMENTS. It appears only in the 1930 – 1940 and 1940 – 1950 analyses.

22. BOLLA, BOLLB, and BOLLC. These are dummy variables used in the analysis of all five decades that reflect the decade during which the boll weevil infestation first began in a county. They are based on Map B.1 and have the same principle behind them as BOLL1 and BOLL2.

23. COTTON PRICE. This is the price of cotton at the initial census point in time. It was coded from the Historical Statistics of the United States, 1780 – 1970.

24. $\triangle$COTTON PRICE. This variable is the percentage change in the cotton price over the decade. Formally it is (COTTON PRICE t_2 – COTTON PRICE t_1)/COTTON PRICE t_1.

25. INCOME PER CAPITA. This is the per capita income in the northeastern United States at the beginning of the decade as calculated in Perloff et al. (1960).

26. $\triangle$INCOME PER CAPITA. This is the change in the per capita income in the northeastern United States over the decade. Formally it is (INCOME PER CAPITA t_2 – INCOME PER CAPITA t_1)/INCOME PER CAPITA t_1.

From the point of view of data comparability over time, one can conclude that only MANUFACTURERS and $\triangle$MANUFACTURERS are potentially difficult. Of course, the other measures could contain measurement error that is systematic. Further, they may not be good measures conceptually. For instance, rural population is defined as persons living in places with a population less than 2500. This may really not be strictly a "rural" population. Nonetheless, given the fact that the various measurements span 50 years, one can conclude that the concepts are relatively constant. Of course, one does not really know how potential biases in the administration of the six censuses utilized here have affected the results. Therefore, all results remain tentative.

The Measurement of
Net Migration

This appendix is concerned with the measurement of net migration in this study and contains three parts: (a) a presentation of the measure of net migration based on forward census survival rates; (b) the presentation of how net migration was actually estimated for each decade; and (c) a comparison between the three methods of estimation used.

The measure of net migration used here is based on the forward census survival rate method (Shryrock and Siegel, 1971; Hamilton, 1959, 1967; Price, 1955; Lee *et al.*, 1957). The basic formula for computing the forward census survival rate is in Eq. (1).

$$M_{x+t} = P^t_{x+t} - sP^0_x, \qquad (1)$$

where x is an age group, t is the interval between censuses, P^0_x is the population aged x at the first census, P^t_{x+t} is the population at the next census at age $x + t$, s is the survival rate from x to $x + t$, and M_{x+t} is the net migration for the $x + t$ age group. If one sums over all age groups, then one has the total net migration. Utilization of this method requires an estimate of s and a knowledge of the age structure at both census points. The estimate of the survival rate comes from Lee *et al.* (1957).

It is the age structure that presents the most difficulties. Age structures at the county level are only available for 1930, 1940, and 1950. The problem, then, is how to estimate net migration for the other three decades. In the section that follows, the exact form of the method used to estimate net migration for each decade is presented. The basic strategy is to use state age structures as estimates for county age structures. Before proceeding to a decade-by-decade presentation, it is of interest to consider this strategy more closely. Using Eq. (1), the following can be noted:

$$\sum^{x} M_{x+t} = \sum^{x} (P^{t}_{x+t} - sP^{0}_{x}) \tag{2}$$

$$\sum^{x} M_{x+t} = \sum^{x} P^{t}_{x+t} - \sum^{x} sP^{0}_{x} \tag{3}$$

$$\sum^{x} M_{x+t} = P^{t} - \sum^{x} sP^{0}_{x} \tag{4}$$

where Σ^{x} refers to summing the age groups. To estimate the net migration, one needs only the total population of age $x + t$, the age structure at the first time point, and the survival rates. In each of the decades, then, an age structure at the first time point is required. Since various subpopulations have different survival rates, it would be important to have age structures that reflect this. Here, age structures are considered separately by race and sex. The basic strategy of this measure is based on the following available data. First, for each county, the number of white men and women and black men and women at the first census decade point is known, and the number ten years of age and older at the second census decade point is also known. Using state age structures by race, sex, and census survival rates, one can compute the proportion of white and black men and women who survived from t_{1} to t_{2} for the state. This proportion is multiplied by the appropriate subpopulation at t_{1} in the county yielding an estimate of the number of survivors in the subpopulation (ΣsP^{0}_{x}). Then, the sP^{0}_{x} of the relevant subpopulation is subtracted from the P^{t} of that subpopulation and gives an estimate of $\Sigma^{x}M_{x+t}$ for that subpopulation. The net migration estimates are summed over the subpopulations and yield a net migration estimate for the county. This technique is modified slightly by inclusion of an urban — rural distinction that will be considered in a moment.

In the decade 1900 — 1910, the following data were available: (a) for 1900, the number of white men and women and the number of black men and women in the county; (b) the number of white men and women and black men and women in the county who were ten years of age and older in 1910; (c) a set of census survival rates by race, sex, and age for the decade 1900 — 1910; and (d) a state age structure with the following age breakdowns for 1900 by race and sex: 0 — 4 years, 5 — 9, 10 — 14, 15 — 19, 20 — 24, 25 — 29, 30 — 34, 35 — 39, 40 — 44, 45 — 49, 50 — 54, 55 — 59, 60 — 64, 65 — 69, 70 — 74, 75 and older. The census survival rates for all decades are broken down into 14 categories: the percentage of those surviving from

$0 - 4$ to $10 - 14$ years, $4 - 9$ to $15 - 19$, $10 - 14$ to $20 - 24$, $15 - 19$ to $25 - 29$, $20 - 24$ to $30 - 34$, $25 - 29$ to $35 - 39$, $30 - 34$ to $40 - 44$, $35 - 39$ to $45 - 49$, $40 - 44$ to $50 - 54$, $45 - 49$ to $55 - 59$, $50 - 54$ to $60 - 64$, $44 - 49$ to $65 - 69$, $60 - 64$ to $70 - 74$, $65 - 75+$. In order to utilize the survival rates, it was necessary to sum the age groups to those older than 65. The following calculations were then performed.

$$ps_{r,s} = \left(\sum_{s_{r,s,a}}^{a} P_{r,s,a}^{0,st} \right) / P_{r,s}^{0,st} \tag{5}$$

where s is the survival rate by race (r), sex (s), and age (a) and $P_{r,s,a}^{0,st}$ is the population at the first decade point by state by race (r), sex (s), and age (a); $ps_{r,s}$ is the proportion who survived by race and sex and $P_{r,s}^{0,st}$ is the total population by race and sex at the first decade point. This produces an estimate of the proportion of persons by race and sex who survived by state. Then these proportions were used within states to obtain an estimate of the number of persons by sex and race who would have survived in each county. These numbers are used in Equation (6) to arrive at estimates of net migration by race.

$$M_r = (P_{r,\text{male}}^t + P_{r,\text{female}}^t) - (ps P_{r,\text{male}}^0 + ps P_{r,\text{female}}^0), \tag{6}$$

where $P_{r,\text{sex}}^t$ is the population at the second time point that was 10 years or older by race and sex, ps is the proportion who would have survived given that the county age structure was similar to the state age structure, and $P_{r,\text{sex}}^0$ is the population by race and sex at the first time point.

The decade $1910 - 1920$ had the following information available: (a) for 1910, the number of white men and women and the number of black men and women in the county; (b) the number of white men and women and black men and women in the county who were ten years of age and older in 1920; (c) a set of census survival rates by race, sex, and age for the decade $1910 - 1920$ with the same age breakdowns as the rates for $1900 - 1910$; (d) a state age structure with the following age breakdowns for 1910 by race, sex, and urban − rural: $0 - 4$ years, $5 - 9$, $10 - 14$, $15 - 19$, $20 - 24$, $25 - 34$, $35 - 44$, $45 - 64$, $65+$; and (e) data on the number and proportion of persons living in a county who were living in urban places (places with populations greater than 2500). Two measures of net migration were constructed for each race. The first was constructed in the same way as the measure used in $1900 - 1910$. That is, the survival rates were multiplied by the state age structure and divided by the relevant total subpopulation to yield the proportion in the state who would have survived by race and sex. In this situation, the state age structure had only nine categories. To apply the survival rates required the following procedure: the survival rates for age groups that were not differentiated in the state age structure were summed and then averaged. The "averaged" survival rate was applied to the state age structure. The proportion who survived in each group was then used at the county level in order to estimate net migration. The procedure at the county level was identical to that in 1900 – 1910.

The second estimate of net migration was based on the notion that urban and rural areas have different age structures. Thus, the survival rates applied to these differing age structures could yield different estimates of net migration. Utilization of the information on urban – rural age structures required an age structure differentiated at the state level by the urban – rural distinction and an estimate of the racial composition of urban – rural places at the county level. The first was available, but the second required further estimation. Consider what is known: the number of persons and the proportion of persons in a county who lived in places with a population greater than 2500 in a county and the proportion of blacks and whites by sex across the state who lived in such places. By using the state estimate, one could estimate the number of blacks and whites by sex in each county who lived in rural and urban places. Using the survival rates, the following proportions can be computed:

$$ps_{r,s,u/r} = \left(\sum^{a} s_{r,s,u/r,a} P^{0,st}_{r,s,u/r,a} \right) \Big/ P_{r,s,u/r} \qquad (7)$$

where s is the survival rate, $p^{0,st}_{r,s,u/r,a}$ is the population at time point 1 in the state by race (r), sex (s), urban/rural (u/r), and age, (a), $ps_{r,s,u/r}$ is the proportion who survived by race, sex, and residence, and $P^{0,st}_{r,s,u/r}$ is the total subpopulation by race (r), sex (s), and urban/rural (u/r). The net migration by race is estimated in the following way:

$$M_r = (P^t_{r,male} + P^t_{r,female}) - [ps_{r,s,urb}(U_{r,s}P^0_{r,s}) + ps_{r,s,rur}(R_{r,s}P^0_{r,s})] \qquad (8)$$

where M_r is the migration rate by race, $P^t_{r,s}$ is the population at the second point in time by race and sex, $ps_{r,s,u/r}$ is the proportion of persons in the state who survived by race, sex, and urban/rural, $U_{r,s}$ is the proportion urban in the state by race and sex, $R_{r,s}$ is the same number for persons who are rural in a county, and $P^0_{r,s}$ is the population by race and sex at the first time point. This yields an estimate of net migration based upon the differential age, sex, and race structures of cities and rural areas.

The decade 1920 – 1930 has the following data: (a) the number of black men and women and white men and women in 1920; (b) the number of black men and women and white men and women ten years of age and older in 1930; (c) the number and proportion who lived in urban and rural places; (d) a set of census survival rates identical in structure to those mentioned previously; and (e) a state age structure differentiated by race, sex, urban, rural farm, rural nonfarm, and age. The age structure contains 16 categories identical to those in the 1900 age structure. In order to estimate net migration, two summations were necessary. First, those 67 years of age and older were summed into one category. Second, rural farm and rural nonfarm were summed in order to preserve the urban–rural distinction. Two measures of net migration were produced. The first was based solely on an application of the survival rates to the state age structure without regard to the urban–rural distinction, and the second utilized the urban–rural distinction. Both measures were calculated in the fashion suggested for the 1910–1920 measures.

The 1930–1940 and the 1940–1950 data structures contained exactly the same data as the 1920–1930 data file. Two measures of net migration identical in construction to those in the 1920–1930 data set were created. One additional measure of migration was also constructed. For 1930 and 1940, the age structure of each county was available by race and sex. The age structure contained 16 categories identical to the 16 categories of the state age structure in 1900. Thus, the survival rates could be directly applied to the county level data. This produced a measure that can be called a "true" net migration measure based on the census forward survival rate method.

In the analyses done in this study, all of the measures of net migration were converted to rates in the following fashion: $NMR_r = NM_r/TOTPOP_{r,t1}$ * 100, where NMR_r is the net migration rate by race, NM_r is the total net migration by race, and $TOTPOP_{r,t1}$ is the total population by race at the first decade point. The net migration rate is directly interpretable as the number of persons per 100 by race who moved in or out of the county. All analyses in this study had net migration rates as dependent variables. The analyses presented in this project were done for one measure in 1900–1910, two in 1910–1920, 1920–1930, and three for 1930–1940 and 1940–1950. The analyses in Chapter 9 were done using two separate sets of measures. The analyses that appear in the tables were all based on the census forward survival rate method applied to state age structures that were differentiated by race, sex, and urban–rural, except for the 1900–1910 analysis, which was based only on the state age structure that was differentiated by race and sex. The 1900–1950 analysis presented in Chapter 9 utilizes these same measures.

Given this choice of measures, it is a matter of some curiosity as to how well these measures tap the same things. Here, two tables are presented that attempt to justify the methodological choices. Table C.1 presents the zero-order correlations between the three measures of net migration used in this study. A rapid glance at this table reveals two conclusions. First, the measures using state age structures are almost perfectly

TABLE C.1

*Correlations among Three Measures of Net Migration Rates
across Four Decades by Race*

Measure	1910-20		1920-30		1930-40		1940-50	
	Blks	Whts	Blks	Whts	Blks	Whts	Blks	Whts
I[a], II[b]	.997[d]	.998	.998	.999	.998	.999	.999	.999
I, III[c]					.946	.962	.963	.971
II, III					.971	.964	.981	.984
	n=799		n=824		n=804		n=804	

[a] The measure is based on a straight application of the state age structure to each county.

[b] This measure utilizes information on the urban/rural age structure of the state.

[c] This measure is based on county age structures and reflects a direct application of the forward census survival rate method.

[d] Zero-order Pearson correlation coefficient.

correlated. This suggests that the proportion which survived is relatively constant across rural—urban age structures. Second, both measures utilizing the state age structures are almost perfectly correlated with measures using county age structures. This implies two things: (a) the state age structure differentiated by race and sex is not a bad approximation for county age structures; and (b) the proportion which survived within a county is not much different than the proportion which survived across the state by race and sex.

High zero-order correlations suggest that the three measures are co-varying. They do not "prove" that the measures are tapping the same dimension. In order to get a sense of how the three measures behave in a regression framework, Table C.2 is presented. Table C.2 contains the results of a weighted least squares regression of various variables on three net migration rates estimated for blacks during 1930 — 1940. All of the possible tables are not presented here since they would be redundant. Table C.2 is a fairly representative comparison of the three measures in a regression framework. A quick glance at the table reveals that the regressions are shockingly similar. All coefficients that are significant in one regression are significant in all three regressions. Further, the signs on the coefficients all go in the same directions. Even the constants have similar values. This suggests that, at least for blacks during the 1930 — 1940 decade, the measures produce remarkably similar results.

TABLE C.2

A Model of the Net Migration Rates of Blacks for Counties in the South, 1930–1940
Using Three Measures of the Net Migration Rates[a]

Variable[b]	I[c] b	I[c] SE(b)	I[c] β	II[d] b	II[d] SE(b)	II[d] β	III[e] b	III[e] SE(b)	III[e] β
TENANTS	-71.226*	2.778	-.488	-72.162*	2.676	-.444	-70.800*	2.688	-.428
ΔTENANTS	1.272*	.361	.121	1.174*	.199	.125	.789*	.187	.199
ΔOWNERS	3.154*	.607	.082	3.654*	.674	.054	3.624*	.658	.051
COTTON	-98.791*	8.258	.316	-131.396*	12.958	-.297	-120.978*	13.264	-.294
ΔCOTTON	94.266*	12.425	.216	125.698*	19.105	.188	115.227*	15.202	.203
ΔBALES	-1.920	1.234	-.038	-.746	.549	-.040	-1.568	.944	-.037
ΔSURPLUS	-.549*	.049	-.178	-.572*	.085	-.168	-.564*	.044	-.166
URBAN	21.843*	1.502	.422	18.820*	1.306	.418	19.271*	1.304	.428
ΔURBAN	4.136*	1.165	.012	6.103*	2.301	.012	5.013*	2.244	.010
BIG CITY	6.469*	1.245	.227	5.583*	1.141	.254	5.519*	1.138	.251
NEAR BIG CITY	12.942*	1.458	.202	12.075*	1.229	.282	12.110*	1.224	.313
MANUFACTURERS	.039*	.003	.142	.049*	.012	.086	.045*	.082	.065
ΔMANUFACTURERS	2.838*	.458	.136	2.532*	.765	.122	2.682*	.777	.130
TEXAS	-3.169*	.258	.068	-2.207*	.292	-.041	-1.352*	.311	-.021
OKLAHOMA	-18.324*	1.441	-.325	-14.927*	1.352	-.296	-14.969*	1.343	-.297
TRACTORS	-.011*	.001	-.116	-.009*	.001	-.079	-.011*	.002	-.099
ΔTRACTORS	-.585	.399	-.028	-.653	.408	-.023	-.869	.488	.024
PAYMENTS	-.030*	.001	-.438	-.035*	.0008	-.435	-.034*	.0011	-.377
Constant	29.942			31.153			30.062		
R²	.863			.859			.896		

[a] See appendix C for discussion

[b] Variable names defined in Table 8.1.

[c] Net migration rate based on a straight application of the state age structure to each county.

[d] Net migration rate utilizes information on the urban/rural age structure of the state.

[e] Net migration rate based on county age structure.

This conclusion also applies to the analyses for the decades 1930 – 1940 and 1940 – 1950.

All in all, then, one can conclude that the measures of net migration based on state age structures are producing results that are nearly identical to those produced using county age structures. While one can conclude little about such estimations before 1930, it is not unreasonable to assert that the measures based on state age structures produced reliable, interpretable results before 1930. The similarities after 1930 are most likely due to the very reasonable proposition that the proportion which survived from county to county by race and sex using national census survival rates is not that different from the proportion which survived within a state using such rates by race and sex.

Weighted Least Squares
Regression

The major analytic tool utilized in this study is a form of weighted least squares regression. This appendix has three parts that attempt to justify and explain the use of this technique. First, an intuitive discussion will be presented to explain what the problem is. Then, a relatively formal statistical technique is presented. Finally, the actual application of the technique is presented.

In Appendix C, the measure of the dependent variable of this study was discussed at some length. Here the crucial issue is the fact that the variable is the net migration rate. This presents potential problems because such rates can take on enormous values. Most of the rates with large values reflect the fact that the base populations are very small. That is, a county with a net migration of 200 and a base population of 20 has a rate of increase of 1000 per 100 people (200/20 × 100), while a county with a net migration of 10,000 and a base population of 50,000 has a rate of increase of 20 per 100 people (10,000/50,000 × 100). While the second county has enormous growth, it is overshadowed by the growth of the first. Upon inspection of some of the data, it was found that roughly 10 – 15 counties in each decade had rates greater than 100. The effect of these counties in the regressions was to create large standard errors and insignificant coefficients. Since these cases are outliers, they are responsible for the large standard errors. One has two choices with outliners: One can throw them out, or one can re-weight the data to minimize their effect. Throwing them out implies that one believes that the measure is distorted for some unknown reason. It can be argued that this is not the case here. The net migration rates are large because they represent large proportional changes. Therefore, it seems more logical to re-weight the data.

Choosing such a scheme requires a statistical model and some reasons as to why such a statistical model is appropriate. Intuitively, the central difficulty is that as the net migration rate increases, the error increases. This implies that the error is related to the net migration rate. Why is this so? Because the net migration rate is sensitive to the size of the base population in the county. Since a number of the independent variables in the model are also dependent on the size of the base population, it follows that they too are systematically related to the errors. From an econometric point of view, the basic difficulty is that the errors are heteroskedastic. To correct this difficulty, a weighted least squares solution is applied.

More formally, the regression model posited here can be presented in the following way. The conditions of the model are

1. $y = X\beta + \omega$
2. X is a $T \times K$ matrix with rank K
3. X is nonstochastic
4. $E(\omega) = 0$

5. $V(\omega) = \Omega$, where $\Omega = \begin{bmatrix} \sigma_1^2 & 0 & \cdots & 0 \\ 0 & \sigma_2 & & \\ \vdots & & \ddots & \\ 0 & & \cdots & \sigma_n^2 \end{bmatrix}$

Ordinary least squares estimation of such a model produces estimators that are unbiased and consistent, but they are no longer minimum variance unbiased estimators (Neter and Wasserman, 1975:131). Minimum variance unbiased estimators require the use of the generalized least squares estimate of β which in this case can be written as

$$\hat{\beta} = (X'\Omega^{-1}X)'X'\Omega^{-1}y \tag{1}$$

where

$$\Omega^{-1} = \begin{bmatrix} 1/\sigma_1^2 & 0 & \cdots & 0 \\ 0 & 1/\sigma_2^2 & \cdots & \\ \vdots & & \ddots & \vdots \\ 0 & & \cdots & 1/\sigma_n^2 \end{bmatrix} \tag{2}$$

Weighted least squares is just a specialized case of generalized least squares (Theil, 1971:244).

The problem in applying a WLS (weighted least squares) solution is that Ω is unknown. In order to estimate (1), an estimate of Ω is needed. The solution utilized here is suggested in Theil (1971:246), Neter and Wasserman (1974:131−133), and Mosteller and Tukey (1976:346−379). In order to estimate Ω, an OLS (ordinary least squares) estimate of β is produced. Using these $\hat{\beta}$'s, y's are generated and thus $\hat{\sigma}_i^2$'s can be obtained. Using these $\hat{\sigma}_i^2$'s in the $\hat{\Omega}$ matrix produces:

$$\hat{\beta} = (X'\hat{\Omega}^{-1}X)^{-1}X'\hat{\Omega}^{-1}y, \tag{3}$$

$$\hat{\Omega}^{-1} = \begin{bmatrix} 1/\hat{\sigma}_1^2 & 0 & \cdots & & 0 \\ 0 & & \cdots & & \\ \cdot & \cdot & \cdot & \cdot & \cdot \\ \cdot & & \cdot & & \cdot \\ \cdot & & \cdot & & \cdot \\ 0 & & \cdots & & 1/\hat{\sigma}_n^2 \end{bmatrix} \tag{4}$$

A simple transformation of the data re-weights the data and removes the effects of heteroskedasticity.

In practice, this transformation is achieved in the following way. OLS estimates of $\hat{\beta}$ are produced, y_i's are estimated, and $\hat{\sigma}_i^2$'s obtained. Then the data are transformed in the following manner:

$$y_n/\hat{\sigma}_n = \Sigma^i \beta_i(X_{ni}/\hat{\sigma}_n) + W_n/\hat{\sigma}_n \tag{5}$$

The application of OLS to Equation (5) implies that the values $y_1, x_{11}, \ldots, x_{1i}$ of each observation are weighted inversely proportional to the standard deviation of the corresponding disturbance. The result is a minimum variance unbiased estimator. In this study, it was found that the parameter estimates were unaffected by this transformation, but the standard errors of the various variables were reduced. This is what one would expect if the data were heteroskedastic. Thus this provides empirical support for the statistical model posited here.

The Logic behind the Analysis of Chapter 9

Basically, the structure of the data for this analysis is as follows. Let

$$y_{ik} = X_{ijk}\beta_j + W_{ik} \tag{1}$$

be the equation for the weighted least squares model for the ith county, with jth independent variables, and for the kth decade. If the income per capita measures and the price of cotton measures were included in the model above, they would be constants. That is, each would form a column in the matrix X_{ijk} with the same value for the ith county within the kth decade. Now consider the following:

$$
\begin{bmatrix} y_{i1} \\ y_{i2} \\ y_{i3} \\ y_{i4} \\ y_{i5} \end{bmatrix} = \begin{bmatrix} X_{ij1} \\ X_{ij2} \\ X_{ij3} \\ X_{ij4} \\ X_{ij5} \end{bmatrix} \beta_j + W_{ik} \tag{2}
$$

This model implies stacking the data and treating the observations on each county's migration rate across time as a vector. Similarly, the matrices with the values of the independent variables are also stacked. There are two important features of this model. First, the variables describing conditions in the North and the price of cotton are no longer constants. In this model, these variables are constant within decades but they vary across decades. This allows one to assess whether or not shifts in these factors caused shifts in the net migration rates of blacks and whites over time. Second, the parameters estimated no longer reflect the possibility that the parameter of any given variable changes over time. Instead, they reflect a parameter that is a "weighted average" of the parameter describing the effect of any given variable in each period.

The logic of this analysis answers the following theoretical question: "Do the levels of and percentage changes in income per capita in the Northeast and in cotton prices affect the net migration rates of blacks and whites from counties of the South net of other variables in the model from 1900 to 1950?" There are a number of difficulties with both this conceptualization and this statistical model. These issues are considered because they affect how "seriously" one can take the results of this analysis.

The important issue to be raised concerns the model of the error structure. Here, the technique used is still the weighted least squares technique presented in Appendix D. This implies the assumption that the data are heteroskedastic. That is, each observation is assumed to have an error that is systematically related to the X's in such a way that large values of some of the X's will produce large errors. By stacking the data, two other potential components are introduced into the error structure. These components reflect (a) the fact that there are successive observations on the same units (i.e., five observations per county) and the errors within each unit could be correlated; and (b) the fact that we observe five separate decades (and processes within each decade) that are not specified in the equation produces errors correlated across decades. This error could potentially bias the equations. For a variety of reasons, the technique applied is the weighted least squares technique described in Appendix D. We must be wary of this application, however, because it is a potentially improper specification of the error structure.

References

Armes, Ethel
    1910   *The Story of Coal and Iron in Alabama.* Birmingham: University of Alabama Press.

Arnett, Alex M.
    1922   *The Populist Movement in Georgia.* New York: Columbia University Press.

Baldwin, Sidney
    1968   *Poverty and Politics.* Chapel Hill: The University of North Carolina Press.

Banks, Enoch M.
    1905   *The Economics of Land Tenure in Georgia.* New York: Columbia University Press.

Benedict, Murray
    1953   *Farm Policies of the U.S., 1790–1950.* New York: Twentieth Century Fund.

Benedict, Murray and Oscar Stine
    1956   *The Agricultural Commodity Programs.* New York: Twentieth Century Fund.

Binkley, Wilfred
    1962   *American Political Parties: Their Natural History.* New York: Alfred Knopf Inc.

Blicksilver, Jack
    1959   "Cotton Manufacturing in the Southeast: An Historical Analysis." Bulletin No. 5, Studies in Business and Economics, Bureau of Business and Economic Research. Atlanta: Georgia State College of Business Administration.

Boeger, E. A. and E. A. Goldenweiser
    1916   "A study of the tenant systems of farming in the Yazoo-Mississippi Delta." U.S. Department of Agriculture Bulletin 337. Washington, D.C.: U.S. Government Printing Office.

Bowers, Claude
    1929   *The Tragic Era: The Revolution after Lincoln.* Cambridge, Mass.: Houghton–Mifflin Company.

Boyle, James
    1935   *Cotton and the New Orleans Exchange.* Garden City, N.J.: Country Life Press.

Brannen, C. O.
    1924 "Relation of land tenure to plantation organization." Bulletin No. 1269, Department of Agriculture. Washington, D.C.: U.S. Government Printing Office.
Brooks, Robert
    1914 "The agrarian revolution in Georgia, 1865 – 1912." Bulletin of the University of Wisconsin History Series, Vol. 3.
Campbell, Christiana
    1962 *The Farm Bureau and the New Deal.* Urbana, Ill.: University of Illinois Press.
Cherry, Frank T.
    1965 "Southern In-migrant Negroes in North Lawndale, Chicago, 1949 – 59: A Study of Internal Migration and Adjustment." Unpublished Ph.D. dissertation, University of Chicago.
Clark, Thomas D.
    1944 *Pills, Petticoats, and Plows.* Norman, Oklahoma: University of Oklahoma Press.
    1946 "The furnishing and supply system in southern agriculture since 1865." *Journal of Southern History* XII (February): 28 – 46.
Cohen, William
    1976 "Negro involuntary servitude in the South, 1865 – 1940." *Journal of Southern History* XLII (February):31 – 60.
Conrad, David E.
    1965 *The Forgotten Farmer.* Urbana, Ill.: University of Illinois Press.
Coulter, Ellis M.
    1947 *The South during Reconstruction, 1865 – 1877.* Baton Rouge: Lousiana State University Press.
Crampton, John
    1965 *The National Farmers Union.* Lincoln: University of Nebraska Press.
Davis, Lance E. (ed.)
    1972 *American Economic Growth.* New York: Harper and Row.
Day, Richard
    1967 "The economics of technological change and the demise of the sharecropper." *American Economic Review* 57:427 – 449.
DeCanio, Stephen J.
    1974 *Agriculture in the Postbellum South: The Economics of Production and Supply.* Cambridge, Mass.: M.I.T. Press.
Dillingham, Harry and David Sly
    1966 "Mechanical cotton picker and Negro migration." *Human Organization* 25 (Winter):344 – 351.
DuBois, W. E. B.
    1964 *Black Reconstruction in America.* Cleveland: World Publishing Co.
Dunning, William A.
    1907 *Reconstruction, Political and Economic, 1865 – 1877.* New York: Harper Bros. Inc.
Eldridge, Hope T. and Dorothy S. Thomas
    1964 Population Redistribution and Economic Growth, United States, 1870 – 1950, Vol. III: "Demographic Analyses and Interrelations." Philadelphia: American Philosophical Society.
Ezell, John
    1963 *The South since 1865.* New York: Macmillan Company.
Farley, Reynolds
    1968 "The urbanization of Negroes in the United States." *Journal of Social History* II (Spring):246 – 258.

Farmer, Hallie
    1930   "The economic background of southern populism." *South Atlantic Quarterly* XXIX (January):77–91.

Fite, Gilbert C.
    1950   "Recent progress in the mechanization of cotton production in the U.S." *Agricultural History* 24 (January):20–32.

Ford, Arthur M.
    1973   *Political Economics of Rural Poverty in the South.* Cambridge, Mass.: Ballinger Publishing Co.

Fulmer, John L.
    1950   *Agricultural Progress in the Cotton Belt since 1920.* Chapel Hill: University of North Carolina Press.

Gardner, John, and William Cohen
    1971   "County Level Demographic Characteristics of the Population of the United States, 1930–50." ICPSR (ed.) Chicago, Illinois: Center for Urban Studies (producer). Ann Arbor, Michigan: Inter-university Consortium for Political and Social Research (distributor).

Going, Allen
    1951   *Bourbon Democracy in Alabama, 1874–1890.* Montgomery: University of Alabama Press.

Goldenweiser, E. A. and Leon Truesdell
    1924   *Farm Tenancy in the United States.* Washington, D.C.: U.S. Government Printing Office.

Goldman, Ralph M.
    1966   *The Democratic Party in American Politics.* New York: Macmillan Company.

Goldstein, Sidney
    1958   *Patterns of Mobility, 1910–1950: The Norristown Study.* Philadelphia: University of Pennsylvania Press.

Goodrich, Carter
    1934   *Migration and Economic Opportunity.* Philadelphia: University of Pennsylvania Press.

Goodwyn, Lawrence
    1978   *Democratic Promise.* Chapel Hill: University of North Carolina Press.

Gray, Lewis
    1957   *History of Agriculture in the Southern U.S. to 1860.* Washington, D.C.: Carnegie Institue of Washington.

Greenwood, Michael
    1975   "Research in internal migration." *Journal of Economic Literature* XIII (June): 397–433.

Grubbs, Donald H.
    1971   *Cry from the Cotton.* Chapel Hill: University of North Carolina Press.

Hackney, Sheldon
    1969   *Populism to Progressivism in Alabama.* Princeton, N.J.: Princeton University Press.
    1971   *Populism: The Critical Issues.* Boston: Little, Brown, and Co.

Hamilton, C. Horace
    1939   "The social effects of recent trends in the mechanization of agriculture." *Rural Sociology* VI (March):3–19.
    1959   "Educational selection of net migration from the South." *Social Forces* 36 (October):33–42.
    1964   "The Negro leaves the South." *Demography* 1:273–295.

Hammond, Mathew
  1897 *The Cotton Industry: An Essay in American Economic History, Part I: The Cotton Culture and the Cotton Trade.* New York: Macmillan Co.
  1925 "The extension of the cotton belt and the New South (Chap. 12)." In Louis Schmidt and Earle Ross (eds.), *Readings in the Economic History of American Agriculture.* New York: Macmillan Co.
Hays, Samuel P.
  1957 *The Response to Industrialism, 1885–1914.* Chicago: University of Chicago Press.
Hechter, Michael
  1975 *Internal Colonialism.* Berkeley: University of California Press.
Herring, Harriet L.
  1940 *Southern Industry and Regional Development.* Chapel Hill: University of North Carolina Press.
Hesseltine, William
  1936 *A History of the South, 1607–1936.* New York: Prentice-Hall.
Hicks, John D.
  1931 *The Populist Revolt.* Minneapolis: University of Minnesota Press.
Holland, Stuart
  1976 *Capital versus the Regions.* New York: St. Martin's Press.
Hoover, Calvin B., and B. U. Hatchford
  1951 *Economic Resources and Policies of the South.* New York: Macmillan Co.
Horn, Stanley
  1939 *Invisible Empire: The Story of the KKK 1866–1871.* Montclair, N.J.: Patterson Smith Co.
Hunt, Robert L.
  1934 "A History of Farmer Movements in the Southwest, 1873–1925." Unpublished Ph.D. dissertation, University of Wisconsin—Madison.
Inter-university Consortium for Political and Social Research
  1974 U.S. Bureau of the Census. County Level Census Data, 1900–1950. Ann Arbor, Michigan: Inter-university Consortium for Political and Social Research.
Jansen, Clifford J.
  1970 *Readings in the Sociology of Migration.* New York: Pergamon Press.
Johnson, Arthur M.
  1956 *The Development of American Petroleum Pipelines: A Study in Private Enterprise and Public Policy, 1862–1906.* Ithaca: Cornell University Press.
  1967 *Petroleum Pipelines and Public Policy, 1906–1959.* Cambridge: Harvard University Press.
Johnson, Charles, Edwin Embree, and William Alexander
  1935 *The Collapse of Cotton Tenancy.* Chapel Hill: University of North Carolina Press.
Keat, Russell, and John Urry
  1975 *Social Theory as Science.* London: Routledge and Kegan Paul.
Kennedy, Louise
  1930 *The Negro Peasant Turns Cityward.* New York: Columbia University Press.
Key, V. O.
  1949 *Southern Politics in State and Nation.* New York: A. A. Knopf Co.
Kile, Orville
  1948 *The Farm Bureau through Three Decades.* Baltimore: The Waverly Press.
Kirwan, Albert
  1951 *Revolt of the Rednecks: Mississippi Politics 1876–1925.* Lexington: University of Kentucky Press.

Kolko, Gabriel
  1963   *The Triumph of Conservatism: A Reinterpretation of American History, 1900 – 16.*
         New York: The Free Press.
Kousser, J. Morgan
  1974   *The Shaping of Southern Politics, 1880 – 1910.* New Haven: Yale University Press.
Kuznets, Simon
  1966   *Modern Economic Growth.* New Haven: Yale University Press.
Lange, Dorothea and Paul Taylor
  1969   *An American Exodus.* New Haven: Yale University Press.
Lee, Everett
  1966   "A theory of migration." *Demography* 3:47 – 57.
Lee, Everett S., Ann R. Miller, Carol P. Brainerd, and Richard Easterlin
  1964   Population Redistribution and Economic Growth, United States, Vol. I. "Meth-
         odological Considerations and Reference Tables." Philadelphia: American Philo-
         sophical Society.
Link, Arthur S.
  1947   *Wilson: The New Freedom.* Princeton, N.J.: Princeton University Press.
Logan, Fremise
  1964   *The Negro in North Carolina.* Chapel Hill: University of North Carolina Press.
Lynd, Staughton
  1967   *Reconstruction.* New York: Harper and Row.
Mandle, Jay
  1978   *The Roots of Black Poverty.* Durham, N.C.: Duke University Press.
McConnell, Grant
  1953   *The Decline of Agrarian Democracy.* Berkeley: University of California Press.
McCune, Wesley
  1956   *Who's Behind our Farm Policy?* New York: Praeger Press.
McKibben, Eugene, and R. Austin Griffen
  1938   "Changes in farm power and equipment: Tractors, trucks and automobiles. *W. P. A.*
         National Research Project Report A-9. Philadelphia: Works Progress Adminis-
         tration.
Montgomery, Robert H.
  1929   *The Cooperative Pattern in Cotton.* New York: Macmillan Company
Mosteller, Frederick, and John Tukey
  1977   *Data Analysis and Regression.* Reading, Mass.: Addison-Wesley Publishing Co.
Myrdal, Gunnar
  1944   *An American Dilemma: The Negro Problem and Modern Democracy.* New York:
         Harper Bros. and Co.
NAACP
  1969   *Thirty Years of Lynching, 1889 – 1918.* New York: Negro Universities Press.
Neter, John and William Wasserman
  1974   *Applied Linear Statistical Models.* Homewood, Ill.: Richard D. Irwin, Inc.
Nevins, Allan
  1927   *The Emergence of Modern America, 1865 – 1878.* New York: Macmillan Co.
Newman, Dorothy
  1965   "The Negro's journey to the city." Parts I and II. *Monthly Labor Review* 88:502 – 507,
         644 – 649.
Nourse, Edwin G., Joseph Davis, and John Black
  1937   *Three Years of the Agricultural Adjustment Act.* Washington, D.C.: The Brookings
         Institute.

O'Connor, Harvey
  1933 *Mellon's Millions.* New York: The John Day Co.
O'Connor, James
  1973 *The Fiscal Crisis of the State.* New York: St. Martin's Press.
Odum, Howard
  1936 *Southern Regions of the United States.* Chapel Hill: University of North Carolina Press.
Omari, Thompson P. K.
  1955 "Migration and Adjustment Experiences of Rural Southern Negroes in Beloit, Wisconsin." Unpublished Ph.D. dissertation, University of Wisconsin-Madison.
Perloff, Harvey S., Edgar S. Dunn, Jr., Eric E. Lampard, and Richard F. Muth
  1960 *Regions, Resources, and Economic Growth.* Lincoln: University of Nebraska Press.
Peterson, William
  1969 *Population.* New York: Macmillan Co.
Poulantzas, Nicos
  1968 *Political Power and Social Classes.* London: New Left Books.
Price, Daniel
  1955 "Examination of two sources of error in the estimation of net internal migration." *Journal of the American Statistical Association* 50 (271):689–700.
Ransom, Roger, and Richard Sutch
  1972 "Debt-peonage in the South after the Civil War." *Journal of Economic History* 32 (September):641–669.
  1977 *One Kind of Freedom.* Cambridge: Cambridge University Press.
Raper, Arthur
  1936 *Preface to Peasantry: A Tale of Two Black Belt Counties.* Chapel Hill: University of North Carolina Press.
Ravenstein, E. G.
  1885 "The laws of migration." *Journal of the Royal Statistical Society* 48 (Part 2):167–235.
  1889 "The laws of migration." *Journal of the Royal Statistical Society* XII (June):241–301.
Reid, Joseph
  1973 "Sharecropping as an understandable market response." *Journal of Economic History* (March):114–120.
Reid, Whitelaw
  1965 *After the War.* New York: Harper Torchbooks.
Rhodes, James F.
  1902 *History of the United States from the Compromise of 1850 to the Final Restoration of Home Rule in the South in 1877.* New York: The Macmillan Company.
Rice, Lawrence
  1971 *The Negro in Texas, 1874–1900.* Baton Rouge: Louisiana State University Press.
Richards, Henry
  1936 *Cotton and the AAA.* Washington, D.C.: The Brookings Institute.
Rossi, Peter
  1955 *Why Families Move: A Study in the Social Psychology of Urban Residential Mobility.* New York: The Free Press.
Saloutos, Theodore
  1960 *Farmer Movements in the South, 1865–1933.* Berkeley: University of California Press.
Schwartz, Michael
  1976 *Radical Protest and Social Structure.* New York: Academic Press.

Scott, Emmett
  1920 *Negro Migration during the War*. New York: Oxford University Press.
Shyrock, Henry, and Jacob Siegel
  1971 *The Methods and Materials of Demography*. Washington, D.C.: U.S. Government Printing Office.
Shugg, Roger
  1939 *Origins of Class Struggle in Louisiana*. Baton Rouge: Louisiana State University Press.
Siegel, Jacob S. and Horace C. Hamilton
  1952 "Some considerations in the use of the residual method of estimating net migration." *Journal of the American Statistical Association* 47 (September):480 – 483.
Simkins, Francis Butler
  1947 *The South, Old and New, A History, 1820 – 1947*. New York: A. A. Knopf.
Sjaasted, Larry A.
  1962 "The costs and returns of human migration." *Journal of Political Economy* LXX (October):80 – 93.
Speare, Alden, Sidney Goldstein, and William Frey
  1975 *Residential Mobility, Migration, and Metropolitan Change*. Cambridge, Mass.: Ballinger Publishing Co.
Stampp, Kenneth
  1966 *The Era of Reconstruction, 1865 – 71*. New York: Alfred Knopf Co.
Stinner, William F. and Gordon F. DeJong
  1969 "Southern Negro migration." *Demography* 6 (November):455 – 471.
Stouffer, Samuel
  1940 "Intervening opportunites: A theory relating mobility and distance." *American Sociological Review* 5:845 – 867.
  1960 "Intervening opportunities and competing migrants." *Journal of Regional Science* 2:1 – 26.
Stover, John F.
  1955 *The Railroads of the South 1865 – 1900*. Chapel Hill: University of North Carolina Press.
Street, James H.
  1957 *The New Revolution in the Cotton Economy*. Chapel Hill: University of North Carolina Press.
Taeuber, Conrad, and Irene Taeuber
  1958 *The Changing Population of the United States*. New York: Wiley Press.
Tannenbaum, Frank
  1969 *Darker Phases of the South*. New York: Negro Universities Press.
Theil, Henri
  1971 *Econometric Theory*. New York: John Wiley & Sons Inc.
Thomas, Dorothy S.
  1958 "Age and economic differentials in interstate migration." *Population Index* 24:313 – 325.
Tindall, George
  1967 *The Emergence of the New South, 1913 – 1945*. Baton Rouge: Louisiana State University Press.
Todaro, Michael
  1969 "A model of labor migration." *American Economic Review* 59 (March):138 – 148.
U.S. Bureau of the Census

1864   8th Census of the United States, Agriculture. Washington, D.C.: U.S. Government Printing Office.

1872   9th Census of the United States, Compendium. Washington, D.C.: U.S. Government Printing Office.

1883   10th Census of the United States, Compendium. Washington, D.C.: U.S. Government Printing Office.

1896   11th Census of the United States, Report on Farms and Homes. Washington, D.C.: U.S. Government Printing Office.

1902   12th Census of the United States, Population, Vol. II. Washington, D.C.: U.S. Government Printing Office.

1902   12th Census of the United States, Agriculture, Vol. VI, Part II. Washington, D.C.: U.S. Government Printing Office.

1916   "Plantation Farming in the United States." Washington, D.C.: U.S. Government Printing Office.

1918   "Negro Population 1790 – 1915." Washington, D.C.: U.S. Government Printing Office.

1975   "Historical Statistics of the United States, Colonial Times to 1970." Washington, D.C.: U.S. Government Printing Office.

U.S. Department of Agriculture

1876   Report of the Commissioner of Agriculture. Washington, D.C.: U.S. Government Printing Office.

Vance, Rupert

1929   *Human Factors in Cotton Culture.* Chapel Hill: University of North Carolina Press.

1935   *Human Geography of the South.* Chapel Hill: University of North Carolina Press.

1945   *All These People.* Chapel Hill: University of North Carolina Press.

Vickery, William

1977   *The Economics of the Negro Migration, 1900 – 1960.* New York: Arno Press.

Watkins, James L.

1908   *King Cotton: A Historical and Statistical Review, 1790 – 1908.* New York: J. L. Watkins and Sons.

Weber, Max

1968   Economy and Society. New York: Bedminster Press.

Weiner, Jonathan

1975   "Planter-merchant conflict." *Past and Present* 68 (August):73 – 144.

1976   "Planter persistence and social change: Alabama, 1850 – 1870." *Journal of Interdisciplinary History* 7 (Autumn):235 – 260.

Wharton, Vernon L.

1947   *The Negro in Mississippi.* Chapel Hill: University of North Carolina Press.

Williamson, Joel

1965   *After Slavery.* Chapel Hill: University of North Carolina Press.

Woodman, Harold D.

1968   *King Cotton and His Retainers.* Lexington, Ky.: University of Kentucky Press.

Woodson, Carter

1924   *A Century of Negro Migration.* New York: Russell and Russell.

Woodward, C. Vann

1938   *Tom Watson, Agrarian Rebel.* Savannah, Georgia: The Beehive Press.

1951   *Reunion and Reaction: The Compromise of 1877 and the End of Reconstruction.* Boston: Little, Brown, and Co.

1966   *The Strange Career of Jim Crow.* New York: Oxford University Press.

1974   *The Origins of the New South.* Baton Rouge: Louisiana State University Press.

Woofter, Thomas
   1936   Landlord and Tenant on the Cotton Plantation. Work Progress Administration Research Monograph, Vol. V. Washington, D.C.: Work Progress Administration.
   1969   *Negro Migration: Changes in Rural Organization and Population in the Cotton Belt.* New York: Negro University Press.
Woolfolk, George
   1957   *The Cotton Regency.* New York: Bookman Associates.
Zipf, George K.
   1946   "The $P_1 P_2/D$ hypothesis: On intercity movement of persons." *American Sociological Review* 11:667–668.

Index

QUANTITATIVE STUDIES IN SOCIAL RELATIONS

Consulting Editor: Peter H. Rossi

UNIVERSITY OF MASSACHUSETTS
AMHERST, MASSACHUSETTS